Management skills in primary schools

Les Bell

First published 1988 by Routledge
New in paperback 1989
Reprinted 1990
11 New Fetter Lane, London EC4P 4EE

Printed and bound in Great Britain by
Biddles Ltd, Guildford and King's Lynn

British Library Cataloguing in Publication Data

Bell, L.
Management skills in primary schools. –
(Educational management series).
1. Great Britain. Primary schools.
Management
I. Title II. Rhodes, C.D.M. III. Series
372.12'00941

ISBN 0-415-00586-8
0-415-04212-7 Pbk

CONTENTS

TABLES

TABLES

FOREWORD

There are few books published in this country that have been addressed specifically to the management of the primary school; and of those some have been overtaken by events and others have been concerned exclusively with the role of the headteacher. This book approaches the management of change from the perspective of a newly appointed headteacher, but one committed to the principle of corporate management and shared decision making. It therefore takes, uncompromisingly and emphatically, a firm stance on collegiality.

Furthermore, its author - himself an experienced primary phase practitioner and now a highly regarded lecturer and trainer in education management - sees the many strands of managerial responsibility within a school as parts of a coherent whole. It is all too easy for those under pressure from the latest initiatives or innovations to lose sight of a framework within which these can be considered and managed. This book provides just that framework.

One of the disadvantages of simulation in books on management can be that the reader's attention focuses on the differences between what is for him or her the real situation and what the author has proposed as 'reality'. That is not a criticism that can be levelled at this book. The school and the members of staff which readers will find on these pages are there to provide a setting within which all the issues of primary school management can be considered; they are not there as puppets for the author to manipulate.

This is a book that contains a wealth of practical advice: a commonsense book that does not assume that primary teachers have unlimited time and resources. Nevertheless, the author does not hold back from pointing out the heavy and time-consuming responsibility involved in school management today. This is a book for the practitioner and the practitioner-to-be; and, both for its unobtrusive scholarship and its potential contribution to the better management of our primary schools, it is a welcome addition to this series.

Cyril Poster

ACKNOWLEDGEMENTS

This book is dedicated to all my friends and colleagues in primary education, many of whom have contributed to it directly or indirectly by sharing their experiences with me and by being active participants in many management courses. Unfortunately they are too numerous to mention but my debt to them is none the less for that. I do owe singular debts of gratitude to four colleagues in particular.

To Chris Rhodes, Headteacher of Sydenham County Middle School who has written the second chapter, helped me to integrate the Rosemary Lane case study into the book, and provided invaluable advice and comment on earlier drafts.

To Derek Wilmer, Senior Inspector of Schools in Warwickshire for providing me with the opportunity to run my very first management course for primary headteachers in 1976 and for his support and encouragement ever since.

To Angela Bird, Headteacher of Woodlands Infant School, Solihull, for her help in making my perspectives on school management relevant to smaller schools, especially to infant schools, and for her insistance that I should always make explicit the practical applications of management theory. This I have tried to do throughout the book.

To Kingsley Bungard, Director of the Professional Development Unit, Silsoe College, Cranfield Institute of Technology, for sharing with me over several years his insights into management training and for working with me in applying these insights to the management of schools. Much that is written here has been strongly influenced by his approach to the professional development of those with management responsibility in schools.

I am also grateful to: Paul Chapman Publishing Limited for permission to reproduce the material from Everard, K.B. and Morris, G. Effective School Management which appears on page 194; Gulf

Publishing Company and Dr. Robert Blake for permission to reproduce the Managerial Grid which appears on page 50; Open University Press for permission to reproduce Table 5, E203, Unit 30, Curriculum Design and Development which appears on page 55; SCDC Publications for permission to reproduce the material on page 225 from Management in Action by Graham Pountney, Longmans Resources Unit for SCDC Publications, York, 1985 and for permission to reproduce the material on pages 221-2 from Primary Mathematics critical appraisal instrument, D. Lumb et. al., Longman Resources Unit for SCDC Publications, York, 1984.

Chapter 1

THE CONTEXT OF PRIMARY SCHOOL MANAGEMENT

The Manager in the Primary School

This book is for and about those teachers who have managerial responsibility in the primary school. It is intended to provide an analysis of those responsibilities and, at the same time, to offer practical guidelines for the development of effective strategies which might enable the primary school manager to cope with the increasing demands which confront most colleagues in primary schools today. The basic premise of the book is that most, if not all, teachers in our primary schools ought to have a direct and developing part to play in the management of the schools in which they work. Clearly the overall responsibility for the total organisation and administration of any school rests with the headteacher working through and with the governing body of the school. This situation is almost immutable and will remain so in spite of the changes contained in the 1986 Education Act, and those which are to be the subject of new legislation in 1987/88. Nevertheless, for reasons which will be examined later in this chapter, it is becoming increasingly clear that the whole staff of each primary school is expected to have collective responsibility for the content of the curriculum in their school, for the teaching methods adopted in their classrooms, and for the routine decisions which are taken about the education of the children in their care. This situation is the logical extension of the movement towards greater accountability in schools which began with the Great Debate and the green paper, Education in Schools: A Consultative Document (HMSO 1987b). It is also a theme developed at length by H.M. Inspectorate and summed up in their publication, Education Observed 3: Good Teachers (DES, 1985b) where it is argued that:

> ...teachers need to work together collectively to produce an atmosphere in the school which encourages children to respond in a positive and responsible fashion...The value of clear objectives for each lesson, and the need for pupils to understand these objectives are often demonstrated...References to the importance of professional team work occur frequently in school reports. Typical is the comment in a primary school report: "The members of staff work as a team so that they can offer leadership and guidance in areas of the curriculum that might present difficulties to individual teachers. In this way weaknesses and omissions are assessed and, as far as it is possible, remedied." The Middle School Survey recorded the influence on the quality of work exerted by teachers with delegated responsibilities who were "involving colleagues in cooperative planning by working alongside teachers in the classroom, by identifying needs for in-service training and, in particular, by demonstrating through personal example what could be achieved." These comments emphasise the importance of professional team work for maximum curricular strength and mutual support.
>
> (DES 1985b, paras. 13-30)

These observations by H.M. Inspectorate are not merely descriptions of existing practices in those schools which have recently benefited from a general inspection, although accurate descriptions of practices observed since 1983, when reports made by H.M. Inspectors were first published they certainly are. These comments go further than describing existing practice since they provide us with an extensive working definition of what constitutes a model of good practice in our schools from the perspective of H.M. Inspectorate. These elements are what HMI regard as essential basic features in any well run and effective school. They constitute those features which, increasingly, H.M. Inspectors and their local counterparts, will expect to find in the schools which they visit. In many schools such practices can be found as a normal and well developed part of the life of the school. Other schools are at the point of developing their own individual responses to expectations such as these, while some schools have not yet crossed that particular threshold. It is clear, however, that whatever steps a school may have taken towards meeting the requirements which are implied in these observations, one of the inevitable consequences of moving in the direction indicated in Good Teachers (DES 1985b) is that the responsibility for managing the school devolves to the whole staff of that school to some significant degree and that, in such circumstances, they all must regard themselves as managers in their primary school.

This, then, is the context within which the management of our primary schools has to take place. This book will argue that all primary school teachers should play a full part in various aspects of the management of their school and that, increasingly, they will be expected so to do. The revision of teachers' salary and career structure contained in The Education (School Teachers' Pay and Conditions) Order (1987b), with its provision for a Main Professional Grade, and its commitment to Assessment and Performance Appraisal may or may not have facilitated this process. However, it would have resulted in each teacher having an individual job description specifying, the particular responsibilities of the job held in the school. These responsibilities for the MPG Teacher include, among other things:

> Advising and co-operating with the headteachers and other teachers...on the preparation and development of courses of study, teaching materials, teaching programmes, methods of teaching and assessment and pastoral arrangements...
>
> Contributing to the selection for appointment and professional development of other teachers...
>
> Co-ordinating or managing the work of other teachers.
>
> Taking such part as may be required of him in the review, development and management of activities relating to the curriculum, organisation and pastoral functions of the school.
>
> (DES, 1987b, Schedule 3, paras. 3.1-3.12, page 5)

The conditions of employment for headteachers identify an even more specific element of managerial activity. This activity includes representing the school in its relationships with the LEA and Governors, formulating the overall aims and objectives of the school, participating in the selection and appointment of staff, determining, organising and implementing an appropriate curriculum, reviewing the work and organisation of the school as well as evaluating standards of teaching and learning together with:

> Providing information about the work and performance of the staff employed at the school where this is relevant to their future employment.
> Supervising and participating in any arrangements within an agreed national framework for the appraisal of the performance of teachers who teach in the school.
> Ensuring that all staff have access to advice and training appropriate to their needs...
>
> (DES, 1987b, Schedule 1, Paras. 4.1-4.23, pages 2-3)

These responsibilities echo those descriptions of good practice which were identified by H.M. Inspectorate in Good Teachers (DES 1985b). With the possible exception of the explicit references to performance appraisal the essential features are almost identical, stressing as they do that teachers have a responsibility which is broader and more far-reaching than might be the case if their only concern was for the work which goes on within the classroom. (See Table 1) Such wider responsibility involves working more closely with colleagues for the benefit of all, especially the children. It also involves most teachers in the general management and organisation of the school in which they work. As Marland (1986) suggests:

> In England and Wales, despite some recent centralist tendencies, a significant proportion of the key decisions are made within the school, often by teachers who hold ´posts of responsibility`. This elevates the management skills of the teachers, as opposed to their pedagogical skills, into very great importance.
>
> (Marland, 1986, p.1)

Table 1 THE TASKS OF THE MANAGER IN PRIMARY SCHOOLS

GOOD TEACHERS (DES 1985b)	BAKER (DES 1987b)
Setting clear objectives	Advising and cooperating
Planning with colleagues	Selecting and appointing
Establishing a consistency of approach	Professional development
Providing leadership	Co-ordinating and managing
Giving guidance	Reviewing the curricular and pastoral functions
Assessing	
Cooperating as a team	Appraising performance
Developing colleagues	

The extent to which teachers recognise this and the degree to which they become involved in the work of their school above and beyond a direct concern for the pedagogical aspects of teaching depends, in part, on the organisation of their particular school. It also depends on the individual teacher's understanding of the nature of management and of the relationship between management and the work of the teacher in the primary school. What management means within the broad context of primary school education, and how management practices may be identified within such an organisation, become the focal point of concern. To answer such questions, even with reference to the smallest primary school, is no easy matter since the concept of management and the application of management skills in schools raises a series of complex issues.

What has to be Managed?

Drucker (1968) drew our attention to the complexities of management when he divided the process of management into two specific tasks.

> The manager has the task of creating a true whole that is larger than the sum of the parts, a productive entity that turns out more than the sum of the resources put into it...The second specific task of the manager is to harmonize in every decision and action the requirements of immediate and long-range future. He cannot sacrifice either without endangering the enterprise...He must, so to speak, keep his nose to the grindstone while lifting his eyes to the hills...
>
> (Drucker 1968, pp. 408-9)

More recently Morgan, Hall and Mackay (1983) have suggested that those tasks which commonly face managers in a school setting can be subsumed under four headings; technical, conceptual, human relations and external relations. Technical tasks are those which are specific to the primary purpose of the school, that is the education of its pupils. Conceptual tasks includes those tasks which are directly concerned with the controlling and administration of the school such as the deployment of staff and other resources. As Field (1985) has pointed out, however, it is extremely difficult in practice to separate the technical (professional) aspects from the executive (administrative) aspects of these tasks. The human relationships element of these management tasks include the structuring of participation in decision-making and policy making as well as the provision which needs to be made for the development of the staff of the school. The external tasks draw our attention to the key boundary role which is often occupied by the head and the senior staff of any school. They control and direct the flow of information into the school and co-ordinate responses to that information. The increasing, but generally legitimate, interventions in the life of the school on the part of parents, governors, the local education authority and a host of other groups and individuals are also part of this aspect of management. Expressed in terms of what a manager in a primary school may actually be observed to do, these tasks fall into the deceptively simple categories of keeping things going (administration), doing new things (innovation), and reacting to crisis (salvation). Effective management demands that the manager in the primary school achieves an appropriate balance between these three tasks. To the extent that any one of them receives too much attention or too little consideration the total enterprise will suffer. Waters (1979) reminds us, with reference to the newly appointed headteacher, that it is likely to be day-to-day administration of the school which saps the energy and imagination rather than the more demanding tasks with which she should be engaged, if only because these tasks, and the everyday but unpredictable minor crises which litter our lives in primary schools, seem to demand, and therefore receive, more immediate responses. Hence the longer-term concerns and the forward planning which they entail tend to be ignored. Our noses are sharpened on the grindstone of immediacy but our eyes are rarely, if ever, lifted towards the hills which beckon on the distant horizon.

In order to reach that distant horizon the primary school teacher in her capacity as manager will need, according to Everard and Morris (1985) a sense of purpose or mission. This should be derived directly from the cultural ethos of the school which is embedded in the notion that the reason for the existence of any school is to promote the learning of its pupils within an appropriate curriculum, based on an organisational structure which takes into account the tensions which may arise between teachers as autonomous professionals and teachers in their role as managers. This is especially true of those in senior management positions in schools who will always have to recognise that they are, at one and the same time, both the leading professional in any group and the senior manager. This means that the teacher as manager has to strike a balance between the educational good of the many and the short term advantage of the few, between education principles and philosophies and pragmatic necessity especially as determined by externally imposed priorities and a scarcity of resources. Judgements such as these have to be made on the basis of those educational values to which the teachers in the school subscribe, tempered by a realisation that difficult decisions and choices have to be made and by a recognition that only certain things are possible. In order to achieve this balance in primary schools staffed, as on the whole they are, by committed and dedicated professionals, the manager, whether it be the headteacher or a teacher with a curriculum responsibility, has to do more than state and impose a view or a course of action.

The approach to management in the primary school to be developed here, therefore, is not one which is based in the experience of the world of industry and which was recently attacked by Maw, Fielding and others as being totally inappropriate for educational institutions (Maw et.al., 1984). Nor is it based on the dominant model of management training which Campbell (1985) claims to have identified in many training programmes and which he caricatures as:

> ...a set of techniques to be applied by a manager (the head and senior staff) to the managed (subordinate teachers or pupils) in order to regulate change in a direction considered appropriate by the senior staff. (Campbell 1985, p. 109).

These models are, as Campbell argues, entirely inappropriate to the management of contemporary primary schools given the commitment of managers in primary schools to supporting colleagues, delegating responsibilities and developing or facilitating programmes agreed among the staff of the school. Indeed the approach to school management to be outlined here is derived from the basic premise that the contemporary image of good practice as promoted is one which, in Campbell's words, may best be described as:

> ...the collegial primary school, predicated on the two values of teacher collaboration and subject expertise. (Campbell, 1985, p. 152)

As Campbell (1985) argues, however, the very existence of this type of primary school, while being rooted in empirical reality, is a projection of it rather than a description of it. Before the collegial primary school can emerge as a widespread reality the dual obstacles of teacher relationships and working conditions have to be overcome. Teachers' conditions of service:

> seem stuck on the anachronistic assumption that there is no need to provide time, facilities and ideas for curriculum development. (Campbell 1985, p. 158)

A similar view seems to exist about the provision of time and resources for the other aspects of primary school management, most of which, at the moment, have either to be fitted into an already crowded teaching day, or carried out before or after school, except in those schools where creative and imaginative ways are found to provide learning experiences for children while, at the same time, organising time and space for teachers to cope with the longer-term demands of school management. This book is concerned with the other obstacle which Campbell identified, that of teacher relationships. It will focus on those elements of the relationship between professionals which, if developed successfully, may lead to the establishment of a more collegiate ethos within the school since it is based on the premise that, for primary school teachers to cope with the increasing demands which are being made upon them, they must be able to work as a team as well as being effective classroom teachers working in relative isolation from professional colleagues. (See Table 2).

Table 2 WHAT HAS TO BE MANAGED?

Bell (1987)	Morgan et. al. (1983)	Whitaker (1983)	Day (1985)
Administration	Technical	Allocation and application of responsibilities	The Climate
Innovation	Conceptual	The curriculum	Standards of behaviour & achievement
	Human Relations	The Organisation - resources, decision-making, communication	Relationships
Salvation	External Relations		Evaluating, recording & assessing
		The People	

Management Skills and the Primary Teacher

Any discussion of management skills in almost any context may quickly resolve itself into a consideration of two basic issues. These are "What is to be managed?", which focuses attention on the essential nature of the organisation and upon its fundamental purposes, and "How shall it be managed?" which raises questions about the type of skills and abilities which may be useful, desirable, applicable or necessary in the particular circumstances. The issues raised by these two questions are closely interconnected and, in practice, may be totally inseparable in the daily turmoil of primary school life. Nevertheless, it might be useful to consider them here as separate if not discrete questions in order to highlight our concern with the need for all primary school managers to acquire and develop those skills which might enable them to move towards the establishment of an effective team of teachers in their schools.

Whitaker (1983) writing with particular reference to primary school headteachers but, nevertheless, with a more general message, suggests that there are four elements which can be identified in response to the question "What is to be managed?" These are the allocation and application of responsibilities within the school; the curriculum; the organisation of the school including the distribution of resources and the arrangements for communication and decision-making; the people in and connected with the school. He blends these into a model role definition for primary headteachers although he points out that this should be regarded as a point of departure rather than a definitive statement. His list does highlight, however, a number of elements with which all teachers in their role as manager need to be concerned. For example the communication and decision-making processes within any school have to be appropriate to the school and clearly understood by all its members if the staff team is to work effectively together. Similarly the way in which responsibilities are distributed, even at the very basic level of who is responsible for what, is fundamental to the work of every primary school.

In a similar vein but in the course of considering the relationship between management and the professional development of the primary school teachers it has been argued that in order to take account of the need to manage primary schools as accountable, professional, and yet essentially educational institutions, there are a number of areas which must be the concern of every manager in every primary school (Day et. al., 1985). The school's climate is the very first concern since this is the embodiment of a range of policies about how various groups and individuals within the school work together. The curriculum, together with the related teaching and learning processes, are the next two areas of concern because these represent those aspects of knowledge which the school identifies as being important. These are linked to the establishing of standards of behaviour and achievements which are expected of both staff and pupils, together with the arrangements which are made within the school for ensuring that such standards remain relevant and achievable. Teachers should also be concerned with the management of relationships within the school, especially the organisation of staff in such a way as to ensure a unity of purpose although not a commonality of teaching styles within the school. Finally every teacher should be involved in the processes of evaluating, assessing and recording the work of their pupils as well as their own performance and professional development within the overall context of the school. Implicit here is the assumption that, if people are involved in managing the processes which shape their activities, then they are likely to be more committed to their work.

It should be recognised, however, that while the staff of the effective primary school may tend to operate as a collectivity, this does not in any way diminish the ultimate responsibility which the headteacher has for the work of the school. Indeed it should be recognised that the headteacher has the responsibility for creating the opportunities necessary for her staff to be able to agree upon clear objectives for their school and for identifying and implementing the means of achieving them. This includes those arrangements which might be necessary for judging the extent to which the agreed objectives are being achieved and the identification of any further action which may become necessary as a result of this process. Thus the headteacher retains the overall responsibility for the management of the school but, at the same time, has to enable her professional colleagues to play a significant part in that process as the school moves towards that model of the collegiate primary school which has become the embodiment of good practice in recent years.

If the above elements constitute those features of school activity which have to be managed and if it can be agreed that the general direction in which primary schools are moving is towards a more collegial management structure based on teamwork and co-operation, then what of our second question, "How should this be managed?" Hughes (1985) points us towards one set of answers to this question when he reminds us that Fayol (1916) defined the fundamental skills of management as being to forecast and to plan, to organise, to command, to co-ordinate and to control, and that this list was further refined by Gullick and Urwick (1937) to include seven tasks which are recalled by the acronym POSDCORB. These are planning, organising, staffing, directing, co-ordinating, reporting and budgeting. These two lists are derived from industrial practice and, perhaps, fail to take sufficient account of those interactive elements of management which are an essential feature of management where all the parties have professional responsibilities and commitment.

Drucker (1968) is more helpful when he adds motivating and communicating, developing people and organising them to his classification of management skills which also includes the setting of objectives and the evaluation of outcomes. He warns, however, that managing effectively requires more from an individual than some ability to apply such skills to particular situations. As he points out, the function which distinguishes the successful manager in any enterprise is an educational one:

> The one contribution he is uniquely expected to make is to give others vision and ability to perform. It is vision and moral responsibility that, in the last analysis, define the manager. (Drucker, 1968, p. 418)

This is nowhere truer than in the primary school, for here, partly because of its relatively small number of staff and partly because of its prevailing ethos, each member of the primary school staff has a body of professional expertise which can usefully be imparted to colleagues and each member of the same staff can benefit from the expertise of others.

Nevertheless, as recently as 1978, H. M. Inspectorate reminded us that:

> The arrangement whereby a class teacher is responsible for the whole, or the major part of, the curriculum...is often regarded as the traditional form of organisation for teaching in the primary school. (DES 1978)

Yet it was still reported that over three-quarters of the classes in their survey were taught at some time by teachers other than their own class teacher. Normally these teachers would be specialists in some aspect of the primary curriculum. In the Bullock Report (DES 1975) it was argued that each primary school should have a co-ordinator for language teaching. It was pointed out that:

> The task would be a demanding one...the teacher would act as consultant to his colleagues on matters of reading and language. (Bullock, 1974, para. 13.23)

Eight years later the role of the mathematics coordinator was made even more explicit in the Cockcroft Report (DES 1982, paras, 354-8). Here it was expected that the co-ordinator should prepare schemes of work in consultation with the head and the staff; provide guidance and support for colleagues; procure and organise the necessary resources; monitor mathematics throughout the school; arrange in-service training; and liaise with other schools and the staff of the LEA. Clearly this model was derived from the expectations outlined in the Primary Survey (DES, 1978) where it was argued that teachers with specific expertise should recognise that they have duties which go further than keeping up-to-date with their subject:

> Additionally these teachers should learn how to lead groups of teachers and to help others teach material which is appropriate to the abilities of the children. They should learn how to establish a programme of work in co-operation with other members of staff and how to judge whether it is being operated successfully. They should also learn how to make the best use of the strengths of the teachers of all ages and help them to develop so that they may take on more responsibility...Heads need to make quite clear the responsibilities of individual teachers (para. 8.64).

This trend to make more explicit the role of those teachers with curriculum expertise has continued with subsequent surveys. In Education 5-9 it was argued that such teachers might support colleagues by:

> producing guidelines and schemes of work; by leading discussions and organising study groups; by disseminating work done on in-service courses; by working along-side class teachers; by assembling and organising resources; and occasionally by teaching classes other than their own.
> (DES 1982, para. 319)

In the ILEA Report on Improving Primary Schools it was further argued that:

> ...with few exceptions, teachers in charge of classes in primary schools should take a dual role:
> (a) the responsibility, within general school policies, for the coherence of the programme of work of their class, either the whole or the bulk of which they will teach themselves;
> (b) an advisory/consultancy role in some aspect of the curriculum throughout the school.
> (ILEA 1985, p. 68, para. 3.37)

The report goes on to argue that the second function may involve working with colleagues, giving advice, visiting other schools, organising workshops, and the planning and revision of school policy documents. It is at pains to point out that these are processes which rest on negotiation and debate rather than upon dictation and direction (ILEA 1985, para. 3.40). A few of these teachers with specialist areas may teach them all the time but most will not. Some may have non-curricular roles such as the oversight of probationers or staff development and all may be helped by having a written job description. The expectation is clearly stated that such advisory or consultancy roles should not be related to a particular salary scale but, rather, should be part of the work of all but the least experienced of primary school teachers (ILEA paras. 3.43-44). Similarly it is argued in the Report of the House of Commons Select Committee on Primary Schooling:

> Virtually every teacher should act as a co-ordinator in some aspect of school work and the role should not be restricted to those paid above the basic scale.
>
> (Reported in TES, 26.9.86, p. 15)

If we attempt to produce a list of the skills necessary in order that the primary school teacher can begin to carry out the various functions outlined above, then such a list may be seen to have some similarities to those previously quoted which were derived from the work of Fayol, Gullick and Drucker. In _Good Teachers_ (DES, 1985b) we find suggested that the teacher as manager needs to be concerned with setting objectives, co-ordinating cross-curricular activity, and helping with the work of colleagues to extend and improve their performance. _The Education (School Teachers' Pay and Conditions) Order_, (HMSO, 1987a) adds to this performance appraisal and formal arrangements for staff development, together with a responsibility for managing resources. These points are reinforced by the _Primary Survey_, (DES 1978), but added to them we find the requirement to analyse the work of colleagues with a view to providing help where necessary and the opportunities for further development where appropriate. _The Bullock Report_ (1975) also recognises the importance of such a consultancy role while the planning of schemes of work and the mobilising of resources are emphasised by both _The Cockcroft Report_ (DES, 1982) and _Improving Primary Schools_ (ILEA 1985).

With this in mind we might agree with Rust who argues that the seven most important management skills for teacher managers are analysing, planning, organising, directing or commanding, controlling, co-ordinating and evaluating (Rust 1985). While most of these skills do have relevance for the primary school manager it is unlikely, however, that activities such as commanding or controlling will often be directly employed since, as _Improving Primary Schools_ (ILEA 1985) is at pains to point out, the work of the primary school manager depends on negotiation not dictation and upon debate not direction. Analysing the work of the school, planning, organising and co-ordinating work with colleagues together with the range of staff development activities which might include the selection, appraisal and deployment of staff should all take place within the framework of a collegiate concern for and agreement about the objectives of the school. It is only on the basis of common objectives that the work of the school can be assessed and evaluated. Therefore the most significant feature of primary school management is the context within which it takes place.

Any consideration of primary school management and the skills which it requires must, of necessity, include an examination of the role of analysis, setting objectives, planning, organising and co-ordinating, staff development and school evaluation. These will all be considered in subsequent chapters of this book. Our concern here, however, is to emphasise the context within which these activities must take place, that is within and through that group of professionals who constitute the staff of the primary school working together as a team. It is clear from our discussion of the research and observations of primary school practice above, that teamwork is an essential element of effective management in the primary school. It is only through such teamwork that those areas which we identified as needing to be managed can, in fact, be managed succesfully. It is only through the teamwork which might, eventually, lead to a fully collegiate approach to management in the primary school that the extensive and demanding range of duties and responsibilities which confront the staff of every primary school can, in practice, be met.

ACTIVITIES

1. Examine the ways in which you are involved in the tasks of the manager in the primary school which are listed in Table 1.

2. In what ways are your colleagues involved in the same processes?

3. How are the items in Table 2 managed in your school?

Chapter 2

PRIMARY SCHOOLS AND THEIR MANAGEMENT : AN EXAMPLE

This case study was written by C.D.M. Rhodes

In the previous chapter it was suggested that power and responsibilities within the school should not be centred on one person, but divided among as many of the staff as possible so that all feel involved in the decision making process and understand the rationale behind school policies. New policies will be more likely to succeed if they have been arrived at through consultation and discussion. True understanding of a final decision can only come if all those who will be involved in the implementation of a new policy have been party to the debate and weighing of argument that have led to its formulation. The head who respects the professionalism of her staff will want to make them aware of the complex issues which lie behind most school policies. Thus, if a primary school is to be managed successfully, the headteacher and her staff need to have a commitment to negotiation and discussion. The head can only gain from sharing important questions with her staff. Working alongside those actively involved with translating policies into practice, she is far more likely to make a wise decision than if she plans in isolation. The staff, in their turn, will respond positively to the fact that they have been genuinely involved at an early stage. Even if some of their ideas are eventually discarded, they have been heard, consulted and their professionalism respected. The object of this chapter is to look at some of the practical problems which might face the new head of a school where the idea of collegiate management is unknown, and to examine the strategies that she might employ in order to introduce it. Our medium, through which we will explore these ideas, is the imaginary Rosemary Lane County Primary School.

PRIMARY SCHOOL AND THEIR MANAGEMENT : AN EXAMPLE

The School and the Staff

Let us suppose that Hackthorne College of Education closed in 1974. Its playing fields, less than a mile from the centre of Middleford in the County of Centralshire, were sold as building land. Planning permission was given for new housing and for a Primary School - Rosemary Lane. By the present date, it is a firmly established area. The 221 children who attend the school come either from the new owner-occupier homes or from the late Victorian property which surrounds them. Forty-six per cent of the school roll are children of Asian origin and usually speak Punjabi at home. The school staffing allocation of 9.2 includes an extra teacher funded under Section 11 of the 1966 Local Government Act. There are three Infant classes: reception and two parallel middle/top Infant classes. The Junior-aged children are in four classes, one for each age band. The school building is single storey and of traditional design, with classrooms off the two corridors which lead left and right of the main assembly hall. The layout of the building tends to reinforce the separatism which exists in the school. Each teacher sees her room, and class, in isolation. The idea of a progressive spiral of curriculum continuity and method does not mean much to the staff of Rosemary Lane. They would subscribe to the theory, but would be uneasy and uncertain about the practice.

Ann Welton, the headteacher, aged 47, has been in post since the beginning of the current term. It is her second headship, and she is regarded by the County as having sound managerial skills. The school undoubtedly presents her with a considerable managerial challenge. The staff are unused to the idea of collective management and a collegiate approach. In the past they have had few staff meetings, and these were more monologues than an opportunity to exchange views. One of the reasons that Mrs. Welton was appointed was her commitment to the concept of staff involvement in the decision-making process. She plans to strengthen the curriculum by encouraging consultation and delegating leadership responsibilities among as many of the staff as possible. She hopes to create a climate within the school wherein the staff will all feel that they are part of a greater whole, rather than class teachers working in isolation. She wants them to move towards agreeing common objectives for the school, and to be clear in their understanding about how they hope to achieve those objectives as a team.

A brief mention should be made at this point about the layout of the headteacher's room. Many headteachers' rooms are small, and opportunities for a variety of layout of furniture are limited. However, Mrs Welton will be aware that visitors get an immediate impression of her attitude to them from the physical environment in which she works. If she sits behind the desk, protected by battlements of penracks and files, she will find purposeful conversation a lot harder than if she sits on equal terms with only a small coffee table between her and her guest. On other occasions, it is useful to be able to sit side by side at a table so that it is possible to examine papers with a colleague, and have something firm on which to write. This will also set a professional tone.

The head plans to develop the whole concept of team discussion. On some occasions it will be appropriate for these discussion groups to be drawn from the teachers who work in a particular part of the school. The detailed planning for the introduction of a new Infant reading programme, for example, need not involve the teachers working with the older Junior children. On other occasions, the topic will need to be discussed by teachers drawn from right across the primary age range. On crucial issues, the complete staff will come together as the decision-making body.

The school is presently organised as shown in Table 3.

Table 3 THE ORGANISATION OF ROSEMARY LANE PRIMARY SCHOOL

Mrs Ann Welton	Headteacher	
Mrs A. Butlin	Reception	26 pupils
Miss J. Gill	Assists Mrs Butlin	Scale 1 (Sect. 11)
Miss E. Danby	Middle/top Infants	30 pupils
Mr P. Smith	Middle/top Infants	30 pupils
Mrs N. Cass	1st year Juniors	34 pupils
Mr V. Johns	2nd year Juniors	34 pupils
Mrs E. Arnold	3rd year Juniors	35 pupils
Mr T. Jowett	4th year Juniors	32 pupils Deputy Head
Mrs P. Chalmers	Remedial reading	Part-time (0.2)

Ann Butlin, aged 40, has been on the staff for six years, and has always been responsible for the reception class. This term she has 26 children. She successfully combines old and new ideas in her teaching, and has coped extremely well with the new admissions policy which has enabled children to start school at the beginning of the academic year in which they have their fifth birthdays. She has a lively and extrovert personality, is loyal to the school and is well liked by the parents. Her own work is meticulous and well prepared.

Jaswinder Gill is 26 and in her second year of teaching. She is a fluent Punjabi speaker, and was appointed to the school under Section 11 of the Act. She works with Mrs Butlin in the reception class, mainly with the children whose mother tongue is not English. She has a group of five children who started school with no English at all. She regrets that she does not have any official contact with any of the other classes because she feels that she does have something to offer. She feels that most of the staff see her as a superior classroom helper rather than as a professional colleague with a status equal to their own. There is some justification for having this feeling although the deputy head has recently started to discuss multi-cultural issues with her. Her family is influential in the district. Her uncle is involved in local politics and has expressed public support for moves to establish Asian languages alongside French, German and Spanish in the County's secondary schools.

Miss Emily Danby is aged 56 and in excellent health. She has a class of vertically grouped middle and top infant children. She has worked in the school, and in the same room, since it opened in 1977. She was with Mr Moss, the previous head, when he was head of Ermine Street JMI. She plays little part in the life of the school outside of her own classroom. She is very defensive about her work, and visitors to her room are closely chaperoned. She will unpick children's needlework and resew it after school if it does not meet her standard. Prior to October 1987 she held a Scale 2 post, but no clear responsibilities appear to be attached to it.

Peter Smith, 35, has the parallel class of thirty middle and top Infants. He has never taught this age range before, and is finding it a lot more difficult than he imagined. Many of his problems are organisational. The term started with children in groups, but this quickly broke down, and queues of children with work to be marked have become a regular feature in his classroom. He is very keen to succeed as he sees his failure to get shortlisted for the headships of small village schools as due to his lack of experience with younger children.

Norma Cass has overall responsibility for the three Infant classes and receives the appropriate allowance. However, the former head asked her to take a lower Junior class during the current year so that Peter Smith could have an opportunity to extend his experience. At the time she saw it as a good chance to break down some of the artificial separation which had grown up between the Junior and Infant departments. She likes her class of 34 first year Juniors, but has increasing reservations about what is occurring in her department now that she does not have an immediate impact on its day to day happenings. The Junior and Infant wings of the building are separated by the hall, office and staffroom area. Mrs Cass has a strong public service motivation. She is Chairperson of the PTA, and is the teacher-governor. She is a good, enthusiastic teacher. There is much original work in her classroom, and the children are stimulated to a high standard. The room is well organised and busy. Miss Danby and she have little educational philosophy in common, but respect each other's professionalism.

Victor Johns, aged 37, has the second year Junior class. He too has a clear teaching style and a highly organised classroom. He has become very interested in developments in CDT, has been on several courses, and would like an opportunity to share his enthusiasm with his colleagues. He is the only member of the staff who makes regular use of the school BBC micro-computer. He is the school representative for the National Association of Teachers, and showed great tact during the period of industrial action. He has special responsibility for resources and audio-visual aids.

Elaine Arnold, responsible for the third year Junior class, will be leaving the staff at the end of the current term. She has been appointed to St. Alban's Church of England Combined School with responsibility for games and PE. She is a keen and enthusiastic teacher whose energies will be missed.

The deputy headteacher is Tom Jowett. Aged 47, he has now given up all idea of becoming a head himself. He is extremely conscientious and tends to lack a sense of humour. He is very anxious to please, but is clearly uncertain how to react to the new head. He became quite alarmed when Mrs Welton announced that the stockroom was to be left unlocked in future, and that staff could help themselves. He tends to keep himself to himself, and prefers to communicate with colleagues through an official message book. He is a strong supporter of school uniform, and is feared by many of the younger children who see him as the authority figure. The staff tend to find relationships with him difficult, and refer quite small matters direct to the head, effectively isolating the deputy.

Paula Chalmers teaches two mornings a week. She left teaching in order to have her baby and now, at 29, is anxious to work her way back into fulltime teaching. Her present teaching role is remedial reading, under which she withdraws small groups of children for regular reading practice and support teaching.

Samantha Hockley is one of Emily Danby's oldest friends and shares a flat with her. Her duties as classroom helper are hearing children read, making the tea and washing up afterwards. She works each morning from 9 a.m. to lunchtime.

There are few curriculum documents in the school. Work in many classrooms is formal and text-book based. The children work hard and are well motivated. They are given regular reading tests, and the staff tend to see the results of these tests as the indicator of their own success in their classrooms.

The Curriculum

Work in what the timetable calls "English" consists largely of comprehension from printed texts, spelling and creative writing. All the classes, except Miss Danby's, have a good selection of County Library books which are changed every six months. The reading scheme for the younger children is *One, Two, Three and Away*. The older children use *Reading 360*, but not the support or language extension materials. There does not appear to be any clear policy on taking books home, or on the degree of parental involvement in home reading. Drama is limited to class assemblies. Mrs. Cass has produced a handwriting scheme for the school which is followed more in the Infant classes than in the Junior. There is no central pool or library of books, fiction or non-fiction. Class teachers have been allowed to spend an annual amount of capitation in order to build up classroom stocks as they see fit.

Officially, maths work in the Infant classes is based on the Nuffield scheme. Mrs Cass has produced a school guideline for her department. Miss Danby, however, prefers to use her own scheme, based on a series of home produced graded work cards. She calls this her "sum ladder". The children are very competitive in their progress and can tell you where everyone else is on the ladder. Practical work appears to be rather superficial in both the vertically grouped Infant classes. Junior work is based on formal published schemes. Mrs Arnold and Mr Johns both use TV material. Maths equipment is ordered by each teacher from their annual allocation of capitation. There would appear to be some shortfalls, and some expensive over-duplication. Mrs Arnold has a good Maths corner in her room, and has made a lot of her own apparatus. She has made some good work-cards to go with them. Mr Jowett studied Maths as his main subject at college, and might be willing to give some curriculum leadership although he has recently developed an interest in the LEA's new multi-cultural educational policy.

Topics in history and geography are left to the discretion of each class teacher. Junior work tends to be in one of four chronological time bands, concluding in the fourth year with the early industrial revolution. There is a lot of copying out of reference books, and very little evidence of first hand experience. Mr Jowett, a keen walker, bases a lot of his classwork on and around a termly "expedition". Infant work arises from themes and general projects.

There is no school science scheme as such. The staffroom library contains quite a good selection of texts. Much of the work labelled "environmental" is little more than nature study. Miss Danby's classroom contains an excellent display made by herself and Mrs Hockley in 1979. It consists of examples of all the wild flowers to be found in the area. Much of Mr Johns's work in CDT has a scientific basis.

Each day starts with an assembly of the whole school. On four mornings a week this is conducted by the head, and on the fifth by a class. This is dreaded by the majority of the class teachers who regard it as too competitive. RE class lessons are left to the class teachers. All the staffroom Assembly books are Christian rather than intercultural in content and suggestion. Miss Danby, a Christian Scientist, has elected not to attend assembly and works in her classroom. She is willing to produce a secular class assembly so that her children do not feel left out. No RE is taught in her class.

Many of the staff are uncertain about PE, and look to Mrs Arnold for advice. Most of the lessons appear to be enjoyed by the children and contain evidence of good organisation. Long-term aims are less clear. Work in CDT is limited to pictorial illustration and some models. Mr Johns, Mrs Arnold and Mrs Cass are the exceptions, in that art and craft work is included as a natural extension of the general work of their classes.

The Management Issues

The particular management tasks likely to face the head of a Primary school like Rosemary Lane are the appropriate deployment of the teaching staff, educationally sound groupings of children, efficient use of the building and physical resources, an effective communication system with all those involved in or connected to the school and, above all, the creation of a climate of professional discussion between staff, leading to shared decision-making.

Any headteacher, newly appointed or well established, should carry out a periodic review of the whole school. There are several published documents, such as the ILEA self-assessment programme, which give an excellent framework in which to work. Some of the issues they raise will be discussed in a later chapter. As a result of such exercises, the head, together with the whole teaching staff, identifies a number of needs, and ranks them into an order of priority. The next stage will be a carefully structured and agreed plan of action indicating the direction in which the school is to go. Consultation, with its consequent feeling of involvement, and effective communication are essential ingredients at this stage.

The establishment of a sense of corporate identity must be Mrs Welton's first priority as the new head. She has to break down the isolation in which the staff have always worked. She will have identified, for herself, aspects of the school which would benefit from change. Indeed, the staff will be expecting her to have ideas different from those of her predecessor. Quite a few of them will feel threatened, to a greater or lesser extent, by the thought of alterations in the established order of things, by worries about their status in the eyes of the new head, or by the need to form a whole new set of relationships if the group dynamics of the school are to change. Others will be looking forward to change, seeing it as a challenge, as long overdue. Many will be aware of national initiatives to raise standards and of the various HMI curriculum discussion papers. Detailed examination of one of these documents might well be introduced by Mrs Welton as the basis for her first piece of whole-school in-service work.

It is important that Mrs Welton quickly establishes a practical framework in which decision-making and consultation can take place. She might well decide to hold a staff meeting with that as the sole item on the agenda. She would explain what collegiate management actually involves, and invite suggestions as to how future decisions will be made. She will probably find that all the staff will want to be informed, and to know what the issues are, but not necessarily all will want to be involved in detailed planning. Everyone will want to play a part in discussing matters which concern the major policies in the school, but will expect specialists to provide a lead in curriculum matters. For example, the complete staff might decide that the Maths work in the school should be reviewed. A small representative working party would be set up to look at the matter in depth, and would then report back to the whole staff. Ideally, everyone would receive a written report a few days before the second staff meeting, so that they all came to the meeting prepared. This may sound laborious, but if trouble is taken in order to approach matters in a professional and prepared manner, then purposeful discussion is more likely, and the eventual decisions stand a greater chance of being implemented positively. Decision-making, based on ill-prepared, rushed, or inadequate information, will fail. Worse still, it will call into question the whole credibility of the consultation process. The giving out before a meeting of written papers allows colleagues to absorb them and consider them carefully. Even Miss Danby, who would be likely to be opposed to a new Maths scheme, may be more receptive when she has read a well-reasoned and informative discussion paper.

An essential feature of a well-managed school must be the clear, fair and understood distribution of authority. The status and role given to Tom Jowett, the deputy head, by the previous headteacher was low in terms of real authority. He had no job description or agreement on areas of responsibility.

Mrs Welton will have seen the establishment of a sound professional relationship with her deputy as one of her earliest priorities. There must be a re-definition of his place in the structure of the school. This will be one of the most important statements Mrs Welton will be making to the staff about her management style.

Starting as she means to go on, Mrs Welton will set down on paper her own understanding of the sort of job description her deputy should have, and set it alongside her impression of the reality of the current situation. At the same time she will invite Tom Jowett to write down his own ideas: how he sees his job and responsibilities at the present time, and the type of role he would like to have in the future. She will arrange a suitable time for them to come together to discuss this formally. By the simple strategy of asking Mrs Chalmers, the non-class teacher, to look after Mr Jowett's class for the morning, Mrs Welton will be demonstrating the high priority she places on their having an in-depth and uninterrupted discussion. Additionally, by giving him an agenda of topics she plans to cover at their meeting, he will approach it with greater confidence. He will have had time to formulate his thoughts and will feel less threatened. There is nothing to be gained from springing important topics on an unsuspecting audience. If Mrs Welton is really committed to collegiate management, she will want a dialogue with her deputy and, for this to be successful, he must have time to prepare. It is clearly central to the success of her plan for Mr Jowett to be committed to her ideals. A new, positive and challenging job description, with genuine responsibilities, will appeal to him. At the same time, Mrs Welton must demonstrate her willingness to listen carefully to his point of view, and to attach considerable importance to what he has to say. If his ideas do not match her own, she will need to consider them carefully and be prepared, if necessary, to modify her own proposals. After all, Tom Jowett has a large resource of knowledge about the staff and children in the school. On his side, Tom will expect her to have a clear leadership style, but will find her willingness to discuss major issues with him as a new and welcome experience.

By inviting Tom Jowett to spend a morning working with her, Mrs Welton will demonstrate that he is a valued and important member of the management team. Prior to their meeting, Mrs Welton prepared her own draft outline of a job description for her deputy. She asked Tom to bring his own perception of his role to the meeting, and to be prepared to discuss his own ideas for his future. By listening carefully, and by holding a full discussion unpressured by time, Mrs Welton will establish common ground and a secure foundation of understanding on which to build their future relationship. Obviously, this will not be Mrs Welton's first long conversation with her deputy, but this will be the first with a formal agenda, and with the clearly understood objective that it will conclude in an agreed statement of Tom's future role and responsibilities. Once the job description has been finalised, it is important that it is checked for accuracy and written down. It is all too easy to leave a meeting with a total misconception about what has been agreed. As a skilled manager, Mrs Welton will want to get the staff accustomed to the idea that the agenda for all meetings or discussions will be known in advance. There will be a clearly defined purpose, and the meeting will end with some form of summary and a permanent record of what had been agreed. A suggested non-threatening conclusion for this particular meeting with Tom might be for Mrs Welton to say: "I've made a note of all the points we've agreed, Tom. I'll read them over to you to see if I've got the details correct... Good. I'll get Cathy to type them up so that we can both have a copy."

Any negotiated job description or, indeed, other form of common agreed proposals, should have an adjustment mechanism built into them. This will permit agreed alterations, refinements and improvements to be made when necessary. Evaluation and modification are key factors in successful planning. Ann Welton might well be thinking of introducing the job description process which she used in her previous school. At the beginning of each term she asked each teacher to prepare a statement about any extra responsibilities they would be carrying during the course of that term. These were discussed with her and amended through discussion where necessary. At the end of each term, the staff reviewed what they had written earlier and added notes on how things had gone in reality. This led to effective and realistic setting of targets for the following term.

Once Mrs Welton and her deputy have agreed on his future role within the management structure of the school, she will need to have a long talk with each of the other members of staff. She will want to establish a pattern of personal relationships on which she can build her plans for the future. She will also want to ensure that her staff are deployed in the most effective way. The needs of the children must be paramount, but Ann Welton has also to remember that each member of staff has real needs of his or her own. She will need to evaluate these needs. External factors may well dominate a teacher's life, and affect his or her professional work in school. Miss Danby is worried about her elderly invalid mother, Mr Smith is frustrated by his lack of promotion, Miss Gill is under family pressure from her grandparents to leave teaching, marry and have a family. All the staff will have strong motivational needs. They will all want to feel valued and successful in their jobs. Mrs Welton recognises this and, so far as is possible, she will deploy the staff in order to meet those needs. She cannot alter their ambitions, hopes and fears, but she can change the allocation of responsibilities and organisation of the school. Her long-term plans will seek to meet the needs of the children, while taking careful account of the needs, strengths and weaknesses of the staff.

Mrs Welton knows that Jaswinder Gill is unhappy in her present role. She feels undervalued and urgently wants a change. Mrs Welton will have an opportunity to meet Jaswinder's needs when she plans for the next school year. If she gives her a wider teaching role, this would not only bring benefits to the whole multi-cultural life of the school, but would enhance Miss Gill's self-image as well. A more influential position in the school, or one with a more acceptable professional status, would be making an important statement about her own standing in the school, and would affect the Asian children's own perceptions of their position in society.

Headteachers have to balance the understandable desires of staff to work in new areas with the needs of the children who might find themselves being taught by an inexperienced teacher. Peter Smith is anxious to gain first-hand experience with five to seven year olds, but is it correct to give him a class of this nature, and to move the experienced head of department away from her normal sphere of influence in order to give Peter a younger class? Mrs Welton will need to talk through his future position in the school very carefully and, in the short-term, consider urgently what support strategies should be made available to him. She must also discuss with Mrs Cass how her year in the Junior department could be used to wider advantage. Mrs Cass has clear leadership potential and considerable professional expertise. Her knowledge, her standing within the school and her genuine ability to communicate effectively with colleagues could well make her an ideal curriculum activist ready to lead a purposeful working party.

Mrs Welton must come up with some solutions herself. One way through the dilemma facing her concerning the frustrations of Miss Gill and Mr Smith, would be to propose a new role for Mr Smith in the following September. If Mrs Welton can find some good in-service support for Mr Smith he could be asked to take over the Section 11 role within the school, and to tackle the school's total needs as a multi-cultural school within a pluralist society. His long experience with the older children would allow him to teach and plan with confidence, and his ambition to work with younger children will give him the necessary incentive to identify needs and devise strategies to meet them. Miss Gill could then be given a class in her own right, and would no longer see herself as the token Asian or bilingual nursery help.

Next to the children themselves, the staff are the school's most valuable resource. More and more teachers are recognising that the professional demands made on them by new curricular areas cannot be met by each teacher working in isolation. Increasing importance is being given to methods of working which encourage teachers to share expertise, use their own talents and interests to support colleagues, and welcome into their classrooms other teachers who are able to offer curriculum strengths which they might not have themselves. Mrs Welton must ensure that all the staff have opportunities to observe or work alongside their colleagues. This is especially important for those who carry curriculum responsibilities. She will either have to take more classes herself or introduce other strategies. She might want to consider children occasionally coming together in larger groups, or classes combining to hear a story well read, or to enjoy singing or listening to music together. Cooperative methods and team teaching will create opportunities to deploy staff more effectively.

Rosemary Lane School cannot be organised so that each subject area is taught by a specialist. Mr Johns cannot be timetabled to teach Science to every class, but it is essential that good science is taught throughout the school. Therefore the head and staff will need to evolve a method of working so that Mr Johns´s enthusiasm for the subject, and his willingness to support colleagues with ideas and resources, can be used to the best advantage. This will be an ideal subject for the agenda of a staff meeting. The various options could be listed in a short paper attached to the agenda. A school in-service day run by Mr Johns with plenty of practical work, or a series of after-school workshops, or the daytime deployment of the staff in order to free Mr Smith to lead lessons or work alongside a less confident colleague, or perhaps a bid for the support and help of the County advisory teacher for science are all possibilities which might be considered.

Mrs Welton will then need to broaden the discussion in the staff meeting to encompass the whole concept of school-based INSET work. Recent Government initiatives correctly challenge teachers to identify for themselves the needs of the school to establish priorities and to make bids for the necessary finance to service the training itself. She will probably find that the staff will generate enough ideas to keep them busy for the next three years.

The headteacher´s own time is a possible resource which could be used to support specialist teachers. By a careful examination of the way in which she organises her time, Mrs Welton will decide how much she can afford to be a teaching head, and where this precious resource could best be used. Teaching Mr Johns´s class so that he can work alongside a colleague who has asked for support with a science topic is one possibility here. By efficient management and good staff development it should be possible to make each member of staff feel confident across the whole width of the curriculum. Teachers will not see themselves as specialists in ivory towers with information and techniques too valuable to be shared with others, but as colleagues supporting each other in their common desire to provide only the best for the children in their charge. Considerable managerial skills are needed to effect this mutual support and sharing of expertise. We have seen that the new head of Rosemary Lane might well decide that an early priority for the school will be a re-examination of its policy on Maths. She will have to decide whether to take on this responsibility herself because it is such a vital part of the curriculum and because she wants to put her own authority clearly behind it, or whether the key worker should be a member of staff with day to day opportunities to evaluate any new methodology, and the facility to demonstrate good practice through the example of his or her own classroom. Will staff talk more openly with a colleague than with the headteacher? In fact, what role should the head have in curriculum development? Mrs Welton might well decide to raise this as an item on the agenda of a future staff meeting.

How will Miss Danby react to a change in the Maths policy for the school? Should she be wooed to the new ideas, or just told to use them? Should she be left alone because it is better for her children to be taught in an old-fashioned way, rather than suffer being in a class where the teacher has been made to use materials which she distrusts and fails to understand, and makes every difficulty in order to demonstrate that the new ideas are not going to work? But can Mrs Welton permit some children to start a scheme in the reception class, spend two years with Miss Danby, and then pass into a lower Junior class where the other half of the class have been following the official school guidelines and have a body of mathematical language and working methods which are completely different?

When one considers class size, Rosemary Lane is fortunate in that its roll falls neatly into seven class units. The top and middle Infants are grouped into two parallel classes. The new head will have to examine the long- and short-term implications of this policy, especially as one of the classes is taught by a teacher likely to be resistant to change. Parents are understandably wary about vertical grouping, and, where it exists, headteachers have to ensure that parents understand the policy and do not feel their children disadvantaged. Whatever eventual form her educational groupings take, Mrs Welton will have to ensure an efficient match between the children's needs and the structure she has designed for them. Among the key issues, on which she and the staff should concentrate, are good classroom organisation, a wide variety of well-chosen resources and a meaningful record system. Additionally, the staff will need to be skilled observers, seeking to identify the types of working situation and challenges most likely to produce the best learning conditions. In recent years, headteachers have had to be prepared to consult, inform and negotiate with a far wider range of people than ever before. During the industrial action of the mid-1980s many heads had to find new ways of working with teacher colleagues. Skills were learned, and working practices evolved, that stood all parties in good stead long after the end of the official action.

Another recent development has been the increasing involvement of governors in the day to day life of the school, and the growing status of parent and teacher governors. Mrs Cass takes her responsibilities as the teacher governor very seriously, and is speaking with increasing frequency and independence at governors' meetings. The Rosemary Lane governors have increased the number of their termly meetings so that they can hold an additional session each term at which an adviser or local authority officer is invited to speak to them on an agreed curriculum or policy matter. Headteachers who still seek to keep their governors quiet with reports packed with detail about drains and sports reports but which never mention major curriculum or management issues, are courting disaster. Governors are becoming increasingly confident in the exercise of their power. The wise headteacher will see that they are fully informed and genuinely consulted, while retaining her integrity as the professional manager of the school.

This chapter has attempted an overview of the main management issues in primary schools. Many of these will be expanded in later chapters. It is of vital importance to remember that the management of a school has to be seen in practical terms. Headteachers have to be trained in the practical exercise of their management skills. They will undoubtedly build up an important resource of past experience, but that is insufficient in itself. They also need a bank of practical management techniques and strategies to set alongside past experience. This book sets out to provide some of these. If Ann Welton is going to succeed at Rosemary Lane, she will need to have a definite conception of what she understands good management to be. She must accept the absolute necessity of careful planning, genuine consultation, and clear decision-making. She must never forget that Rosemary Lane is not some form of advanced intellectual board game, but two hundred and twenty one children and nine teachers who can never have those years again if she gets it wrong.

She is aware of the changing managerial role of the headteacher. She is no longer the autocrat who dispenses educational wisdom from on high, but the chair of a staff meeting where all the teachers have a right to a voice in the decision-making process. The more she can adopt strategies which include the staff in the planning process, and involve them in thinking through basic underlying educational principles, the more likely she is to take them forward with her. She must encourage them to think and act as the team responsible for fostering and developing the school. She is willing to transfer genuine responsibility from herself to the staff as the professional team. She has accepted that this will increase her managerial responsibility in seeing that the staff use their new power wisely. In three years time she could well be invited to attend a five-week course during term time. Will she decide, by herself, whether to go on the course or not, or will she take the problem to a staff meeting and share the pros and cons with them before making that major choice? If the years have gone well, and she has forged the staff into a genuine corporate management team, they will make the decision together, in the best interests of the school as a whole.

Activities

1. What strategies for staff development would you adopt if you were Ann Welton at Rosemary Lane?

2. On the basis of an analysis similar to that contained in this chapter, identify the main management tasks in your school.

3. Given that you were the headteacher of Rosemary Lane, what strategies might you adopt for dealing with the tasks which you have identified in your response to activity 2?

Chapter 3

HEADSHIP, MANAGEMENT AND LEADERSHIP IN THE PRIMARY SCHOOL

The issues which face the new headteacher of Rosemary Lane are familiar ones. How can she help her staff to make the best use of their individual talents for the benefit of the whole school community? How can she create that climate within which all of the staff, including non-teaching staff, may feel that they are part of a greater whole? How can the activities of the staff and their use of valuable resources be co-ordinated in order to make the most effective use of the facilities which are available within the school? How can agreement be reached on the nature and extent of the changes which may need to be made in the curriculum and organisation of the school? How can the growing pressures for change be met while, at the same time, maintaining a relatively stable environment within the school for both pupils and staff? These issues, or ones of a very similar nature, confront many colleagues in primary schools today.

In a recent survey of the work of deputy headteachers in first schools within one local education authority a number of priorities were identified for the forthcoming year (Fellows, 1985). These included co-operative teaching and staff development, reviewing curriculum policy and organisation, improving intra-school liaison and co-operation, and planning school-based in-service training. There was also an emphasis on giving the responsibility for many of these developments to staff teams and on identifying a range of strategies for increasing the involvement of staff in all aspects of school life. In a similar survey of headteachers` perceptions of primary school organisation and management an almost identical set of concerns were identified (Bell, 1986). One head stated that his main priority was to ensure that his management structure enabled his postholders to exercise their responsibilities across the whole school. In this community primary school over 50 staff were involved in the total work of the school so such a policy was almost an essential for this headteacher. In a much smaller first school the reported job descriptions placed a similar emphasis on the role of postholders in co-ordinating the activities of colleagues through meetings, workshops, informal consultations and by example. The head saw her own role and that of her deputy as being to create a situation in which this could work successfully and to take initiative where necessary in generating change. Priorities were again related to effective use of resources including the deployment of staff, effective curriculum development and coping with demands for change while, at the same time, preserving a relatively stable school environment.

The identification of priorities and the involvement of staff in that process will be discussed in detail in a subsequent chapter. Suffice it to say for the moment that, as one headteacher put it, 'This process requires me to be both team coach and visionary. It is extremely demanding.' There is no doubt that the headteacher in the primary school does carry the ultimate responsibility for the identification of her school's priorities and for establishing the means of achieving them. One headteacher, at least, has real reservations about how realistic are the expectations which many headteachers, especially newly appointed ones, have of themselves. Angela Anning (1983), in an extremely witty and perceptive article, argues that all headteachers suffer from the 'three year itch'. This is not a comment on the private lives of headteachers. Rather it is an assessment of their capacity to change and develop their schools. She argues that, given the ability to define priorities and to pace themselves and their staff, most headteachers can manage the superficial revamping of the school. The environment is usually the first target. Corridors are cleared, flowers and plants arrive, cloakrooms become resource areas and all the dated paraphernalia of a bygone teaching age is exorcised from cupboards and shelves. Next, or even at the same time for the overly energetic and enthusiastic, curriculum guidelines are drawn up by the staff working together or in groups. Parents and governors may even be consulted. The illusion, the writer suggests, comes from believing that at some point you will reach a finishing line. Alas, this is not the case. About three years into her headship the headteacher will realise that all this activity has had little effect in the one area which really matters, generating real, rather than superficial, changes in classroom practice. At this point, she suggests, many headteachers change schools, a decision rationalised as a desire for a new challenge. Others move into peripheral areas of activity such as teacher training or the advisory service. Still others give up, albeit slowly and almost imperceptibly at first. Anning sees this process as one in which complacency sets in. This may indeed be the case in some circumstances. The process of giving up may also involve other, less easily recognisable forms of behaviour. Some headteachers become immersed in the administration of their school. Here, getting things done takes on an overwhelming significance at the expense of doing new things, of thinking and planning. In a similar way it is possible for other headteachers to retreat into reaction. In this situation nothing of significance is done in the school unless it is as a reaction to a crisis or as a response to some form of emergency. Thus, for some headteachers, the three year itch may lead to an over-emphasis on administration or on salvation at the expense of coming to terms with the real changes which may need to be made within the school.

Is there, then, no life beyond the three year itch for the dedicated or the brave? Angela Anning believes that there is. To move beyond that superficial acting out of the roles within schools which she regards as being endemic to the early years of most headships, and the subsequent years of many, will, she states, involve a desperate and dangerous leap, requiring the headteacher and her staff to take risks and to trust each other in order that they may embark upon a journey of genuine self-evaluation leading to genuine change in significant areas of the life of the school. Risk-taking and trust may not be sufficient if the headteacher is to accept the responsibilities placed upon her by her office, while at the same time encouraging, involving and developing her colleagues to arrive at that point at which they are willing and able to play a wider role in the management of their school. The headteacher needs an understanding of her own role, including its management and leadership elements. She must recognise that special care, based on praise rather than blame, encouragement rather than discouragement, and self-evaluation rather than externally imposed criticism, is necessary where one is managing, leading and developing professional staff within the small but complex world of the primary school (Waters 1979).

Headship

The role of the primary school headteacher, like that of many other people in managerial and leadership positions, is a relatively ambiguous one. At first sight the headteacher <u>controls</u> the school within which she works. Yet such control is shared with a number of other individuals and groups to a varying degree. As Harling (1980) has pointed out, the local education authority is required by law to provide efficient and suitable education for children in its area but this obligation is not met by the simple provision of premises, resources and teachers. The conduct of the school, in the widest sense, and the curriculum which it provides and delivers has also to be controlled. Much of this control is delegated to the headteacher. It is not uncommon, however, for chief education officers to state that they have the ultimate responsibility for the control of the schools within their LEA. <u>The Instruments and Articles of Government</u> of ILEA schools includes the following statement:

> The Authority shall determine the general educational character of the school and its place in the education system. Subject thereto, the governors shall, in consultation with the headteacher, exercise the oversight of the conduct and curriculum of the school. (Report of the Committee on Primary Education, chaired by Norman Thomas, January 1985, <u>Improving Primary Schools</u>, p. 21, para. 3.23.)

The same <u>Instruments and Articles</u> go on to clarify the position a little by stating that:

> ...the headteacher shall control the conduct and curriculum, the internal organisation, management and discipline of the school, the choice of equipment, books and other resources, the methods of teaching and the general arrangements of teaching groups..., (quoted in <u>Improving Primary Schools</u>, para. 3.23).

Paisey (1981) identifies similar examples of the legal and administrative framework on which the authority of the headteacher rests. One LEA makes headteachers "professionally responsible" while another vests in the headteacher the responsibility for "the general direction of the conduct and the curriculum of the school", (Paisey, 1981, p. 104). The NUT makes its position clear:

> The head of the school, under the articles of government or rules of management is responsible for internal organisation, management and discipline, and by virtue of his or her position, controls the teaching and non-teaching staff, (NUT 1982 quoted in Winkley, 1984, p. 206).

These statements indicate the nature of the managerial, educational and professional responsibilities which the headteacher carries. They say little about how these duties are to be carried out or about the extent to which others may expect to share with the headteacher the burden of ensuring that the school meets the implied requirements of such instruments and articles. Certainly members of the governing body of the school have a role to play. This role will increase as the terms of the 1986 Education Act are implemented. The same Act will also change the nature of parental involvement in many aspects of the life of the school. We have seen in Chapter One how the changing professional expectations and definitions of good practice are slowly creating situations in many schools in which the role of the primary school teacher is, itself, being subjected to changing expectations. Such formal indications of the nature and scope of those responsibilities which combine to limit the role of the primary school headteacher do not, therefore, give anything like the whole picture of the role of the head since they convey a misleading impression of certainty and clarity which, in practice, is only an illusion of the reality. Nevertheless the primary headteacher does have extensive scope within her school for:

> ...planning a suitable curriculum, establishing the organisation to implement it and a system for evaluating what is taught, (DES 1982, para. 3.I).

The same paragraph goes on to remind the headteacher that it is also incumbent upon her to establish and maintain good communications and relationships with parents, the local community, the LEA, and the head-teachers and staff of other schools.

This formal description of the headteacher's role and related responsibilities embodies the assumption that headteachers have both the skills necssary to meet the demands which are being placed upon them and the authority to ensure that appropriate decisions are taken, implemented and evaluated. Thus the legal or formal foundation of a headteacher's position in the school leads to a set of assumptions about the functional capability of the same headteacher. The role of the headteacher is outlined in Instruments and Articles of Government but it is through interaction with colleagues that the actual role takes shape. It is the professional skills of the individual head which enable her to carry out her duties effectively. In schools it is this functional authority vested in demonstrated competence and ability which is likely to enable the headteacher to meet the legal requirements which Instruments and Articles identify and to meet the expectations established through contact with her staff. Similarly it will be that same demonstration of competence which is likely to be most influential in determining the extent to which other colleagues are able to establish leadership positions within the school based on their own specialist knowledge and expertise.

To suggest that the authority of the primary headteacher is, at least in part, functional is to argue that the role of the headteacher is no longer that of the paternal/maternal figure whose influence over the school depended largely on personal control and a form of moral authority which Coulson identified (Coulson, 1976). The clear assumption which underpins the trends discussed in Chapter One is that the headteacher can no longer claim that this is "my" school. The school has become, or is in the process of becoming, "our" school. The possessive pronoun is now widening to include more than just the staff and pupils of any given school. The argument about how and why this change is taking place is beyond the scope of this particular volume except to the extent that such trends influence the management of primary schools. One significant way in which this trend is influencing primary school management is in its effect on the role of the head and on the ways in which that role is perceived by incumbents and colleagues alike. Coulson himself foreshadowed just such a development when he asked of the primary headteacher:

> ...can he alone function competently [in] ...teacher-training, management, and administration, moral and social values, social work and counselling, home-school relations, curriculum development and so on? (Coulson, 1976, p. 103).

Just how headteachers seek to carry their onerous duties has been the subject of some discussion. This discussion has produced some graphic labels which can be attached to the behaviour of headteachers. Waters (1979) uses terms such as autocratic leader, benevolent despot, and democratic leader. Lloyd (1985) regales us with a typology of headship which includes descriptions of primary headteachers as nominal, coercive, paternal, familiar and passive, while Nias (1980) discusses the attributes of passive, positive and bourbon approaches to primary headship. Pivotal though the position of the headteacher undoubtedly is in the primary school, it is possible that descriptions such as these may soon lead the head into just that situation against which Waters warns us:

> It is important for the headteacher of a smaller school not to engage in a make-believe kind of management in a situation which isn´t big enough to carry the weight of such complex proportions, (Waters, 1979 p. 117).

A description of typologies does not necessarily enable us to identify the key components of the task in hand. What does become clear from such typologies, as well as from the formal descriptions of the headteacher´s role, is that the responsibilities of the head are extensive. They include decisions about the aims and purposes of the school; about the allocation and distribution of resources; about the discipline and conduct of those within the school; about the evaluation and monitoring of the progress and development of those within the school; and the decisions about the control and flow of information into and within the school as well as other boundary related activities. Thus the headteacher, while no longer necessarily the premier professional in all spheres of school activity, is certainly a professional responsible to and for professionals. The general responsibility for the learning of pupils; for the curriculum, its content and the ways in which it is taught; and for the success or otherwise of this teaching and learning and how it is monitored and evaluated are just some of the areas where this professional guidance has to be exercised. This involves the headteacher in a leadership function within the school. It is almost self evident that professional leadership is part of this function but broader aspects of team leadership are also important. These will be discussed in Chapter Six. Finally there is a management element to the headteacher's role. As Waters has reminded us:

> Leadership without managerial skills can be both pointless and ineffectual, and do little for staff. (Waters, 1979, p.21)

Thus the role of the head in relation to those educational processes that take place within primary schools is a dynamic fusion of professionalism, leadership and management. Such a fusion is also to be found in other roles within the primary school to a greater or lesser extent. In the position of headteacher, however, is vested the major, and the legal, responsibility for ensuring the success of the educational enterprise within her institution.

The Primary Headteacher as Manager

Our consideration of the legal foundations upon which the role of the primary headteacher has been developed highlights the formal requirement for the head to control, and be responsible for, the organisation of teaching and learning within the school. Such concerns are no longer the sole province of the headteacher, if they ever were. Others within the school have legitimate claims to influence the direction in which the school may choose to move. It is to the headteacher, however, that the ultimate responsibility falls for the managing of those processes which will enable the school to become and remain what those within it wish it to be. It is the responsibility of the headteacher, in conjunction with her senior colleagues:

> ...to see that things really do get done and to ensure that staff co-ordinate their activities towards the achievement of clearly defined aims and objectives, (Maund, Pountney, Scrivener and Ward, 1982, p. 29).

In Chapter One it was argued that a family of activities could be identified which would help us to understand what the processes of management entailed. We sought to link the fundamental skills of Fayol´s scientific management approach with the creative art of management as espoused by Drucker. Hughes (1985) seeks to simplify and unify these approaches in a three stage model of management in which the main components are:

<u>Planning</u> the identification of problems and the search for and selection of solutions

<u>Organising</u> the processes of implementation including communicating, delegating, consulting and co-ordinating

<u>Controlling</u> the evaluation of the management process and effecting change.

The dominant element in the first part of the process is the need to cope with uncertainty. In the second it is the need to ensure that the processes are carried out effectively even in the relatively small but complex world of the primary school. In the third stage the emphasis moves to the careful and systematic collection of appropriate data on which to base judgements. These factors will all be dealt with in some detail in subsequent chapters within a context identified for us by Griffiths (1979) who reminds us that all interactions within organisations, especially those concerned with management, produce strategies and decisions which are the result of a complex interplay between the expectations and perceived capabilities of individuals and the demands and constraints created by the organisation. This is as true in small schools as it is in large industrial enterprises although, perhaps, in schools we tend not to pay sufficient attention to the inter-relationships between individuals and the context within which they operate as professional colleagues.

This area of interaction, the uncertainty which is typical of it, and the need for negotiation based on both professional and interpersonal skills, has been explored by Campbell (1985) with particular reference to the work of primary school postholders. He argues that knowledge of subject area combined with professional skills and judgement (curriculum skills) together with social skills and the ability to represent his or her subject to outsiders such as advisers (interpersonal skills) are used by postholders in a variety of school situations (Campbell,

1985, p. 53). He recognises that uncertainty is almost inherent in a postholder's position. This may result from ambiguities in the postholder's relationships with class teachers; conflicts over priorities; or from the strains involved in simply being a postholder and carrying out the postholder's responsibilities (Campbell, 1985, p. 68). These same characteristics of primary school organisation which create uncertainty for the postholder may have a similar effect on headteachers who are also called upon both to provide professional leadership and exercise managerial skills.

The spectrum of managerial skills is broader, perhaps, than Campbell or, indeed, Hughes (1985) leads us to expect. Hughes' model tends to concentrate on the planning and implementing of change. This is, as we argued in Chapter One, a significant part of the management of primary schools but it is not the totality of it. Campbell's five fold typology gives a fuller picture of managerial activity. An extension of both can enable us to arrive at a descriptive list of those areas of management activity which form a constellation of skills which are regularly employed as a significant part of the process of managing primary schools. Table 4 provides us with a starting point for just such a list. What emerges from this is the recognition that management of primary schools means more for those involved with it, especially the primary school headteacher, than the simple process of carrying out routine or prescribed tasks in a routine or prescribed way.

Alexander (1984) has warned us, however, of the dangers inherent in too ready an acceptance of models of school management which are mongrel in the sense that they derive their basic premises from industrial rather than educational contexts (Alexander 1984). He categorises non-educational contexts as mechanistic in that they are hierarchical and closed, and that information about performance is passed upwards while instructions and decisions are passed downwards; or they exist in unstable conditions and, therefore, they are organismic in the sense that they demand extreme role flexibility, shared decision-making, omnidirectional communication and an emphasis on all members having an overall view of the purposes of the organisation.

His models, derived from Burns and Stalker (1966) seem to exhibit some, but not necessarily all, of the characteristics of the contemporary primary school as it emerged in our discussion of it

Table 4 THE SKILLS OF MANAGEMENT

advise - to give counsel, to give information

administer - to carry out routine work

analyse - to separate into elements so as to determine their nature, proportion, function

approve - to sanction, to endorse, to express a favourable opinion of

appraise - critically and constructively to discuss professional performance

assess - to form judgements about...based on appropriate evidence

assist - to give help

authorise - to give official approval

change - to introduce a new element into a situation

communicate - to share information

compile - to put together in an orderly form

consult - to seek the opinion of others

co-ordinate - to bring sets of activities into proper order

decide - to form a definite choice between alternatives

delegate - to hand over responsibility to a person acting as one´s representative

develop - to extend and to provide opportunities for staff

evaluate - to judge or determine the worth or quality of

examine - to look at or into critically or methodically in order to determine the facts

implement - to carry into effect

innovate - to change in a deliberate and planned way

initiate - to introduce or start

interpret - to explain the meaning of

monitor - to check for a particular purpose

organise - to arrange into unified and coherent relationships

participate - to share in common with others

plan - to search for problems and identify structured and orderly solutions

praise - to emphasise an individual´s worth or value

recommend - to set forward as advisable

resource - to make adequate provision for

selection - choosing appropriate staff for identified positions

support - to provide for, to help, to encourage

in the first chapter. The approach to management derived from the trends identified in that chapter does seek to foster what Alexander terms "potential consequences" (Alexander, 1984, p. 205). He identifies these as a welcome emphasis on curriculum planning and evaluation; the enhancement of teachers' intellectual autonomy; the promotion of collective discourse on educational matters; the achievement of a higher level of cultural and social awareness; and the generation of a coherent whole curriculum. Nevertheless it is necessary for us to be aware of the dangers of over-bureaucratisation, superficiality in approach, and rigidity in the definitions which are ascribed to desired outcomes from the educational process. (Alexander, 1984, pp. 205-6).

Management for the primary headteacher should not, however, be conceived of as:

> something heads (or potential heads) do to other people. To manage a school is to define, determine and evaluate the lives of the children within it.
> (Alexander, 1984, p. 208)

Management in the context of the primary school involves consulting and involving colleagues in decisions on the basis of their skills and experience. It involves recognising their contributions as professionals and ensuring that they are enabled to make those contributions. Thus the processes involved in the management of the primary school are the concern of all the staff who work within it. The headteacher, by the legal requirements placed upon her, does have certain clear responsibilities. She has to be accountable for the school as a whole. She has to have a clear view about what she wants the school to be like and to cause this to happen through the collective activities of her colleagues. She has to exercise responsible stewardship over resources, their allocation and use. She has to promote effective and appropriate teaching and learning as well as encouraging the search for continual improvement. No headteacher can carry this burden alone. Every headteacher requires the willing co-operation of her colleagues in achieving these tasks. The staff of each and every school has to create its own working arrangements both individually and collectively if the school is to provide the most appropriate education for its children. This is the responsibility which the primary headteacher and her colleagues share. This is not a top down process. Nor is it the domain of the headteacher alone. She has to work with her staff to achieve common objectives. They have to work with her as well as with each other. Management of the primary school, if it is to be done successfully, involves co-operation and team work at all levels. Management is not a dictatorial imposition in the primary school. It has to be a celebration of collaboration between professional colleagues.

Leadership in the Primary School

In order to examine some of the ways in which this process of collaboration between professional colleagues can be fostered it is necessary to explore two further aspects of primary school management. The first of these is the nature of leadership and how appropriate forms of leadership might be identified within an organisation which is seeking to operate in a collegial way. The second, which will be considered in the next section, is the particular problems and opportunities which are presented to those responsible for leading and managing groups of teachers who claim the right to be regarded as professionals and who, therefore, may have established educational practices within their schools which are predicated on the notion of professional autonomy. These two aspects of primary school management are closely related. An individual teacher's approach to either or both of them will, in part, depend on her attitude towards, and understanding of, processes of management.

Management in the primary school context has been broadly defined in the preceding section as the application of a specific group of skills, in conjunction with professional colleagues, in order to achieve a set of common objectives. It is recognised, however, that these objectives may not be clearly and articulately stated although implicit in this approach to primary school management is the belief that this should be the case. What then, do we understand by leadership? What kind of leadership might Ann Welton at Rosemary Lane Primary School be expected to exhibit? What kind of leadership behaviour might she reasonably expect from other members of her staff such as Tom Jowett, her deputy, Norma Cass with her responsibility for the three infant classes, or Victor Johns with his interest in CDT? Each of them in his or her own way has to come to understand the various management processes which may be used in their school and to apply this understanding to their work with groups of colleagues. The relationship between management and leadership is a complex one since it is not always possible in a primary school to make a clear distinction between the communicating, coordinating, planning, evaluating and related activities of management and the emphasis on working with, supporting, developing and encouraging staff which is the province of leadership.

Leadership is more than the simple application of management functions, many of which may have to do with administration and the maintenance of the school. Effective management requires successful leadership since, as was argued in Chapter One and illustrated in Chapter Two, primary schools are having to embrace change rather than stability and, therefore, they are required increasingly to adapt to new circumstances rather than being able to rely on what has gone before. Perhaps, therefore, the style of leadership employed by those whom Coulson (1980) identified as having an 'ego identification' with the school, which resulted in them regarding it as their own property towards which they and they alone exercised a deep sense of responsibility for everyone in it and everything which happened within it, is no longer appropriate. Such people may or may not have been born leaders. They would certainly have claimed the right to leadership through their status position in their schools. Such a form of leadership tends to become ascribed rather than achieved in that its main features seem to be vested in one powerful individual within the school. It is verging on what Paisey (1984) has called congenital leadership: that is leaders who are born rather than fashioned by environment. He also identifies situational leadership which, he argues, focuses on the relative nature of leadership and the extent to which opportunities for leadership are created by specific situations; and management leadership which he suggests is leadership based on holding a particular office such as headteacher. We have described this aspect of school management as the formal definition of the various roles within the school, especially that of the headteacher. This has been presented as a part, and only a part, of management. Opportunities for leadership may be presented to an individual by virtue of her position in the school but holding a particular office provides no guarantee that leadership behaviour will be forthcoming from the incumbent although the expectation is that this will be the case. At its most basic level, therefore, leadership may be understood as attempting to make existing structures within the school work well.

Whitaker's definition of leadership is somewhat more specific. He sees it as:

> ...the influencing of group activity in determining what needs to be done, how it is done, and if it has been successful.
> (Whitaker, 1983, p. 28)

Thus, in Whitaker's view, leadership is concerned with giving purpose and direction to group activity. It is about setting goals, determining how to achieve them and checking that they have been achieved. It might also be thought to be about setting, or helping to set, priorities both in terms of what needs to be done and how resources are allocated to different activities. This approach to leadership has been used as the basis for Management in the Primary School, (Maund, et. al., 1982), a document produced as a follow-up to a series of management courses for primary school postholders and senior managers in Coventry. It is argued that:

> At scale 2/3 level the tendency has been to concentrate on the subject expertise of the postholder; now the emphasis needs to be much more on LEADERSHIP skills...A first stage in the development of leadership skills might be the analysis of the job to be done...Such an analysis should be seen not only in terms of the jobs to be done (KEY TASKS) but also of:
> a) ways to do them (IMPLEMENTATION)
> b) ways of testing their impact (EVALUATION).
> (Maund, et.al., 1982, p. 6)

The processes of analysing the job to be done will be examined further in the next chapter in the context of producing job descriptions. Implementation and evaluation are dealt with in subsequent chapters. The inclusion of these elements in our perceptions of leadership, however, helps us to recognise that leadership is not a quality vested in a special individual. Rather leadership activity is a combination of a concern for the tasks of the school, how they are identified, implemented and evaluated, and a concern for the group of people involved in those processes.

These two related concerns, the concern for the tasks of the organisation and the concern for people, form the basis of many studies of leadership. In most studies concern for people refers to the establishing of warm relationships between people within the organisation while the concern for task refers to the successful accomplishment of whatever the organisational tasks might be from time to time. People in leadership positions will differ in the extent to which they emphasise each of these concerns. Blake and Mouton (1985) have devised a leadership grid which seeks to categorise how such differences in emphasis might produce different types of leadership behaviour, (see Table 5). They suggest that the most commonly adopted leadership style is the Balanced one which they regard as being the result of a compromise between achieving tasks and maintaining good relationships. The leadership style which they see as the most desirable is the integrated one in which there is a high concern for the tasks of the organisation as well as a similarly high concern for the relationships between the people within it. Blake and Mouton suggest that the integrated style, unlike the other styles which they identify, contains no inherent conflict between the needs of the individuals and those of the organisation. This is the position towards which the development of collegiality in primary schools appears to be trying to take us, since a collegiate approach presupposes that all the staff are accountable for the responsibilities which they all will have.

The integrated style identified by Blake and Mouton shares much in common with the positive leadership style identified by Nias in her work with primary school teachers. This type of leader:

> Sets a high professional standard; has a high level of personal involvement in the school
>
> Is readily available, especially for discussion; is interested in individual teacher development
>
> Gives a lead in establishing aims for the school; encourages participation in goal-setting and decision-making
>
> (after Nias, 1980, p. 260)

Table 5 STYLES OF LEADERSHIP (THE MANAGERIAL GRID®)

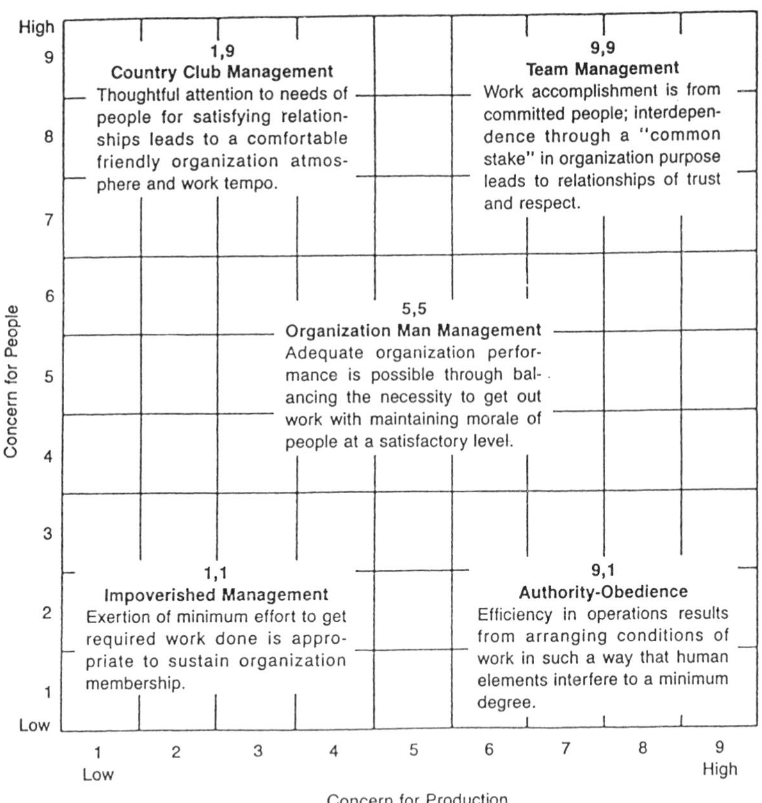

Source: Blake, Robert R., and Mouton, Jane Srygley. The Managerial Grid III: The Key to Leadership Excellence, Houston, Gulf Publishing Company, Copyright c 1985, page 12. Reproduced with permission.

This broad description of the elements of a leadership style still leaves significant scope for different forms of actual behaviour even within the framework of positive leadership. In any given circumstances a leader might:

- o assert her own centrality by taking and announcing decisions
- o involve the group by explaining decisions
- o give the group power by encouraging it to select from a range of options
- o develop group power by encouraging it to suggest solutions
- o submit to group power by devolving decision-making to the group on certain issues within identified parameters
- o act as one of the group where the group defines its own authority over particular issues.

(Derived from Tannenbaum and Schmidt 1958)

A number of factors may influence the choices which a leader may make: the extent to which she feels that it is appropriate that her colleagues ought to be involved in the particular decision, her own self-confidence and her confidence in her colleagues, and her personal inclinations, since some people feel happier when working as members of a group while others feel more comfortable taking responsibility alone. All of these factors will influence how a leader chooses to lead. Her judgement might also be affected by her colleagues. For example she may know that her colleagues prefer to be involved in taking certain decisions or even that they expect to be included in the taking of some decisions. A wise leader will not ignore this. Similarly her colleagues may have significant relevant expertise which demands that they should be involved in some aspect of the school's work. The leader may also be influenced by the specific situation. If it requires a rapid response then involving colleagues may prove difficult. If it requires detailed specialist knowledge then certain colleagues may need to be involved but not others. A decision may have a far reaching impact on the work of some members of the staff. Perhaps they should be involved in the discussions about that decision even if they do not help to make the final choice or determine the preferred solution.

Leadership style, then, is a product of the interaction between a number of factors. Concern for defining and achieving tasks; concern for the inter-personal relationships within the group; choices about appropriate methods of involving colleagues in the work of the group are all part of leadership behaviour. John Adair (1983), in his work on effective leadership, subsumes these points under the headings of:

- o achieving the task
- o building and maintaining the staff team.

His third element of leadership behaviour is one concerned with:

- o developing each individual.

He expresses these in terms of three overlapping circles which indicate that any single element of leadership behaviour can and will combine with any other single element but leadership within any group will only be really effective if all three elements receive sufficient attention. For example the failure to build the team in a primary school successfully can easily result in failure to achieve those tasks which have been identified as important to that school. Similarly, if the development of individuals is entirely sacrificed for the building of a team and the achievement of its tasks, then individual members may soon become disillusioned and de-motivated. As a result tasks will not be achieved and the team will cease to be effective. Therefore the successful leader takes action to:

Achieve
The Task

Build
The Team

Develop
Individuals

Thus it can be argued that the key elements in leadership are the integration of individual, team and school goals. Strategies for achieving this will be discussed in some detail in Chapter Seven. It is clear, however, that this approach requires the leader to understand what motivates her colleagues. She also has to be able to help the team to identify and achieve its goals. She may, as primary schools become more collegial, need to operate through processes of consultation and participation and she will need to maximise the individual´s opportunities as well as her responsibilities for the attainment of the team's goals. Thus, such an approach to leadership requires that the staff of the primary school are involved in the total running of the school. It also requires that headteachers like Ann Welton treat her staff as professional colleagues or, at the very least, seek to develop situations in which they can respond as professional colleagues. It also necessitates that the staff of the school see themselves as professionals, accepting their part of the responsibility for the tasks, the team and the individuals within it.

Managing and Leading Professional Teachers

Most teachers working in primary schools regard themselves, and wish to be regarded by others, as professionals. This has implications for the ways in which schools are managed and for the ways in which groups of teachers work together with leaders. Handy (1984) has suggested that in organisations such as schools which are staffed by professionals, the professionals like to manage themselves. Indeed our commonly accepted notion of what professionalism means contains within it the idea of autonomous groups who exercise control over their own actions on behalf of others, normally their clients. Writers such as Leiberman (1956), Millerson (1964) and Hoyle (1974) have identified a number of characteristics which might be used to identify a profession. These include:

- a body of knowledge on which practices are based
- a lengthy period of training during which knowledge and skills are acquired
- a concern with the welfare of the client
- a high degree of autonomy
- a code of ethics governing professional relationships

How far those occupational groups which are generally regarded as professions actually exhibit any or all of these characteristics is not particularly significant in the context of our discussion of managing professionals in the primary school.

What is important is the extent to which such characteristics shape the expectations of teachers, parents and pupils within the school. It is clear that teachers do undergo training and, in many cases, in-service training. They do have a commitment to their pupils and they do expect to retain a high degree of control over what they do in their classrooms based on this training and this commitment. Such claims to professional autonomy have been described as 'a new despotism' (Musgrove and Taylor, 1969).

It has even been argued that because professionals are self-directed they do not need to be managed. This position is based on the view that either all decisions are group decisions or, alternatively, any decision taken by one professional will be very much like that taken by another (Rust, 1985). This is an extremely simplistic view of professionalism and professionals. Primary schools, even those staffed by the most highly committed and sophisticated professional teachers, are unlikely to exhibit such unity and accord on all matters. Furthermore teachers are often struggling to cope with the pedagogic demands which are made upon them and may not always have the time to devote to management activities even in the most collegial primary school, a point recognised by the *Report of the House of Commons Select Committee on Primary Education*. Thus management of professional people and leadership of professional groups is vitally necessary. Management and leadership tend to mediate between the needs and expectations of the teachers, those of their pupils, and those identified as part of the primary school within which they work. It is the function of the managers in the school and the leaders of groups of teachers to help to break down the physical and social separation which results from the way in which much of a teacher's work is structured. A well-managed school in which professional colleagues share the responsibilities associated with the work of the school and in which different individuals take the lead in different areas of school life, depending on their expertise, can move a significant way towards minimising the professional isolation that some primary school teachers experience.

Professional autonomy or, in Coulson's (1976) words, 'professional independence' is not easily compatible with collegiality which requires a commitment to sharing expertise and to benefiting from the expertise of others. Those primary school teachers who work in situations where teams of teachers share expertise within the framework of a well structured primary school organisation are not likely to be professionally independent. They are more likely to exhibit professional interdependence. This requires that they are treated as professionals by the headteacher and her senior colleagues. It also requires that they act as professionals who

Table 6 RESTRICTED AND EXTENDED MODELS OF PROFESSIONALITY

Restricted professionality	Extended professionality
Skills derived from experience	Skills derived from a mediation between experience and theory
Perspective limited to the immediate in time and place	Perspective embracing the broader social context of education
Classroom events perceived in isolation	Classroom event perceived in relation to school policies and goals
Introspective with regard to methods	Methods compared with those of colleagues and with reports of practice
Value placed on autonomy	Value placed on professional collaboration
Limited involvement in non-teaching professional activities	High involvement in non-teaching professional activities (esp. teachers' centres, subject associations, research)
Infrequent reading of professional literature	Regular reading of professional literature
Involvement in in-service work limited and confined to practical courses	Involvement in in-service work considerable and includes courses of a theoretical nature
Teaching seen as an intuitive activity	Teaching seen as a rational activity

From Hoyle and McCormick (1976) p. 75.

have a concern for the whole school rather than for their own classroom alone. Thus they become extended rather than restricted professionals. While recognising that the essential professional activity of a teacher is her transactions with her pupils Hoyle and McCormick (1976) suggest that the approach of the teacher to this transaction can be based on one of two professional perspectives. A perspective which is firmly rooted in the classroom skills of the individual teacher is not likely to help or encourage that teacher to play a full part in the development of whole school policies or enable her to use her special expertise in giving a strong lead to her colleagues in planning and implementing a programme of work effectively, thus influencing their work and that of the pupils throughout the school. Alternatively professionality which is not limited to classroom skills alone but embraces a wider knowledge and broader approach to educational matters is more likely to provide a sound basis upon which to build a wider contribution to the work of the primary school.

Thus the exercise of headship in the primary school has to take into account the professional orientations of the teachers within the school. Professional teachers have to be managed in such a way as to recognise their claims to professional status while, at the same time, not allowing claims for independence to prevent the development of whole school policies which are founded on interdependence within a group of professional colleagues. If this is true for headteachers then it is equally true for those with other responsibilities within the school. Deputy headteachers, year leaders and teachers with curriculum or other responsibilities all have to understand the importance of professional interdependence and how to achieve it. This requires a knowledge of those specific skills which form our broad definition of management. It also requires the ability to apply those skills in order to achieve the tasks of the group, whether the group be the whole school or a small part of it. The achieving of tasks has to be done at the same time as team building and the developing of individuals within the team. In this way management and leadership of a group of professional colleagues can begin to be effective. Much depends, however, on the expectations which individuals have when they enter the school. For teachers this normally means when they were appointed. Selection and appointment procedures are, in many cases, the starting point of creating an ethos within which groups of professional primary school teachers can cooperate for the benefit of the whole school.

Activities

1. Examine the formal description of the role of the headteacher in the Instruments and Articles of Government. How far does it cover all the key responsibilities of the headteacher?

2. List the expectations held by your staff of their headteacher. What strategies can you suggest for meeting those expectations?

3. Identify ways in which headteachers can provide leadership in a professional group.

Chapter 4

PROFILES, DESCRIPTIONS AND SPECIFICATIONS IN THE PRIMARY SCHOOL

We have seen in the previous chapter that the management and leadership of professional staff in the primary school is a complex matter. Headteachers and others with management responsibilities have to provide a framework within which the tasks of the school can be understood and defined. A range of management skills have to be deployed in order to ensure that these tasks are completed although, given the ever-changing nature of education, perhaps completed is the wrong word. The tasks which face schools have to be addressed in a variety of ways yet it has to be recognised that these tasks are, themselves, subject to review and redefinition over time. The monitoring and evaluation which is necessary in order that this might be done is discussed in a subsequent chapter. This chapter is concerned with the processes of identifying the range of activities which might be found in the primary school. It suggests that a school profile can help with this process. Looking at what is expected of the school is only one part of the picture, however. Examining the capabilities and interests of the staff, perhaps by producing job descriptions, will be considered as an integral part of this process. When the time comes to appoint a new colleague then a person specification might also be useful. We consider the appropriate stages in the selection and appointing of staff within the context of the school profile and the range of available skills and abilities to be found among the existing staff of the school in the next chapter. The main thrust of the argument in this chapter is that effective school management can enable us to make the best use of staff in primary schools provided that it is clear to all colleagues where the school is going and what part they have to play in helping the school to move in that direction. Such understanding comes, in part, from teachers knowing their own individual responsibilities and the expectations attached to them. It may also come from being aware of the roles played by colleagues. As Poster (1976) reminds us, an outsider would scarcely believe how often teachers in a school disclaim all knowledge of what colleagues are doing or of what they might reasonably be expected to do. This lack of knowledge is frequently presented as a virtue. It may, however, lead to isolation and parochialism which can make work in schools extremely difficult, especially when much of that work can best be done on a team basis. In Rosemary Lane, for example, how much more useful to the school might Jaswinder Gill be if her colleagues had a clearer view of her responsibilities. How far do Ann Welton's plans for the future of the school depend on enabling her colleagues to share and develop further the expertise which they undoubtedly have? How can a climate be created in which this understanding and knowledge is made more readily available to all the members of the Rosemary Lane staff? One way forward might be to begin with a school profile.

The School Profile

The school profile is a technique for identifying what the school is doing at the present time and what else it might still need to do. It helps us to see how tasks and responsibilities are allocated and to consider how appropriate is the current deployment of staff. It can help to clarify who is responsible for what, as well as giving an indication of those areas of responsibility which are not being covered. This does not imply that primary schools need to be rigidly organised or that the demarcations between colleagues have to be inflexible since, in primary school teaching, there will inevitably be many areas where responsibilities and duties overlap. A school profile should gather information about the total work of the school. A thorough analysis will specify the unique characteristics which differentiate the work of one teacher from another. This will eventually provide a clear picture of all of those activities which go to make up the work of any school. It should be remembered that the school's environment is dynamic and, therefore, the school must always be changing in order to adapt itself to its environment. One of the major features of the British education system over the past three decades has been its changing nature. We cannot, therefore, sit down on a given day and complete a profile for a school and say "That is that." Profiling is a continuous process. The manager in the primary school must be constantly looking to see how the work of her school needs to be monitored and subsequently changed in order to meet changing needs and demands. A rigorous approach to compiling the school profile which, admittedly, is a time consuming process in the first instance, can be invaluable here.

The full importance of the school profile becomes clear when it is realised that such an analysis will produce information which will not only enable every teacher to know exactly what is expected of her in the performance of teaching duties. It will also clarify the relationship between roles, thus avoiding gaps in responsibility, and help teachers at all levels to acquire a greater understanding of their posts by an analysis of what is involved in them. This can then provide a framework within which key objectives can be set, targets identified and the deployment of staff considered. For individual teachers within the organisation the existence of "non-jobs" may be revealed in which the incumbent has little or nothing to do since other roles overlap incessantly with hers, or in which the incumbent has insufficient authority to carry out the necessary duties and responsibilities. We may define a duty as what a teacher is required to do personally and a responsibility as something which may be done personally or by others but for which the teacher concerned is ultimately accountable. Thus the profile may be valuable in revealing areas in which frustration and irritation exist as a result of "non-jobs", and revealing confusions about duties or responsibilities. The information which makes up the total profile and the information which it reveals may be no more than that which ought to be available to all colleagues within the school. We are suggesting that such information is not collected randomly, hapazardly or irregularly and in an impressionistic or vague form. It should be the result of a systematic process of collecting and recording. Some possible techniques are outlined in Table 7. They combine an analysis of the written evidence concerning what the school is doing with observational and interview evidence which may be more impressionistic. It is important that the whole staff should be involved in this process and that it should be carried out in an open and

Table 7 TECHNIQUES FOR PRODUCING A SCHOOL PROFILE
1. Building up a picture of the work from previous profiles, job descriptions, timetables, schemes of work, teachers´ records, curriculum documents and other written evidence
2. Observations of the teacher in a variety of different settings within the school over a period of time
3. Interviewing the teacher about all aspects of his or her work in the school
4. Structured or open-ended questionnaires given to the teacher, subject co-ordinator, headteacher or other relevant people
5. Self recording of activities in the form of a structured diary but taking into account the different demands at different times
6. Some form of audio or visual recording of a range of teaching and committee work

positive way.

There are three component parts to a full school profile. The first is a profile of the individual members of staff; the second is an analysis of the school itself; the third is an identification of possible areas for future development. The profiles of individual members of staff are related to their job descriptions but provide more useful information and can be used as a basis for constructing or, by negotiation, modifying job descriptions. The profile contains no evaluative or judgemental content. Rather it is a statement of qualifications, activities and interests. As such it is best compiled by the teacher herself although this might be done in conjunction with a colleague. The sections in Table 8 give an indication of what material might be included in such an individual profile although not every teacher will be involved in every aspect of the work indicated in that table.

The outcome of a complete set of profiles will be, at the very least, a clear indication of the division of responsibility within the school. The profiles may also reveal areas in which efforts are being duplicated and areas which are not being covered at all. In a general way the *individual profile* should provide a total picture of what a particular teaching position entails whatever the specifics of it might be. Care needs to be taken to distinguish between the vital components of a position and those aspects of it which are the product of the special interests of the present holder of the post. This information will tend to be either descriptive in the sense that it outlines what a teacher actually does, or personal in the sense that it lists qualifications, experience and interests. Methods 1 and 4 in Table 7 may be the quickest ways of collecting information from a group of teachers but those methods may be less reliable and accurate than other methods. Methods 2, 3 and 5 will take more time but may be more accurate. Method 1 is probably the least threatening of all since it concentrates on written documents while method 3 may be the most necessary in even a medium-sized primary school. Method 6 may be the most costly unless the appropriate equipment is available but it has the virtue of being very accurate and may be especially useful where teaching takes place in a fairly restricted area, around a forge or a kiln, in a small music room or other specialist area. For the most comprehensive form of individual profile, a selection of all the methods should be used with methods 3, 4 and 5 forming the basis of the analysis. The time and effort devoted to this should be determined by how it is to be used in the school.

A further development of the individual profile might be to relate the qualifications and experience part of the profile to the areas of learning and experience listed in *The Curriculum from 5 to 16; Curriculum Matters 2* (DES 1985d, p.16). These form the basis of Table 9. As can be seen from that table, the individual profile indicates in which areas the individual teacher has qualifications, experience or interest. It might also show whether she has a desire to gain some experience or qualifications in any particular area. This approach can then be useful in forward planning, curriculum development and staff development. As *Curriculum Matters 2* reminds us:

Table 8 INDIVIDUAL STAFF PROFILES

Role in the School
- Title and Position
- To whom responsible
- For whom responsible
- For what responsible
- Copy of personal timetable

Teaching Activities
- Subject expertise, age ranges taught and pastoral work undertaken
- Procedures used
- Resources and equipment used
- Record keeping and self-evaluation techniques

Responsibilities and Duties
- Planning activities
- Administration activities
- Staff development activities
- Curriculum and assessment activities

School Responsibilities
- School planning activities
- School administration activities
- School staff development activities
- Curriculum and assessment

Other Activities and Responsibilities
- Involvement with clubs and societies
- Visits, field trips, sporting events
- Courses attended, other professional activities
- LEA curriculum planning and development meetings

Qualifications
- Academic, professional, educational including initial training and further qualifications
- Experience
- Knowledge, skills and interests

> Schools need to examine existing practice to establish the extent to which particular topics, aspects and subjects are already contributing to these areas and to the development of knowledge, skills, and attitudes. They will then be in a position to decide on any changes and additions which may be required. (DES 1985d pp.16-17).

Table 9 A CURRICULUM RELATED STAFF PROFILE

	Qualifications Initial	Qualifications INSET	Experience	Interest	Future Interest
Aesthetic and Creative			✓		
Human & Social		✓	✓		✓
Linguistic and literary			✓	✓	
Mathematical	✓		✓		
Moral				✓	
Physical					
Scientific				✓	
Technological					✓
Spiritual				✓	

The above table is one way of relating what the staff do to the curriculum as it might be. An approach based on the national curriculum subject areas would achieve a similar effect. The ticks on Table 9 show where entries might go for Mr Jowett, the deputy headteacher at Rosemary Lane. His initial training subject was mathematics, an area which he subsequently followed up by holding a post of responsibility before he became a deputy. He is interested in the environmental studies aspects of primary school science and uses this interest in the preparation and teaching of his topic work. His approach to both history and geography as integral parts of the projects he plans also reflect this interest. Like most primary school teachers he has an interest in and experience of language development and literacy. He feels that he would like to know more about the newly emerging technological aspects of the curriculum and he has recently developed an interest in multicultural education. By using ticks here it is not possible to convey any indication of type of training, nature of qualification or length and nature of experience. It is not clear which age groups he has taught nor is it clear what other areas of responsibility he holds or has held. Table 9 could be modified in order to include such details by providing space to write them in and by providing a separate section for other responsibilities.

A similar approach could be adopted to the profile of the school. It might start with a form which lists the nine curriculum areas across the top and the names of the staff down the left side. If sufficient space is provided it will then be possible to show, by subdividing each of the nine sections, which colleagues are qualified in particular areas, which have experience of them, which have an interest in them and which are interested in developing skills in particular areas. This approach can also be adapted to include further curriculum areas which might be of direct concern to the school or the LEA. In some schools it may be thought appropriate to include other areas of school activity such as assessment, record keeping or staff development. By collecting this information it is possible to build up a picture of what a school is doing across the broad spectrum of its activities. This may reveal what is not being done or what is being duplicated. It may lead the staff of a school to focus directly on how well certain areas of experience are taught in the school. Colleagues can explore exactly how far the school provides a curriculum incorporating the areas of experience and how well this curriculum meets the criteria of breadth, balance, relevance and differentiation that are identified in *Curriculum Matters 2* (DES, 1985d). A method of recording this data is to be found in Table 10. It must be remembered, however, that the process of recording the information is only a necessary prelude to its analysis and to the

Table 10 SCHOOL PROFILE

Section ONE	Areas of Experience	Aesthetic/ Creative						Human/ Social						Linguistic						Mathemat-ical						Moral/ Spiritual						Physical						Scientific/ Techno-logical					
NAME		Q	T	R	E	I	FI	Q	T	R	E	I	FI	Q	T	R	E	I	FI	Q	T	R	E	I	FI	Q	T	R	E	I	FI	Q	T	R	E	I	FI	Q	T	R	E	I	FI

Table 10 (cont´d)

Section TWO	Other Curriculum Areas	Multicultural Education						Special Educational Needs						Economic Awareness					
		Q	T	R	E	I	FI	Q	T	R	E	I	FI	Q	T	R	E	I	FI

Table 10 (Cont´d)

Section THREE	Other Areas	Staff Development						Assessment						Library						Relationship with Parents					
		Q	T	R	E	I	FI	Q	T	R	E	I	FI	Q	T	R	E	I	FI	Q	T	R	E	I	FI

key to columns: Q = Qualification T = INSET Training
R = Responsibility for E = Experience in
I = Interest in FI = Future Interest in

An approach similar to this can be found in the Wirral Education Department´s useful document Staff Training Profile and School Curriculum Expertise Profile: Primary Education.

professional debate about how well the school is doing which should follow.

Such a process of discussing the performance of the school in broad terms with reference to the curriculum and to other areas of school life leads naturally into the third aspect of the school profile. As a result of such professional discussions judgements can be made about the strength of the school and about how far it is providing an appropriate curriculum for its children, both in terms of the current documents on the curriculum and in relation to the particular situation of individual schools. It may be that some schools are not covering certain areas completely, or that insufficient curriculum planning has taken place in some of those subjects. This is certainly the case in Rosemary Lane where sparse attention seems to be paid to linguistic skills and where there is no coherent policy on mathematics or multicultural education. Science is not well developed as an integral part of the curriculum and CDT is rather limited in its horizons. In terms of balance and differentiation Rosemary Lane School has some way to go before the staff can feel satisfied with the curriculum that they are offering. It is a broad curriculum but it would be interesting to trace the experiences of individual children as they move through the school to see exactly what they encounter in their time at the school. These, then, are some of the areas which Ann Welton and her staff may wish to consider for the future development of their school.

As a result of discussions based on their school's profile the staff of Rosemary Lane can begin to formulate a <u>coherent plan for the development of their school</u>. A crucial part of this plan will be the existing qualifications, experience and interests of the staff themselves. The individual profiles provide the basis for knowing what these are. It can also be seen from those individual profiles where colleagues might like to develop an interest in the future. In this way the future development needs of the staff can be taken into account as the developmental plan for the school is formulated. It is perhaps too much to expect that the needs of the school will coincide exactly with the wishes of the staff in this matter. It is possible to see where the strengths and the gaps might be in what the school is able to provide and to begin to identify ways of filling those gaps. For example, Rosemary Lane urgently needs curriculum leadership in mathematics and multicultural education. Tom Jowett might be encouraged to provide this in one of those areas. There may be other areas in which no member of staff has expressed an interest. The headteacher then has to decide how this situation might best be dealt with. Does she encourage an existing colleague to develop an interest in, say, PE to replace Elaine Arnold? She may decide that Mrs Arnold's replacement should have an entirely different area of expertise, science perhaps? However situations such as these are resolved, the existence of a school profile does enable decisions to be taken on the basis of the best available evidence rather than on the basis of instinct and guesswork.

The school profile is the foundation upon which a coherent development plan for the school must rest. It enables the staff of the school to identify where changes need to be made and where the school needs to get better at doing what it does. It enables those with management responsibility in the school to examine what steps need to be taken in order to bring about that improvement as well as to consider the resource implications of that process, including the deployment of staff. The object of developing the school is to improve the work of the children and it is here that the evidence of the success or otherwise of the school's development must be sought. The means to bringing about this improvement will be, at least in part, the development of the staff of the school. The basis for that development is where the staff are now. The school and individual profiles, the analysis of the strengths and gaps in the provision which the school is making for its pupils, and the proposed future developments are all part of exploring the existing situation within the school.

Job Descriptions

A further crucial element in the deployment and development of staff in the primary school is the job description since this provides each teacher with a reference point for her own work in the school. Once the school profiles, the individual profiles and the planning for the future have been considered it is advisable to formalise the existing duties and responsibilities for each member of staff in the form of a job description. A job description can reinforce the process embarked upon by the school profile in that it leads to further clarification about who is responsible for what within the school. It should not, however, lead to a rigidity and inflexibility among the staff about how they carry out their professional activities. For all practical purposes, especially when appointing new members of staff, the process of writing a job description can best be understood in two distinct but related parts. These are, firstly, describing the duties and responsibilities attached to a post and, secondly, specifying the qualifications, experiences and abilities required to carry out those duties and responsibilities. The first part of this process is variously described as a job description, job specification or some other similar term whereas the second process is often also called a job specification. This inevitably creates a certain amount of confusion. To avoid this we propose to call the first process a job description and the second process a person specification. The job description therefore, is a description of the duties and responsibilities attached to a post, whilst the person specification is a description of those characteristics for which one would look in somebody fulfilling those duties.

There appears to be broad agreement about what a job description will contain. Everard suggests that it should include:

- Job title
- Brief description of the purpose of the job
- Reporting relationships
- Description of duties

(Everard, 1985, p. 68)

Lyons and Stenning argue that a job description should record the following facts about the job:

- Title of the job
- Indicate to whom the jobholder reports
- Indicate who reports to the jobholder
- The overall purpose of the job
- Each main function to be carried out by the jobholder

(Lyons and Stenning, 1986, p. 60)

Dean takes us one stage further when she suggests that the job description should also contain a detailed statement about responsibilities including how far the teacher is responsible for the work of other teachers, ancilliary staff, equipment, materials and other activities and facilities. (Dean, 1985). It is Goodworth, however who encapsulates the essence of a good job description when he states that it is a detailed description of WHAT is to be done (Goodworth, 1979).

What does not emerge from such lists of contents for job descriptions, however, is the extent to which the job description must be negotiated with the holder of the post and must match her expectations, especially at the staff selection stage. Nothing is more calculated to be a constant source of conflict and irritation than a significant mismatch between the job description and the teacher´s own expectations. The teacher who comes to a school like Rosemary Lane expecting to play a major part in the development and teaching of primary school science but who finds that this is not made possible by timetable constraints may, with some justification, become a thorn in the flesh of those who appointed her if the situation was not made clear on appointment. The same could be true of a teacher who is presented with a job description which bears only passing resemblance to what, in fact, she actually does, or which contains some significant changes to which agreement has not been given. Job descriptions should, therefore, be seen as the property of both the person in the managerial role and of the teachers concerned. The writing of the job desciption should, wherever possible, be based on the actual work which the teacher does and should be done in such a way as to enable that teacher to play a significant part in the process. The final job description should always be agreed with the teacher concerned and should only be changed by agreement on both sides. Thus Ann Welton at Rosemary Lane negotiated his job description with Tom Jowett, her deputy headteacher and together they agreed its content (see Table 11). Clearly the emphasis here is not upon circumscribing the job that Tom Jowett has, nor on limiting his professional freedom or fitting him unwillingly to a set of situations with which he is not familiar.

Taken together job descriptions and person specifications must enable structures in schools to be built on the strengths and interests of the staff. Posts should fit people and not the other way round. By basing the job description on the postholder´s present work, knowledge and skills, development and change is assumed and encouraged. The use of a job description in such a way as to leave little or no scope for new ideas and

Table 11 DEPUTY HEADTEACHER: ROSEMARY LANE COUNTY PRIMARY SCHOOL
Job description agreed between Mrs A. Welton, headteacher, and Mr Tom Jowett, deputy headteacher, for the forthcoming academic year Deputy headteacher: agreed special responsibilities
a. To be classteacher for the third year Junior class. He will be relieved by Mrs Welton for the equivalent of three hours a week in order to carry out his other duties
b. To act as head of the school in the absence of the headteacher
c. To carry out a variety of administrative duties on a rotational basis with other members of staff. These duties will include the ordering and distribution of stationery, the organisation of duty lists, membership of the PTA committee, displays of work in the entrance hall and "housekeeping" for the staffroom
d. To support and induct new members of staff, probationers and students working in the school
e. To foster the development of a multicultural curriculum for the whole school. This will involve attending appropriate in-service training, close liaison with the Section 11 teacher, chairing a staff working party, and the preparation of staff discussion documents. He will also prepare a draft Statement of Intent, and be able to identify positive measures being taken in the school in order to combat racism
f. To develop effective liaison with the appropriate staff at Willingham High School

initiatives, to inhibit staff development or to demand a rigid conformity would indicate an inflexible management style which may prove to be totally unacceptable in the current educational climate. Similarly the use of a job description by the postholder to define the limits of professional activity and involvement would indicate a similarly unhealthy and undesirable approach to education in general and to teaching in particular.

The good job description for schools should concentrate on the _what_ of teaching rather than on the _how_ although _how_ forms a vital part of job analysis and it has a significant place in the person specification. The _what_-based job description enables the head and the teacher concerned to know both what it is expected will be done and what it is agreed must be done. In focusing on the _what_ of a job description it is possible that the product might be similar to that in Table 11. This is clearly concerned with the _what_ of deputy headship. It has obviously been compiled by the process of listing all of the relevant tasks to be performed in that school by the deputy head. It does, however, contain some statements about how the job is to be done. It implies certain unspecified responsibilities for the work of colleagues and that the head is, in some way, part of the pattern of responsibility. How much better if all this was to be made explicit in a job description which spelt out more precisely what the holder of this post would actually do and which indicated exactly where the responsibilities for planning, controlling and evaluating are to be located.

The job description in Table 12 goes further in that direction by listing quite specifically the various areas of responsibility under a group of headings. It even includes a statement about minor responsibility. It represents a general agreement about the boundaries of a particular post within a school. Yet, in spite of being very specific, it is open to question exactly what the major areas of responsibility are and which areas are less crucial to that position in the school. Both of our examples might be improved if they were to be rewritten using the headings in the job description section of Table 13. An effective job description will contain all the information subsumed under those headings. The information in Table 13 comes from the job description of Rosemary Lane's deputy headteacher which is provided in Table 11 but, apart from the "Resources" section there is no information given

Table 12 JOB DESCRIPTION

Title	Deputy Head
Role	To assist the headteacher in the efficient running of the school, and to deputise for the headteacher when appropriate
Responsibility	To the headteacher

Areas of Concern

Management

To be aware of school routine and share in the smooth running of each day
To share with the head the responsibility for ensuring that the School´s aims and objectives are achieved
To share in the policy decisions which effect the efficient running of the school
To help with the allocation of capitation
To give practical help and encouragement to any teacher, especially a new colleague

****

Administration

To share the routine administrative tasks, and to be able to take responsibility for LEA forms, including requisition forms, Accident Book, Registration of Pupils, Building Maintenance forms, School Meals forms

****

Organisation

To organise the staff playground duty rota
To be aware of the Health and Safety regulations and to help promote a safe environment within the school
To be responsible for internal communication
To share in the organisation of school events
To assist the head in setting and maintaining a high standard of behaviour throughout the school

****

Table 12 (Cont´d)

Curriculum

To take curriculum responsibility for Science, formulating aims and objectives with colleagues and producing a scheme of work designed to assist teachers to fulfil the agreed aims and objectives
To assist in the production of other schemes of work
To help in the evaluation of the work of the school
To help maintain high standards of presentation and display of childrens work throughout the school and to organise corridor displays
To share with the head in the professional development of colleagues
To help welcome all visitors to the school

****

Relationships

To help support and encourage all teaching and non-teaching staff in the school
To help promote a happy atmosphere between children and staff
To assist the head with the effective organisation of parental involvement in the life of the school
To assist the head in fostering good relationships within the local community

****

Minor Responsibility

To keep up-to-date with the latest developments in Science by attending relevant courses, reviewing new publications and evaluating new resource materials available

Agreed for 1986/87 ....
Deputy Headteacher

....
Headteacher

---

about how the job is to be done. Those considerations are not a direct part of the job description although they may well form part of the discussion which takes place about it. The amended job description for Tom Jowett makes it clear exactly what his main function is, that is to assist Mrs Welton in the effective running of the school. It then indicates how he will do this in terms of what his particular contributions will be. These can, of course, be changed over time but the implication of this particular job description is that the development of a multicultural curriculum will take at least three years. In that time some of the other duties could be renegotiated if only to provide in-school staff development opportunities for other teachers at Rosemary Lane. The other significant addition to the material in Table 11 is the various attempts which have now been made to describe exactly what is to be done. The number of meetings with the relevant staff of the high school is indicated. The deadline for producing the first set of multicultural guidelines is indicated and the frequency of PTA meetings is shown. This is to avoid the creation of unrealistic and open-ended commitments for the postholder and to clarify the expectations about what has to be done and by when. The use of words like "organise", "plan" and "attend" help to keep the statement of duties concise. Seldom should each duty description be more than fifteen words in order to achieve clarity and precision.

If a job description is to be really useful it must be kept short. It should be concise enough to fit on one side of A4 paper. It is vital to remember that a job description is a device which helps to spell out exactly what is expected of the teachers. It is not meant to be a method of establishing demarcations between people and jobs in the everyday running of the school. It is primarily a method of helping heads and other colleagues to consider the type of person who should be appointed, as a basis for the regular development of teachers, and as a way of clarifying the role of each member of staff. Everybody knows what the work of a deputy headteacher involves until some dispute arises about who is responsible for what and when. Most of the time the central duties are reasonably clear but additional or peripheral duties are often negotiated by individuals and become traditional in a school. In our example the membership of the PTA Committee is one such situation. These need to be made clear.

Table 13 TOM JOWETT´S JOB DESCRIPTION AND PERSON SPECIFICATION

Job Description	Person Specification
Job Title Deputy Headteacher	Job Title Deputy Headteacher
Main Function To assist the headteacher in achieving the aims and objectives of the school and to act as head of the school in the absence of the head teacher	Qualifications Qualified teacher status with emphasis on primary education Evidence of attending courses in school management and in multicultural education
Main Duties To be the class teacher of the third year junior class To develop a multicultural curriculum throughout the school. To produce guidelines for all staff by the end of the next academic year To organise, in conjunction with the headteacher, the induction of new colleagues To be responsible for the integration of new colleagues into the staff team To organise in-service training for colleagues in multicultural education To plan effective liaison with Willingham High School and to organise at least two meetings a year with the staff of the high school who are responsible for pupil transfers To organise duty lists on a termly basis and to amend them daily as required To order and distribute stationery termly To attend the termly meetings of the PTA Committee as a staff member	Experience At least eight years as class teacher in a primary school Recent experience of working with top juniors At least three years as a postholder with curriculum responsibility Evidence of experience in co-ordinating the work of colleagues Evidence of experience in controlling stock Evidence of experience in helping with the professional development of colleagues Aptitudes Evidence of successful class teaching Evidence of ability to work with colleagues, especially newly appointed members of staff Evidence of ability to organise school-based in-service courses Evidence of ability to communicate successfully with pupils across the primary age and ability range Evidence of ability to organise displays of pupils´ work

Table 13 (Cont'd)

Job Description	Person Specification
To organise monthly displays of work in the entrance hall	Evidence of ability to work successfully with colleagues in other schools Evidence of organisational and administrative ability Evidence of ability to work positively with colleagues
<u>Responsible to</u> Ann Welton	
<u>Responsible for</u> Jaswinder Gill in her capacity as Section 11 teacher assisting with the development of multicultural eduction throughout the school The work of all colleagues in the area of multicultural education Pupil transfers to the high school Work displays in the entrance hall Sharing with the headteacher in the professional development of colleagues Sharing in the policy decisions which effect the efficient running of the school Supporting and encouraging all teaching and non-teaching staff Sharing the routine administration of the school	<u>Physical</u> Must pass LEA medical <u>Interests</u> Evidence of interest in team sports Must have current driving licence to drive mini bus Evidence of interest in computers would be an advantage
<u>Resources</u> Three hours non-contact time each week The assistance of Jaswinder Gill for the equivalent of one and a half days each week £200 annually from capitation for three years The equivalent of half a day of secretarial time	

Similarly the number and timing of important meetings also should be specified. All of these things and many more help to make up the _what_ of the job description. Since teaching is, by its very nature, dynamic then job descriptions need to be reviewed regularly. The description and its underlying perceptions will change over time. These changes need to be detected, discussed and recorded with the co-operation and agreement of the postholder to ensure that colleagues are clear about the _what_ of each post within the school.

Person Specification

If job descriptions are about the _what_ of a job then person specifications are about the _who_ of it. On the basis of a person specification it should be possible to identify what kind of person might be best able to fulfil the requirements of the described post. Broadly speaking, therefore, the person specification describes not the post itself but the person who is required to fill it or, in the case of an existing postholder, the abilities which the postholder ought to have or ought to be developing. It would be unfair to appoint a candidate to a post for which he or she was clearly not qualified but it is often forgotten by headteachers, inspectors and governors, who are under considerable pressure to ensure that the work of the school can continue in spite of staffing difficulties, that it is even more unfair to expect a teacher either to teach an unfamiliar topic or subject without adequate time for preparation and/or retraining together with suitable extra support. In the case of Tom Jowett, therefore, Mrs Welton will have to assure herself that he has the experience and qualifications to carry out the duties required of him or she will have to provide opportunities for the relevant in-service training for him. She should not assume that the kind of person that her deputy will have to be is implicit within the job description. The particular attributes and skills necessary to perform the job effectively should be made explicit, if only to act as an indication of where training and development are necessary. Thus the specification for the existing postholder should show what qualities and experience he or she brings to bear on the work being done but should also give some indication of areas for future thought and development to enable performance to be improved, promotion prospects to be enhanced and the needs of the school more fully met. As with the job description, the person specification can and should be reviewed and revised regularly through discussion involving all the parties who may be concerned and, ideally, as part of a regular development process.

The person specification derives, in the first instance, almost entirely from the job description which dictates many of the skills and qualifications which will be required. The job description will certainly determine the minimum qualifications and will also give an indication of basic experience required. Table 13 illustrates in the left column some headings for a flexible framework for writing a person specification for the whole range of positions in primary schools. For the post of deputy headteacher the basic qualifications are specified. The length and precise nature of previous experience is also evident from this person specification. The emphasis is again on clarity, evidence and precision in specifying the requirements which appear in Table 13. It is possible to be even more specific if we so desire. Is experience of a particular type of school or in a particular subject area desirable or essential? Are there particular aspects of the post which may demand experience in working with special equipment or with particular groups of children? Are the records of pupils to be transferred to the new computer and, if so, will the deputy require special expertise or be required to acquire it, especially as he has responsibility for pupils transferring to the high school? Does the school have a large proportion of disadvantaged pupils about whom the postholder may need to have some experience? These and many similar considerations help to shape a person specification similar to that which appears in Table 13. This table also shows how the job description and the person specification may be used in conjunction with one another to give a complete picture of one set of tasks within the school.

Some parts of the person specification, such as the qualifications, may, for the moment, describe what the incumbent actually has when the person profile is being written for an existing postholder but it should be remembered that these may need to be subject to revision if the present postholder leaves. Parts of the specification may also indicate where it might be desirable for the postholder to gain additional qualifications or experience. In Tom Jowett's case he does need more knowledge about current developments in multicultural education, for example. He may do this by attending courses, or by visiting other schools, or a combination of both. In terms of the experience required for the post a person specification should indicate what experience is necessary rather than what experience the postholder actually has. In the case of the deputy head at Rosemary Lane he already has most of the necessary experience in abundance, but some of the more specific experience in new areas will still have to be acquired. If the specification came to be used as a basis for an interview then care would have to be taken to rewrite it with the future needs of the school in mind as well as to avoid the possibility of precluding the appointment of an excellent candidate who does not quite fit the preconceived ideas of the interviewers. It should also be sufficiently explicit to avoid the possibility of fitting a square peg into a round hole.

Profiles, Descriptions and Specifications

Clearly to understand one's own function within the school and to have a similar insight into the work of professional colleagues can only assist in the smooth running of the school. For this reason alone, the processes of completing school profiles, individual profiles and school development plans are beneficial. For similar reasons job descriptions and, ideally, their associated specifications should not be known only to the head and the holder of the post, but shared with colleagues. Such sharing of knowledge can lead to a clearer and more supportive appreciation of what everyone in the school is doing and is trying to do. It can also help to establish the necessary unity of vision or common approach which is so helpful in achieving the aims of any school and in ensuring that those aims do not become divorced from reality. School profiles and job descriptions inevitably raise questions about what teachers are trying to do. This, in turn, helps everybody to develop a more informed understanding of the aims of the school and the ways in which it is hoped that they might be achieved. As a result expectations become more realistic since they are based on knowledge rather than on speculation. Constraints are identified and understood and the criteria for the adoption of particular forms of organisation are open to inspection and debate. Staffing, never easy in schools, may at least be approached on an informed and rational basis with the need for certain new skills becoming clearer and the basis for change understood. The detailed organisation of work within schools may take into account the wishes and aspirations of members of the staff of that school rather than reflect a policy of "as close to last year as it can be". Teachers may then be given the opportunity to gain new insights and experience and to develop new skills and interests within the framework of their existing expertise. Finally these processes should produce a greater awareness of the range of responsibilities and duties within the primary school.

Taken as a whole the process of producing school and individual profiles, and the writing of job descriptions and specifications can make a valuable contribution to several major areas of primary school management and can have benefits for all the staff of the school, as Table 14 shows. Staff development and school development, funded by GRIST as they now are, can play a vital part in ensuring that the most appropriate education is provided for the children in each school while, at

Table 14 THE IMPACT OF JOB ANALYSIS ON THE SCHOOL

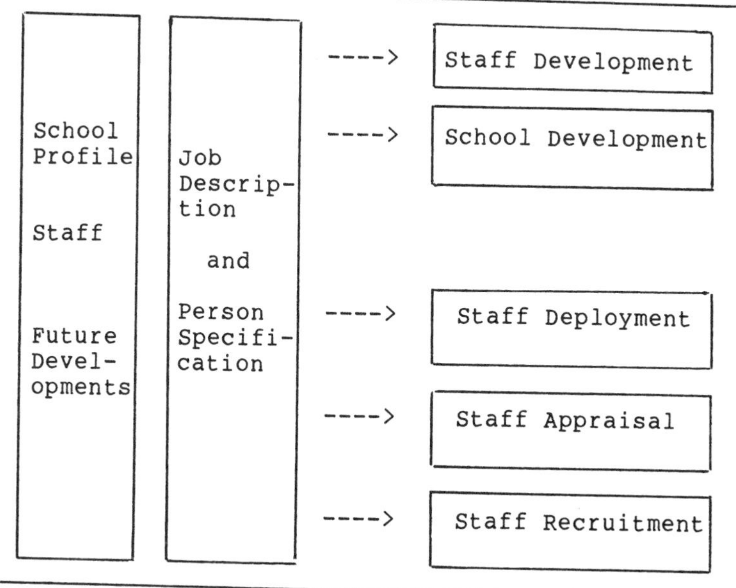

the same time, helping teachers to maximise their own professional skills. A sound and objective base for staff deployment can also be identified from the analysis of the work of the school. Appraisal can take place on the basis of a clear understanding on all sides of what the school is trying to do, how it is trying to do it, and what part each individual is playing in that process. Schools are also provided with a range of information against which to consider the making of new appointments. Any appointment should be made only after a careful analysis of the work of the school and of the existing expertise, qualifications and interests of the staff of that school. Profiles, descriptions and specifications give us just such a framework.

Activities

1. What techniques would you employ when constructing a school profile to ensure precision and conciseness?

2. If you were writing an individual profile for one of your teachers what steps would you take to ensure that it was accurate?

3. Why do you think it is important to spell out "responsibility to" and "responsibility for"?

4. Using the model in Table 14 try to construct a job description for your own post. Now construct the related person specification. Who are you going to consult to see if these are accurate? When and how will you use them?

Chapter 5

THE SELECTION AND APPOINTMENT OF STAFF IN PRIMARY SCHOOLS

In Rosemary Lane it will soon be necessary to consider the steps necessary to replace Mrs Arnold who is leaving to take up an appointment at another school. This situation arises regularly even today, when staff turnover is far less than it once was and when the sight of a new teacher, especially a probationary teacher, is a relative rarity in many primary schools. As the slight increase in the birth rate which was evident in the early 1980s works its way into primary schools this situation may change and more staff may need to be appointed to many schools. In any case there are almost always some staff changes due to promotion, retirement and family commitments. All primary school staff ought, therefore, to be aware of the appropriate stages necessary to fill a vacancy. Such an awareness enables vacancies to be filled to the best possible advantage for the school. It helps to avoid mistakes in staff appointments which can cause genuine unhappiness to many people. It also enables those teachers who are likely to be seeking promotion to make the most of their professional opportunities. It is not intended, however, to emulate the work of Marius Rose whose _Intelligent Teachers' Guide to Preferment_ has amused and informed generations of primary schoolteachers. Nor is it intended to cover the same ground as Waters (1983) who gives detailed guidance about promotion and preferment in primary schools. This chapter will deal with the stages in making an appointment from the point of view of those in the school in which the vacancy has occurred. In so doing, it will cover many aspects of the appointing process which are relevant to those seeking to be appointed to posts in primary schools.

Different Local Education Authorities have always had different procedures for making appointments. These may vary from the situation in which the LEA handles the entire process with minimum involvement of the headteacher to the other extreme where the whole process is delegated to the headteacher (Whitaker 1983). Most headteachers will be involved in the process at some stage and the exact procedure for making appointments is normally described in the Instruments and Articles of School Government. These statements are sometimes not very helpful. In one LEA it is laid down that the headteacher will appoint assistant staff and the governing body will approve the appointment (Poster, 1976). No indication is given about what will happen if the appointment is not approved. Such obvious and necessary safeguards are commonplace. Their effective working depends more on the nature of the relationship between the headteacher and her chairperson of the school's governing body than on the written word.

Frequently headteachers will be required to use the LEA's facilities to advertise a vacancy so that a common style for advertisements can be adopted, with headteachers submitting details to the education office. The applications often have to be returned to the LEA in such cases. Thus considerable time may elapse between the headteacher becoming aware that a vacancy will exist in her school and the same headteacher being able to consider application forms. At this stage the school's pastoral inspector or a relevant subject inspector, together with governors' representatives, may well become involved in drawing up a short list. Today it is a frequent practice, especially for headships and deputy headships, to draw up a long list for consideration from which the short list is then identified. Much depends on the number of applicants. In the case of the Rosemary Lane vacancy this extended procedure was not adopted.

A further factor which may constrain the actions and intentions of the headteacher in the matter of staff appointments is the problem caused by falling pupil numbers. This has required many LEAs to insist that all vacancies must, in the first instance, be open only to teachers who are to be redeployed from their present schools. This drastically reduces the power of the headteacher to make her own choice in appointments and will continue to do so until numbers of pupils in the primary age range increase again. This is starting to happen in many places but the need to redeploy staff has certainly created a new pattern of appointments in the last decade. Nevertheless many of the processes which are used for appointing new staff after an open and unrestricted advertisement are also relevant when consideration is being given to appointing from a group of teachers who are to be redeployed. Therefore selections and appointments will be discussed in this chapter from the point of view of a headteacher who has relative freedom to make her own appointments.

The selection procedures will be discussed under six headings:

(i) Defining the post
(ii) The selection procedures
(iii) Conducting the initial selection
(iv) The interview
(v) Making the appointment
(vi) Induction

These procedures do not, however, take place in isolation within any school. In the previous chapter it was argued that all primary schools should have a school profile based on an analysis of the total contributions made to the school by all its staff combined with an examination of what the school sought to do. This produced a school development plan which enables all the staff of the school to have a clear view about how the school needs to develop in the future. Added to this, job descriptions and related person specifications help to clarify the responsibilities and duties of individual teachers and to indicate the qualifications, experiences and interests required for fulfilling that particular role. It is in the light of information produced by these processes that all appointments need to be considered, and all vacant posts defined.

Defining the Post

Every vacancy presents the headteacher with an opportunity to make a series of choices. Does the post actually need to be filled in its present form? Does it need to be filled at all? Are there other ways of filling the vacancy apart from a full-time appointment? A series of part-time appointments might provide more flexibility, for example. Is the vacancy an opportunity to bring other, much needed skills into the school? Are there teachers on the existing staff who could fill the vacant position or who could be trained to do so? If the answer to this is yes, then what are the implications for filling the post? Do you choose not to fill it at all, fill it with somebody with different skills, or fill it in different ways? Other facts which may need to be taken into account include the age of other colleagues and the possibility of other promotions. Miss Danby at Rosemary Lane is 56 and will retire in four years time when Miss Hockley, now aged 50 might well retire also. Mr Smith may be successful in his attempts to obtain the headship of a small school while Mr Johns may soon be looking for advancement. All these factors need to be considered. There often appears to be a built-in reflex action which leads us to assume that recruitment has to be undertaken simply because a colleague is leaving. Such an assumption must be based on an analysis of the facts and in the light of the school's development plan.

Before a headteacher can think critically about any vacancy she should, therefore, have a clear view about where the school is going and what skills will be needed to help it move in that direction. She may also have to acquire a clear idea of what her departing colleague has actually done, what resources and skills she has used, and what her views are about the post she is leaving. As years go by a particular post may grow or become re-defined. Tradition and practice tend to be more important in defining a post than future needs or current practice. For example Mrs Arnold has gradually taken over more and more of the PE and Games teaching in Rosemary Lane as a result of informal agreements with her colleagues. Mrs Welton may or may not know about this. She may or may not want it to continue after Mrs Arnold has departed. Before she makes any assumptions about this she would be wise to conduct an "exit interview" with Mrs Arnold. (See Table 15)

The exit interview provides the headteacher with the opportunity to thank her departing colleague for her work in the school in the years she has been a member of staff. It is also an opportunity to explore privately the reasons for her departure and to identify those areas of school organisation which may need to be improved. Sometimes these interviews do reveal some problem within the school that should be dealt with. These do need to receive the prompt attention of the headteacher. At the same time the exit interview can lead to a valuable discussion about ways in which the existing post might be changed. This would result in the modification of the job description before the post is advertised. It is also worth seeking the

Table 15 EXIT INTERVIEW - CHECK LIST

PURPOSE

(a) To thank the person for her contribution to the life of the school

(b) To discover the person's true reasons for leaving the school with a view to taking any remedial action if this reason is in respect of:
    Poor recruitment
    Inadequate staff development
    Poor management or supervision
    School policy
    Selection

(c) To secure the member of staff's goodwill and the school's reputation

(d) To identify the main elements of the job which is being vacated and to amend the job description if necessary

(e) To seek advice about the qualities required in a person appointed to the post

PREPARATION

* check resignation letter - reason stated
* check staff records
* where necessary check with other members of staff
* ensure privacy and no interruptions
* allow adequate time

CONDUCT

* put at ease
* state purpose of interview
* encourage and allow member of staff to talk freely about the job, the school and the people
* listen and observe, be alert for clues to underlying reason
* thank member of staff for services rendered and wish her well

FOLLOW-UP

Decide if any action is necessary in the light of information gained and implement accordingly views of the person who is leaving about the skills, experience and qualifications which she feels are now necessary to do the job well. After all, at Rosemary Lane, nobody knows Mrs Arnold's job better than she does herself.

After this interview Mrs Welton may wish to consult her colleagues about the vacancy. She will almost certainly wish to discuss it with Mr Jowett, her deputy, and since she wishes to make certain changes which affect all her staff, they too should be included in the discussion at an early stage. Mrs Welton has decided that there is an urgent need to find a way of providing curriculum leadership in mathematics and that she will, after consultation with her chairman of governors, use the £501 allowance which is now available to her in order to attract a teacher who will give this leadership. Mrs Welton believes that a suitable candidate would be undertaking duties beyond those common to the majority of teachers in her school and would need to be an outstanding classroom teacher. The person appointed may not retain the allowance indefinitely. This would need to be discussed at the interview. As a result of this decision to appoint somebody to give curriculum leadership in mathematics Mrs Welton's existing staff will have to take more responsibility for their own PE and games although there may be a possibility of either finding a teacher with an additional interest in this area or of strengthening this aspect of the curriculum if another colleague leaves in the future. Ann Welton also wants to be able to provide the resources for the incoming teacher to be able to introduce a new mathematics scheme throughout the school especially in the junior department where the work is rather uncoordinated. This will mean that colleagues will have to forego the luxury of ordering their own mathematics stock and equipment. It may also mean that other curriculum areas will only receive the bare essentials for the next two or three years. If the capitation for the school is approximately £15 for each child then Rosemary Lane will receive just over £3,000 annually. A new scheme may cost in the region of £1,200 although many schemes now require the children to have individual work books and the cost of these needs to be accounted for. If the staff of the school is to operate in a collegiate way, based on a team approach to planning and decision-making, all the staff need to be involved in the taking of decisions such as these since they are directly affected by them. Once Mrs Welton has explored with her staff the implications of the proposed appointment then a job description and person specification can be produced, perhaps again involving colleagues in the staff group.

The writing of descriptions and specifications has been considered in detail in the previous chapter. The one produced by Mrs Welton for this particular post followed the principles outlined in that chapter. In addition she sought to take into account the extent to which certain qualities might be necessary to promote and maintain good relationships among the staff group since it was likely that the school would be undergoing a series of significant changes over the next few years (Table 16). She recognised that the new post would call for initiative as well as specific qualifications. The person appointed would need to be able to get on well with colleagues and be able to provide leadership by working with them and encouraging them in their own work in the classroom. School-based in-service training is going to be a vital part of that leadership. Explaining the new developments to parents is also going to be important and so is some experience of bringing about curriculum change in a primary school. Mrs Welton will be heavily involved in the work of the school across the curriculum and would, therefore, rely on the teacher with curriculum responsibility for mathematics for developments in that area and to ensure that successful changes were implemented.

In drawing up the job description and person specification Ann Welton has considered the nature of the job to be filled and what particular competencies are needed to perform it. Some of the duties will be a permanent part of the post, the overall responsibility for mathematics, for example. Others, the teaching of a fourth year junior class, may change over time. This will need to be pointed out to candidates at interview or in the further particulars. The job description cannot be regarded as a legal extension of a teacher's contract. It is an internal agreement about duties in a particular school and a guide to identifying relevant competencies. Some of those competencies are general in the sense that they might reasonably be expected of anyone applying for a similar post. Evidence of successful classroom teaching, experience of particular age ranges and ability to communicate with and work with colleagues come into this category. Another set of competencies are specific to this post. Those involve knowledge of and experience in

Table 16 JOB DESCRIPTION AND PERSON SPECIFICATION FOR A NEW POST IN ROSEMARY LANE PRIMARY SCHOOL

Job Description	Person Specification
<u>Job Title</u> Teacher scale A with curriculum responsibility for mathematics	<u>Job Title</u> Teacher scale A with curriculum responsibility for mathematics
<u>Main Function</u> To act as class teacher for fourth year junior class and to be responsible for mathematics throughout the school	<u>Qualifications</u> BEd or equivalent with mathematics as a specialism <u>OR</u> PGCE with mathematics as a specialism Evidence of attending INSET courses in primary school mathematics
<u>Main Duties</u> To be the class teacher of the fourth year junior class To prepare a new scheme of work in mathematics To provide guidance and support to all colleagues in implementing the scheme To monitor work in mathematics throughout the school including record keeping and progress assessment To assist colleagues in diagnosing children's learning difficulties in mathematics	<u>Experience</u> At least five years as class teacher in a primary school Recent experience of teaching top juniors Experience of involvement in curriculum change in mathematics Experience of coordinating the work of colleagues Experience in providing school-based INSET in mathematics
To identify support strategies to improve the performance of children with learning difficulties in mathematics To arrange school-based INSET in mathematics for colleagues To liaise with head of mathematics at Willingham High School over work done in final year of the primary school To organise necessary resources for mathematics and to inform colleagues of what is available and how it might best be used	<u>Aptitudes</u> Evidence of successful class teaching Evidence of ability to work with colleagues and to provide curriculum leadership Evidence of ability to organise resources Evidence of ability to diagnose learning difficulties and to identify strategies to cope with them Evidence of ability to communicate with colleagues in other schools

Table 16 (Cont´d)

Job Description	Person Specification
Responsible to Ann Welton Responsible for The work of all colleagues in mathematics School-based INSET in mathematics Providing support for child ren with learning difficulties in mathematics Advising the head and gover nors on new developments in mathematics Resources Two hours non-contact time each week The resources to fund a new mathematics scheme up to £1,500 over two years The equivalent of half a day secretarial time to help with preparing material Two hours of classroom helper time each week for one year to help provide materials in the infant department	Aptitudes (cont´d) Evidence of ability to communicate with parents Evidence of ability to keep up-to-date with developments in primary school mathematics teaching Physical Must pass LEA medical examination Interests Must be interested in and committed to multicultural education Interest in PE and games would be an advantage

this particular subject area and the commitment to multicultural education which is an important part of the ethos of Rosemary Lane. Other competencies may well be expected of somebody applying for the post but could, if necessary, be acquired after appointment. The special skills required to provide detailed analysis of the special needs of children with learning difficulties in this area and the ability to organise resources might come into this category since both can be learned. The former would require a relevant in-service course while the latter might only require careful coaching from Mrs Welton or her deputy. Other competencies are merely peripheral. The interest in PE certainly fits this description and might be omitted entirely were it not for the special circumstances surrounding the appointment. Thus it is becoming clearer which competencies are essential for this post, which are desirable but not essential, and which are of only marginal importance. This analysis will provide Mrs Welton with a framework for ordering her priorities when she comes to consider the candidates who have applied for the post, since they should all receive a copy of the job description and the person specification when they are sent application forms and further particulars. So should those people who are to be asked to provide references.

The Selection Procedures

An essential initial part of the selection procedure has already taken place by this time, although possible candidates are not aware of it; nor are potential members of the interviewing panel with the possible exception of the chairperson of the governors and the school's pastoral inspector. The job description and the person specification have been written. These two sets of information will, when they arrive in the hands of potential applicants, lead a significant number of them to decide not to pursue their application because they do not suit the requirements of the post. Before this can happen, however, the advertisement has to be produced and placed in the appropriate publications. These may be the LEA's own bulletin and/or any of the usual educational journals, depending on the policy of the LEA.

The advertisement itself can be relatively brief. The basic information will include a brief outline of the post; the name of the school; any special information about the school; the address from which application forms can be obtained; the closing date; the date when the successful candidate will be expected to take up her appointment. If the appointment is for a limited period or subject to certain conditions then this should also be stated. The general principles which guide the drafting of an advertisement are: firstly that it should contain sufficient information to enable those candidates who are suitably qualified and experienced to apply for the post and secondly that it should be brief enough to be assimilated easily. Thus the advertisement for the vacancy at Rosemary Lane would read as follows:

> Rosemary Lane County Primary School (221 on roll)
> Required for the above school from the start of the Autumn Term an enthusiastic and experienced class teacher, (Main Professional Grade + A allowance for suitable candidate) to be responsible for a class of fourth year junior children. The successful applicant will be expected to initiate curriculum work in mathematics, and to be responsible for its development and implementation throughout the school. A firm commitment to multicultural education is essential.
> Application forms and further details may be obtained from ....
> The closing date for applications is Friday 13th May.

This advertisement provides prospective applicants with all the vital information except that Rosemary Lane is a mile from the city centre. This might discourage those candidates who are seeking rural or suburban employment. The size of the school may not always be relevant but in an authority with a mixture of large and small schools many teachers may be attracted by the possibility of working in a larger school. Alternatively some teachers may wish to develop their skills in a smaller school. The size of the school does give some indication of how many colleagues will form the staff group with whom the successful candidate will be working. Much more information about the post will, of course, be contained in the job description and person specification which should be sent to each applicant. Relevant information about the LEA, the school and its surroundings may be included in the further particulars.

If the post is advertised only within the LEA then much of the formal detail about the LEA may be omitted although it is surprising how often colleagues find it helpful to be reminded of such matters especially where an LEA is subdivided into areas or regions. As for the school itself it is not easy to summarise all the information that a prospective applicant may wish to have. The school handbook, while obviously written for parents, will contain much relevant information and should be made available to applicants. If there is a staff handbook then this too should be provided. The existing staff of the school might like to provide a list of the information which they think that a prospective colleague might find useful. This could be incorporated into a document about the school. The Post Project Report suggests six headings under which information ought to be provided for applicants for secondary headteacher posts. These headings are a useful check list for all posts in any school. They are:

(a) The School and its Situation
This heading includes information about the history, size, organisation, age range, site and buildings, catchment area and community use of school.

(b) Staffing
Here information is provided about the number and deployment of teaching and non-teaching staff and their responsibilities.

(c) Parent-Teacher Links
This should include information about links, both formal and informal, between the school and parents, and should indicate the expectations about teacher involvement in PTA where relevant.

(d) Curriculum
Here there should be a brief statement about the curriculum relevant to the particular post including pupil groups and the role of colleagues. Also included should be an indication of provision for children with special needs.

(e) LEA Support and Provision for Staff Development
Information here should include details of courses and other activities at the teachers' centre, the role of the inspectors and other facilities which may be available.

(f) Community Links
Links with the wider community including contact with volunatary agencies.

(Adapted from Morgan, Hall and Mackay, (1984), pp. 28-29).

Morgan, Hall and Mackay (1984) provide an extremely detailed account of the necessary planning for staff appointments which goes far beyond the scope of this chapter but which colleagues involved in making a series of crucial appointments would find invaluable. All the above information together with that in the appropriate handbooks and with the possible addition of a map of the catchment area, ought to provide most candidates with the information necessary in order to enable them to decide whether or not to submit an application. This decision should be based on how far the potential applicant thinks, on the basis of the available evidence, that the post would suit her if she was successful and, of equal importance, how far she thinks that she is suitable for the post as advertised. Thus the selection process does not start with the interview. The advertisement, the further particulars, the job description and person specification are crucial in the very early stages of making an appointment. These details give clear criteria for prospective applicants against which they can judge their own suitability and upon which the initial screening of applications can be based. Much depends now on how far the application forms themselves enable the selectors to identify and assess the relevant information.

The application form is more valuable than is generally realised. If carefully designed and interpreted, it can provide a wealth of information about a candidate. Conversely, it will prove to be a blunt instrument if these conditions are not fulfilled. Its principal purpose is to ask pertinent questions and elicit relevant information, thus enabling the selector to identify candidates who correspond closely to the person specification. Subsequently, it can serve as a framework around which the interview may be built. Lastly, it can be kept as a record of the member of staff´s background. This is its least important function. Unfortunately, an application form is liable to be regarded as part of a standard routine. The procedure tends to obscure the real purpose. There is no point in a person filling in a form if it is obvious that she fails to meet one or more of the essential requirements of the post. Similarly, there is little point in inviting a person to attend an interview if careful study of her career record would show that she is unlikely to be suitable for the post. The candidate´s time is valuable too! The application form is, therefore, a method of asking and answering questions by correspondence. The selector should already have a clear idea from the person specification about the criteria by which she will differentiate between candidates. The application form needs to be designed with those criteria in mind.

Many headteachers will have little or no control over the shape of the application form since most LEAs issue a standard form to candidates. It is possible in such situations to request a letter of application from candidates which might cover some of the areas not included in the standard form. In such cases, or where no standard form exists, it is only fair to indicate in the further particulars those areas which it is felt appropriate for the candidate to comment upon in her application. Much of this will be evident from the job description and person specification. The combination of an application form and the letter of application should give the candidate the opportunity to demonstrate her suitability for the post in terms of the duties and responsibilities demanded of the successful applicant and in terms of the specifications for the person required. Where no standard form is used the headings for the application form should include those necessary to collect the relevant personal and professional details, including professional and in-service details. Candidates should be clear about what they are being asked and have room for adequate replies. It ought to be made clear whether or not a supporting letter is expected. The example of an application form in Table 17 can be adapted to suit most purposes and most posts although for very senior posts a more flexible approach may be useful to enable candidates to develop their ideas more fully in a letter of application.

Conducting the Initial Selection

When the application forms start to arrive the final stages of the selection process are uppermost in the mind but the forms should be considered very carefully. Ann Welton will certainly want to involve her deputy in screening the applications. She may also want to involve other colleagues, Mrs Cass for example, since she will be concerned with the mathematics work in the infant department as part of her overall responsibility for that area. The pastoral or subject inspector and the chairperson of governors may also need to be involved in the screening stage. The screening should start by inspecting the factual sections, qualifications and experience, to ensure that the candidate meets the basic requirements for this post. There is nothing to be gained by spending time on a detailed analysis of the application of a candidate who lacks one

Table 17 EXAMPLE OF APPLICATION FORM HEADINGS

APPLICATION FOR POST OF:	Teacher with curriculum responsibility for Mathematics	AT: Rosemary Lane County Primary School

FULL NAME:

PRESENT ADDRESS:	TEL NO:

AGE:	DES NUMBER:	NATIONALITY:

MALE/FEMALE:	MARITAL STATUS:	AGES OF CHILDREN:

Do you hold a current driving licence? YES/NO	Groups:	Endorsements:

EDUCATION: School/College/University	Dates	Qualifications

IN-SERVICE COURSES	Dates	Qualifications

DETAILS OF EMPLOYMENT

Are you currently employed? YES/NO	If YES, state notice required by your present employer:

Give details of all full time and part time employment below, working back from your current or most recent post

From Mth/Yr	To Mth/Yr	Employer´s name and address	Position, brief description of post and institution	Reasons for leaving

Table 17 (Cont´d)

Have you ever been dismissed or asked to resign? YES/NO	If YES, give details:

Interests (Hobbies, Club membership etc.)

HEALTH RECORD:

Give details of any disabilities or any illnesses which have caused you to be absent from work for more than four weeks:

REFEREES:

Candidates are asked to provide the names of three people to whom reference may be made concerning their suitability for this post:

Name: Position:
Address:
Relationship to candidate:

Name: Position:
Address:
Relationship to candidate:

Name: Position:
Address:
Relationship to candidate:

FURTHER RELEVANT INFORMATION

Candidates should submit a letter in support of their application of no more than 1,000 words indicating how they meet the specifications for this post (see Job Description and Person Specification). Forms should be typed or completed in black ink.

essential attribute. So those who are not well qualified in primary school mathematics ought to be discounted immediately for this post however interesting they may appear from other points of view. After the first reading of the forms the candidates can be placed in three provisional groups: unsuitable, possible and probable. If a number of people are involved in the screening, disagreements will frequently occur at this point. In order to find the best possible candidate it is advisable to leave each candidate in the most favourable grouping proposed for her at this stage. A second and more rigorous consideration of the forms will follow in order to draw up what has become known as "the long list". In some LEAs this implies that the candidates on that list will be called for an initial interview or some other form of selection procedure. In others it means that references will be taken up for the long list candidates. In either situation the form of the analysis is similar. An assumption is made that the pattern of a person's previous behaviour contains a reasonable guide about her future performance. This tends to be a more reliable assumption for older candidates than for those who are younger. However, for most applicants, it is possible to learn a significant amount about the candidates, especially where they have included supporting letters. We can see the use she has made of opportunities, the handicaps she has overcome, her interpretation of the requirements of the post for which she has applied and her assessment of how far and why she meets the specifications, and the extent to which she has proved herself compatible in different social groupings. These are some of the trends and tendencies which may be apparent from her past record. Taken together, they can serve as a valuable guide when considering the post for which she has applied. It is important to bear in mind that even a well designed application form will not contain all the parts of the jig-saw puzzle we are attempting to piece together. Inevitably there will be some gaps in our knowledge, perhaps vital ones, which remain unfilled. This additional information will have to be gleaned later by personal interview. Even so, these tentative deductions about the candidate are of considerable value especially as they are made without the interplay of personalities which occurs in the face-to-face situation of the interview. On the strength of these tentative conclusions some candidates will be eliminated. The remainder will need to be considered further.

It is desirable at this point to inform those candidates whose application is not being pursued that this is the case, a step not normally taken in educational appointments. The advantage of doing this is twofold. Firstly the candidates not being considered further are informed well in advance and can therefore make other career choices. Secondly the candidates who are being given serious consideration might be visited in their own school or can be invited to visit the school informally prior to drawing up a list for interview. Candidates may then wish to withdraw or it may be decided after an initial encounter that the applicant should not be pursued further. The preview of the school is important for both the candidate and the school staff. It provides an opportunity for people who may be working together to become acquainted. Some LEAs will not bear the additional expense of a school visit which is not a direct part of the interview. In this case the visit and the interview should be as separate as it is possible for them to be. For example the visit to the school might take place in the morning and be organised by a senior member of staff who is not involved in the interview. Visits to the school by the candidate need to be well planned (see Table 18). This needs to include a tour of the buildings, especially the rooms where the candidate will work. There should be an opportunity to see the school in operation and for the candidate to receive more information about the particular policy objectives and specific needs of the school. In the case of the Rosemary Lane post the fourth year classroom and the mathematics area together with an examination of the books and equipment for number work throughout the school need to be included. There should also be an opportunity to meet other members of staff with whom the new colleague will work closely, ideally in a social setting rather than in a work setting. Coffee or lunch provide opportunities for this although with some appointments there may need to be time for a detailed and structured discussion of the post and the school. There should always be time for a discussion with the headteacher. It would be naive for anyone to assume the visit is not part of the process of assessing and selecting candidates but, at this stage, the candidate is less likely to be under the kind of stress that an interview might produce. The visit gives the candidate time to make sure that she would be happy accepting the post if it is offered.

Table 18 A STRUCTURE FOR THE CANDIDATE´S VISIT

<u>Information Required</u>
- application form
- job description/person specification
- plan of visit indicating time/place/person on staff responsible for meeting candidate

<u>Structure of Visit</u> (Head)
9.30-9.45 in Head´s Office
- Introduction
- welcome and coffee
- explain structure of visits
- deal with initial questions

<u>Tour of School</u> (Deputy Head)
9.45-10.30
- general tour
- return to
  - o meet key staff
  - o talk to pupils
  - o see key areas
  - o examine key facilities and equipment

<u>Meet Staff</u> (Deputy Head: in Staff Room)
10.30-11.15 Coffee prepared
- meet all staff
- meet present holder of post
- meet other key staff again

<u>General Discussion</u> (Head in Office) 11.15-12.15
with deputy and key staff
- answer candidate´s questions
- provide more relevant information
- give candidate a summary sheet of policy information including plan of school
- depart or lunch

By this stage references may have started to arrive. A reference is only as useful as the information contained in it. It can be made more useful by requesting specific kinds of information. All referees should be sent the same information about the post as the candidates receive. The letter requesting a reference should draw the referee´s attention to the significant parts of that information. The most significant elements of the job description and the person specification should be indicated. In the case of the Rosemary Lane appointment referees will be reminded of the main duties of the post and asked to comment on each part of the person specification with reference to the particular candidate. This gives a clear structure to the reference and leaves the referee in no doubt about what is being asked and what the criteria for the appointment will be. Structuring the request for the reference in this way will then enable Mrs Welton, her chairperson of governors and her pastoral inspector to differentiate between candidates on criteria which are directly related to the post to be filled. At the same time the referee has the opportunity to mention other factors which may be relevant but which do not come into the description or the specification.

To date careful records need to have been kept on each stage of the procedure. This becomes even more important as the references arrive because all possible evidence will be necessary to enable the most important short (or long) list to be drawn up. This is a complex process of consultation. Exactly who becomes involved may depend on LEA policy but it is likely that the headteacher, the chairperson of governors and the pastoral inspector will be included. Others, such as the deputy head, the subject adviser or another representative of the governors may also play a part. The usual procedure is to read through the applications and references with the object of eliminating the unsuitable candidates and identifying the probable interviewees. The criteria for making these choices should, as far as is possible, relate to the job description and person specification. It is easy to allow prejudices to cloud judgements at this stage. Handwriting and general presentation are important but should never be the main criterion for selecting or rejecting a candidate for interview. Not all good teachers have neat handwriting and not all good mathematics postholders can set out an application form to perfection. Relate the significant choices to relevant criteria. It is worth attempting to codify information at this stage. Table 19 provides an example of how this might be done for the Rosemary Lane mathematics Post. Once each person involved in drawing up the short list has completed such a form then there exists a basis for logical and rational debate about the merits of the various candidates. The essence of using such a form is to identify clear reasons for making judgements.

The Interview

The size of the short-list which results from the discussions of the applications will depend on the next stage in the process. For many senior posts LEAs are now following the recommendations of the Post Project (Morgan, et al., 1984) and identifying a long list from which a short-list will be selected by using a series of job-related exercises and simulations. This may even be done in other cases. Candidates may be asked to teach a class, to analyse relevant documents or to show how they might produce, say, a mathematics curriculum for the school. In such situations the initial list of candidates might be as long as fifteen but if the short-listed candidates are all to be interviewed with a view to making an immediate appointment then the number involved should be no more than a third of this. It becomes almost impossible to remember with any degree of clarity the performance and characteristics of any more than five candidates in an intensive interview. At Rosemary Lane the candidates proceeded straight to the interview. There are still some important arrangements to be made before the interview can take place. Candidates need to be invited to the interview. The letter of invitation should contain some basic information:

- Where and when the interview will be held
- travel arrangements, parking and if appropriate, accommodation
- the exact time and duration of the interview
- The names and positions of the interviewing panel
- Other details of the programme including catering arrangements and visits
- How and when the decision will be made
- How candidates will be notified
- How candidates may claim expenses and the appropriate rates
- Candidates should be asked to reply in writing stating that they intend to attend for interview, indicating approximate time of arrival and any special arrangements that may be necessary

On the day of the interview the preparation becomes more detailed. The candidates should be met

Table 19 CHECKLIST FOR ANALYSING APPLICATIONS

Teacher with curriculum responsibility for mathematics at Rosemary Lane County Primary School	Name of candidate & present post	Name of candidate & present post	Name of candidate & present post	Name of candidate & present post
<u>Qualifications</u> Teaching Certificate BEd or similar first degree PGCE Higher Degree Other advanced qualification INSET courses				
<u>Experience</u> Infant Junior Other Involvement in curriculum change in mathematics Co-ordinating work of colleagues Providing school-based INSET in mathematics				
<u>Aptitudes</u> Successful class teaching Providing curriculum leadership Organising resources Diagnosing learning difficulties and identifying strategies to cope with them Communication with colleagues in other schools Communication with parents Knowledge of recent developments in primary mathematics				

Table 19 (Cont´d)

	Name of Candi-date & Present Post	Name of Candi-date & Present Post	Name of Candi-date & Present Post	Name of Candi-date & Present Post
Interests Commitment to multi-cultural education PE/Games				
Other Comments				
Physical Any indications of ill health				
RANK ORDER OF CANDIDATES				
FINAL RANK ORDER OF CANDIDATES AFTER DISCUSSION				

List of those invited for Interview

and welcomed. Refreshment should be available and there should be suitable waiting accommodation provided. Sitting in the staff room at morning break is hardly the way to prepare for an interview. The interview panel also need to be prepared. Each member of the panel will require the application form, letter of application and references for each candidate to be interviewed as well as copies of the job description and the person specification. Each member of the interviewing panel should have a timetable for the day and the briefest details about each candidate. The Chairperson should be responsible for welcoming each candidate and for introducing the panel to her. The process for recording information about the candidates should be discussed and agreement reached about who will concentrate on which areas in order to avoid unnecessary duplication of effort. It is not wise to restrict each interviewer to one question for reasons which will be discussed below so a time limit should be agreed which is long enough to allow the candidate to explore the particular area fully but short enough to ensure that the interview does not overrun its allotted time which should be realistic. Thirty minutes is hardly long enough for a group of five to interview one candidate. Far better to allow slightly too long for each interview than to allow too short a time.

The interviewing panel may contain some or all of the shortlisting group. If this is the case then there will already exist a shared view of the candidates as they appeared from the application form. There will also exist a shared view of what is being sought in the ideal candidate. This will derive from the job description and the person specification but will also be a result of the interaction between the shortlisting group in terms of the weightings they may have give to various types of experience and to various aptitudes. For example it might have already been established that a BEd is marginally preferable to a PGCE even where both involve mathematics. It might also have been established that evidence of providing successful leadership to colleagues in a professional context is more important than having had direct experience of curriculum change in mathematics. The assumptions about the importance of each individual item on the job specification is given a numerical expression in the "IMPORTANCE WEIGHTING" column on the Interview Analysis Sheet (Table 20). These weightings were, in this instance, proposed by Mrs Welton and accepted by the shortlisting group. Thus more importance is being attached to junior experience than any other form of experience and successful class teaching and curriculum leadership are the two most important aptitudes. Such assumptions may need to be shared with all panel members before the interview starts. If, as they should, all members of the panel have copies of the job description, person specification, application forms and references then this might be done by the headteacher reviewing the qualities and experience required and drawing attention to the apparent strengths and weaknesses of each application. In this way strengths can be explored and apparent weaknesses probed during the interview. Clarifying such issues is a vital part of the preparation of the panel of interviewers of which the headteacher

Table 20 INTERVIEW ANALYSIS SHEET

Teacher with special responsibility for mathematics	Importance Weighting	Mr Brown Actual Score	Mr Brown Weighted Score	Mrs Green Actual Score	Mrs Green Weighted Score	Miss Lilac Actual Score	Miss Lilac Weighted Score	Mr White Actual Score	Mr White Weighted Score
Teaching certificate	2	1	2	0	0	0	0	0	0
BEd or similar	5	0	0	2	10	1	5	0	0
PGCE	4	0	0	0	0	0	0	0	0
Higher degree	2	0	0	0	0	0	0	2	4
Other advanced INSET courses	3	1	3	2	6		3	3	9
		Sub Total	5	Sub Total	16	Sub Total	8	Sub Total	17
Experience									
Infant	3	0	0	1	3	1	3	0	0
Junior	4	1	4	1	4	0	0	1	4
Other	1	0	0	0	0	2	2 (Special)	0	0
Curriculum change in maths	2	1	2	2	4	0	0	0	0
Co-ordinating work of colleagues	3	2	6	4	12	3	9	1	3
Providing school-base INSET	3	1	3	2	6	1	3	1	3
		Sub Total	15	Sub Total	29	Sub Total	17	Sub Total	10

Table 20 (Cont'd)

Teacher with special responsibility for mathematics	Importance Weighting	Mr Brown Actual Score	Mr Brown Weighted Score	Mrs Green Actual Score	Mrs Green Weighted Score	Miss Lilac Actual Score	Miss Lilac Weighted Score	Mr White Actual Score	Mr White Weighted Score
Aptitudes									
Successful class teaching	5	2	10	4	20	5	25	3	15
Providing curriculum leadership	5	2	10	4	20	2	10	1	5
Organising resources	1	1	1	3	3	4	4	1	1
Diagnosing learning difficulties and identifying strategies	2	1	2	4	8	5	10	2	4
Communication with colleagues in other schools	1	0	0	0	0	1	1	0	0
Communication with parents	1	1	1	2	2	3	3	1	1
Recent developments in mathematics	3	1	3	3	9	3	9	2	6
		Sub Total	27	Sub Total	62	Sub Total	62	Sub Total	32
Interests									
Commitment to multi-cultural education	4	5	20	3	12	4	16	5	20
PE/Games	3	4	12	0	0	2	6	1	3
		Sub Total	32	Sub Total	12	Sub Total	22	Sub Total	23

Table 20 (cont´d)

Teacher with special responsibility for mathematics	Importance Weighting	Mr Brown Actual Score	Mr Brown Weighted Score	Mrs Green Actual Score	Mrs Green Weighted Score	Miss Lilac Actual Score	Miss Lilac Weighted Score	Mr White Actual Score	Mr White Weighted Score
<u>Other Comments</u>									
Suitability as colleague	5	3	15	4	20	5	25	4	20
Ambitious	1	2	2	3	3	3	3	5	5
Interested in PTA	2	1	2	3	6	2	4	4	8
		Sub Total	19	Sub Total	29	Sub Total	32	Sub Total	33
Total Weighted Scores			98		148		141		115

<u>Discussion Points</u>

<u>Candidate Appointed</u> MRS GREEN

<u>Notes</u> The weighting on this table is provided as a guide to interviewers. The scoring on this form should be on a 1-5 scale where, on the basis of the evidence, 5 is the highest unweighted score which can be awarded to any candidate in any category, 3 indicates an average rating and 1 is low. The weighted score for each item is arrived at by multiplying the actual score for each item by the figure in the IMPORTANCE WEIGHTING column. Thus, on the available evidence Mrs Green was given an actual score of 4 for her success as a class teacher. This has an importance weighting of 5. Therefore her weighted score is 20.

will be but one. The optimum size is five if the interview is to remain flexible and useful. Preparing the panel is one way in which the headteacher is able to guide and influence its decisions if she so wishes.

The objectives of every selection interview are threefold. The first, and most obvious, is to establish whether the candidate is suitable for the post and, if so, in what particular ways her talents can best be used to mutual advantage. The second objective is to ensure that the candidate has an accurate picture of the job for which she is being considered. If she is a strong contender for the post it is doubly important that she should be given a full understanding of what that job entails. It is pointless to gloss over aspects which the interviewer thinks may be unattractive. If, in fact, they are unattractive to that candidate, it is far better that she should withdraw her candidature. A new teacher who believes she has been misled is unlikely to stay in the post for long or to be a valuable member of staff while she remains. The third objective is to conduct the interview in such a manner that the candidate feels she has had a fair hearing, whether she is appointed or not.

The prime purpose is to choose the most appropriate candidate for the post based on all the available evidence. The application forms, letters of application and references form the initial evidence upon which the selection is based. The interview is usually the final stage in the process. Evidence tends to fall into the categories of essential and desirable. During the initial phases it is relatively easy to separate the two categories since most of the time only written evidence is being considered. In the interview stage the personality and appearance of candidates can play a very significant part in blurring the distinction between the two categories. Interviewers in primary schools, apart from the headteacher perhaps, may have very little practical experience of making appointments and may, therefore, need careful guidance as to the criteria to be used in the selection process. A sheet similar to that given in Table 19 can be produced to enable interviewers to focus on the qualities, experience and interests being sought. Such a form can be available in every school as a blank to be filled in each time an appointment has to be made. It might look like the form in Table 20. Each interviewer will complete a form during the interview. For some of the sections the scores are easily determined. The qualifications section, for example could almost be a yes/no answer except that the grading of the qualification might be important. Thus Mrs Green had an upper-second class honours degree with mathematics as her main subject while Miss Lilac had a pass degree. Mr White's PGCE was for maths and science in the primary age range. In some of the other sections reaching an agreement on the basis of the interview and other evidence is more difficult and more subjective but a process such as this can concentrate the discussion on relevant criteria and on how different judgements were made on the basis of those criteria. It makes the interviewers consider relevant evidence in a similar way. Thus, although all may not be agreed on the evidence about Mrs White's success as a class teacher the debate can be about the evidence which might be used to make an evaluation rather than about peripheral issues. In many interviews a main concern may be whether or not an individual will fit into the existing staff. All of the candidates scored well on this but the total weighted scores indicate that the person who might fit into the staff best of all may well not be the successful candidate. Much depends on what the interviewers are looking for. In this case Mrs Welton wants strong curriculum leadership. Here Mrs Green is the strongest candidate although Miss Lilac may be marginally the better class teacher and she has additional special school experience which enables her to score higher in the area of diagnosing learning difficulties and identifying strategies to cope with them. Mr Brown's strengths appear to be in areas which are not central to the role which Mrs Welton may want him to play in the school. Mr White, on the other hand, is the best qualified of the candidates but is rather short on experience. For Mrs Welton, then, the choice is between Mrs Green and Miss Lilac. Other interviewers shared this view but only after a long dicussion about the commitment of all candidates to multicultural education and the inability of Mrs Green to offer PE and Games.

The approach advocated here involves judgement based on a thorough evaluation of the evidence at every stage. The success or failure of this method, however, depends largely on the interviewing skills of the panel. Interviewing can only be done well in the appropriate environment. Whenever possible interviews should be held in the school. The physical setting has quite an important bearing on the degree of rapport which can be established. An office used for interviewing should be reasonably noise-proof and the furnishings should not be too distracting. Chairs should be so arranged that the interviewers do not appear to be dominating the candidate. With a little forethought, it is seldom necessary for the interviewers to address the candidate across an enormous desk, or from a higher chair, or to have artificial light blazing into the eyes of the guest. Easy chairs and coffee tables are suitable for most interviews but where a desk is used be sure to clear away all irrelevant documents before the interview. Above all, the environment should be clean, tidy, uncluttered and free from interruptions. There should be complete freedom from telephone calls and other interruptions whilst the interview is in progress. These arrangements are essential if the interviewing panel is to do its job properly. Concentration is essential!

Interviewing involves a range of quite specific skills. These skills need to be employed to ensure that a dialogue takes place between the candidate and the panel with the major part in the dialogue being taken by the candidate who must be allowed to show herself in her best light. If the candidate is doing most of the talking then members of the interviewing panel must be doing most of the listening. It is by listening to the candidate that the panel will identify most of the relevant evidence about her. Listening takes place on three levels. The first is actually making sense of the current response to the immediate question. The second is relating that response to what has gone before and to what may follow later. The third enables the interviewer to form judgements about accuracy, consistency and even commitment. Good listeners will try not to interrupt and will avoid thinking of their next question while the candidate is talking. The next question will often be related to something that the candidate has previously said and this can only be achieved by accurate and active listening.

Active listening involves observing. This is the skill of making judgements about the candidate on the basis of her non-verbal behaviour, including eye contact, facial expression, tone of voice and gesture. Many candidates are nervous at interview. This is natural. Other factors do have an effect on the interviewing panel. Appearance is one such factor. The image which a candidate presents to the panel is important. What to wear and how to look can be a matter of fine judgement and is certainly one on which different members of a panel may have different views. How significant all of these non-verbal signals are is open to debate. What is clear is that they do influence opinion and, since this is the case, they should be discussed openly by the panel in order that their relevance or otherwise to the post under discussion can be explored.

If listening and observing provide evidence upon which judgements can be made it is the skill of questioning which can trigger the responses from candidates to provide the evidence. (See Table 21) Goodworth (1983) suggests that the interview is not an interrogation and, therefore, interviewers must reflect deeply about the type of questions they wish to use. He argues that all interviews should be based on open questions, that is those questions which require the candidate to give explanatory answers. Such questions almost always begin with words such as What, Why, How, When although Which and Where may also be employed. Thus for this post questions might be employed such as:

- What experience have you had of providing school-based in-service courses?
- Why did you choose the Kent Mathematics Project for your mathematics scheme?
- How did you involve your colleagues in making that choice?
- Which other schemes were examined?
- When did you make your choice?

Such questions may be followed by probing questions which enable the interviewer to explore further the issues raised by the candidate. For example:

- What difficulties did you encounter in setting up your in-service day?
- How did you overcome them?

OR

- What are the main strengths of the Scottish Primary Maths scheme?
- Can you give me some examples from your work with children?

Challenging questions, those which set problems rather than those which are deliberately antagonistic or aggressive, may also be used. For example: "You have seen the mathematics equipment. How would you improve it?" At the end of a particular sequence of questions it can be useful for the interviewer concerned to summarise briefly what has been said and to get agreement from the candidate that her views have been clearly represented and understood.

Normally interviewers should avoid closed questions which require a short or a yes/no answer. These do not require candidates to discuss or explain their views. Such questions should be avoided unless they are being used to confirm information or as a precursor to a probing question. Leading or assumptive questions should always be avoided. Thus questions such as "Do you agree that it is important to keep accurate records?" simply invites an affirmative answer and reveals nothing about the candidate except that she agrees with a bland statement of intent. An open question might follow: "How would you set about keeping accurate records?" This question could have been asked independently of the closed question even if it had to be rephrased slightly. Valuable time has been wasted in a relatively short interview by asking an ill-conceived question. Similarly those questions which contain an assumption reveal little: "You have worked with the Kent Maths Project for three years so I can take it that you will have no trouble in explaining its strengths to colleagues?" What candidate who is even half awake is going to refute that assumption?

The flow of the discussion is largely in the hands of the interviewers. The chairperson must be in control of the situation throughout, however light may be her touch. If each interviewer has expressed herself clearly at the outset, so that the candidate knows in advance what sort of response is expected she will usually receive relevant answers to her questions. If she does not, the candidate can soon be directed back to the right lines. Simple openings, "I was most interested in...", or "I'd rather we concentrated on....", will work wonders on the person who has wandered away from the point.

The good listener will always find a link question from among asides and comments on previous subjects, "You mentioned just now that... Could you tell me a little more about...?" A comparative question will frequently suffice, and, at the same time, introduce a demand for self-insight, "How did

Table 21 QUESTIONING TECHNIQUES IN INTERVIEWS

The most important rule to remember is:

> Ask OPEN questions as much as possible
> The candidates must do most of the talking

OPEN questions may require explanatory answers. They may be:

GENERAL	
"Tell me about your present job?"	- To get the applicant to start talking and feel at ease
"Can you tell us about some of the curriculum leadership initiatives you have taken in your present post?"	
PROBING	
"You say that you regard the Cockcroft Report as the most important single document about mathematics teaching How have you reached this conclusion?"	- how/what/why questions are good ones,to explore points
"Tell me more"	- to encourage the applicant
"Can you add to that?"	- to carry on talking, expanding on what she has said
"Give me some examples"	
CHALLENGING	
"You've seen the equipment in each room. How would you set about increasing its use by all staff?"	- one or two mildly challenging questions will show whether the applicant can apply her experience. Do not overdo it or imply criticism

Summary questions MUST be brief. They can:

1. Help to ensure that the candidate's views are being correctly understood and interpreted
2. Bring one phase of questioning to a close and open another one

Table 21 (Cont´d)

The following types of question do not yield much useful information. Use them as little as possible:

<u>CLOSED</u> (Yes/No) "Are you familiar with school television programmes?"	- only use closed questions when you want to confirm points. They do not encourage the applicant to open up
<u>LEADING</u> (Cued) "Do you agree that it is important to keep accurate records?"	- do not use this type of question. You learn nothing from it
<u>ASSUMPTIVE</u> "You spent a year in a mixed age class so can I take it that you will have no trouble organising children´s work?"	- do not make assumptions - evidence of ´experience` is not necessarily evidence of skill

that work compared with ...?" The interview should not be closed without the candidate being given an opportunity to ask questions and to volunteer information which she feels has not been adequately taken into account. This can be achieved quite simply by asking "Is there anything else you would like to know about this post?" and by posing a question such as "Are there any other important aspects you would like to raise?" At the end of the interview the candidate should be reminded of how and when the decision will be reached and communicated to her and, above all, thanked for her interest in the post. These points had all been covered by Mrs Welton in a workshop on interviewing which she and her pastoral inspector had held for the school´s governors.

Making the Appointment

By the end of the interviews each candidate will have assimilated further information about the post and each member of the interviewing panel will be faced with the task of digesting and interpreting an array of information about each candidate. If the interview has been conducted properly the candidate will have a detailed picture of the school, the post and the people with whom she will be working if appointed. Gaps in the panel´s knowledge about the candidates will have been filled in and they will have noted the performance of each candidate under similar circumstances. All of this information has now to be processed. The framework for this is the person specification and the related forms which each panellist will have filled in on each candidate.

Most interviews are organised so that the panel can reflect upon each candidate briefly after she has been interviewed in broad terms of strengths, weaknesses and any specific circumstances which might influence the decision of the panel. At this point the interview analysis sheet should be completed by each member of the panel. When the final stage of reaching a decision begins the chairperson should remind the panel of the job descriptions and person specification highlighting the essential requirements to be taken into account when appointing. Each member of the panel should review the information on each candidate, and, on the basis of a comparison between this information and the essential requirements of the post, note down the name of any candidate that they think ought not to be appointed. This done, these names can then be shared. If there is general agreement the reasons for this elimination can be examined. Once such a candidate has been eliminated he or she should no longer enter into the discussion. It is tempting here to ask if there is a consensus about which candidate should be appointed. However this can often lead to a poor or second best choice being made. The total available evidence ought now to be considered by all the panellists for each candidate until they can be placed in an agreed rank order. This process ensures that the merits of all the appointable candidates are carefully considered.

The Interview Analysis Sheet helps in this process because it relates directly to the person specification for the post and it is a combination of professional judgement and measurement of relevant attributes, experience, qualifications and interests. Further discussion might be developed by encouraging the panel to:

- o assemble the facts of the candidate´s career in chronological order;

- o superimpose her explanations and attitudes using quotations of her actual words when possible;

- o examine the trends and behaviour patterns;

- o consider her progress and rate of development in relation to her peers. Compared with people from a similar background and with similar opportunities, has her progress been below average, about average or better than average?

Whilst the interview is in progress and afterwards, the interviewer will formulate working hypotheses about the candidate and then search for evidence in past and present behaviour to confirm or refute those hypotheses. A useful technique is to visualise the candidate at work in typical situations and to consider how she might behave: "I can see her coping convincingly with curriculum development in this school". The interviewers aim is to build up a coherent picture of the salient features of the candidate's life. Only a few bare bones have previously been apparent from the candidate's own written statements. It is all too easy at this point to forget the person specification and the job description, especially when faced with candidates who have wide ranging strengths and qualities. It is an essential function of the chairperson to remind the panel of the main requirements of the post for which the candidates have been interviewed. It would be unfair to the candidates and deleterious to the school if an appointment is made on any other criteria. Better not to appoint than to appoint somebody who is not suitable for the post as advertised. From time to time during the discussion of candidates it may be necessary for the chairperson to bring the panel back to the essential features of the post and the main requirements of the person to be appointed. People continually have to be linked with tasks.

Once the decision has been made the selected candidate can be informed. If the candidates are still waiting then the successful person should be invited to re-enter the interviewing room and the other candidates asked to wait a few moments longer. Here the onus is on the interviewers to ensure that the candidate has a clear picture of the post which she is being offered, the duties and responsibilities that go with it and the salary scale. The discussion of salary can be held to be legally binding at this stage so care has to be taken with the offer, especially if the candidate's appointment has still to be ratified by the LEA or is subject to any conditions such as satisfactorily completing a medical. Details such as date of appointment, visits to the school and so on may all be raised at this point although the candidate may well have to seek permission from her present employer for these if they are outside the normal agreements. If the candidates have already dispersed then the preliminary offer and discussion may take place by telephone although no appointment can be agreed except in writing.

At this point the unsuccessful candidates should be told that the post has been filled and thanked again for their interest. Some of them may find it helpful to have some feedback on the interview. This is often done by the LEA representative who may know the candidates from inside the authority. If at all possible this feedback should be positive, constructive and encouraging. Sometimes each candidate is given the opportunity to discuss her performance informally with the appointing panel although this is very time-consuming for all parties. All the papers relating to the appointment should be kept for a period of time in case there are any queries about the appointment. This can often happen in LEAs where redeployment is an integral part of the process of staff selection and appointment. The papers pertaining to the successful candidate should be retained as the start of her personal file, but all the notes made on all the candidates during the interview should be collected up and destroyed (not consigned to the waste paper basket) by the headteacher.

Induction

The appointment process does not end when the successful candidate has accepted the post. The appointment is, in fact, the start of another process, that of induction. The induction process should begin by informing the existing staff that the appointment has been made. At Rosemary Lane, therefore, Mrs Welton informed her colleagues that Mrs Green had been appointed, that she would take up her appointment on the first day of the next term and that she would be visiting the school in two weeks' time. The note also included a few details about their new colleague for the staff. A little nearer the time she will, of course, arrange for colleagues to meet Mrs Green on her first visit. She

Table 22 CHECKLIST FOR INDUCTION INFORMATION

1. Terms of employment and conditions of service
   - Normally provided by LEA but may need checking and explaining
   - Salary and methods/date of payment
2. School Organisation
   - Details of start/break/meal/finish times and dates of terms
   - List of duties and playground supervision
   - Basic routines for entering, leaving building, playtime, lunchtime, visits, out of school activities
   - Staff meetings and parent meetings
   - Fire drill and first aid material
   - Arrangement of staff facilities, provision of and payment for refreshments
3. The School
   - Names and responsibilities of staff including ancillaries, helpers, caretaker and secretary
   - Policy on marking, discipline, pupil and staff records, registers, dinner money, absenteeism
   - Arrangements for children with special needs
   - Layout of the school
   - Organisation and allocation of classrooms and other facilities such as the hall, library and special equipment
   - Arrangements for consulting and being consulted by other colleagues, headteacher and parents
   - Governors' meetings and names of governors
   - Arrangements for Assembly
4. The Post
   - Timetable and working arrangements
   - Curriculum documents
   - Stock and equipment availability and ordering
   - Responsibilities and duties
   - Agreed targets and priorities
   - Staff development and further training
   - Arrangements for staff review interviews
   - Communication within the school
5. The Locality
   - Details of catchment area including transport and shopping facilities
   - Other local amenities
   - Teachers' Centre
   - Community involvement in school
   - Accommodation and nearby schools

will also involve the existing staff in the induction process.

For all new appointments the initial visit to the school after appointment may be rather difficult especially if there are unsuccessful candidates on the staff. The first visit should, therefore, be more social than inductive, enabling the new colleague to become familiar with the buildings and to meet her fellow teachers and the children she will be teaching. The first visit also provides the new member of staff with the opportunity to ask questions and deal with her own immediate concerns which may have arisen since the interview. In the case of Mrs Green she is taking on a new role. She will want to talk this through in detail with the headteacher and may wish to arrange several discussions between the appointment being made and starting her new job. The first visit is also a good opportunity to check that the new colleague has such documents as the school handbook, the staff handbook, and to give her recent newsletters, curriculum guidelines, and copies of timetables, equipment lists, and details of any stock ordering that may have to take place before the start of the next term. Some of this may have been provided as part of the material sent out to the applicants for the post but it is advisable at this stage to ensure that the new colleague has a <u>complete</u> set of relevant information.

The initial visit might be followed by several more, one of which may be a formal induction day when all the relevant details of appointment are covered by various members of staff in various ways. In Rosemary Lane this took place for Mrs Green on the day before term started and involved Mrs Welton, Mr Jowett and Mrs Cass. Much of the basic information about the school had already been given to Mrs Green prior to her interview and she had learned much about the basic organisation of the school, the arrangement of classes and the available resources. She was, however, provided with the information outlined in Table 22. In future Mrs Welton decided to compile a pack of information of this kind which could be presented to new colleagues or given to visitors where this was appropriate. This induction day enabled Mrs Green to check that she had all the information which she needed to start her new post in the best possible way. She had information at her finger tips or could find it quickly and she had organised her room to her satisfaction. She could now concentrate on her professional responsibilities.

Mrs Green is well on the way to becoming an important member of the staff team at Rosemary Lane. She is clear about why she was appointed and about what her duties and responsibilities are. She can begin to give the curriculum leadership which she was appointed to provide. How then might she set about doing this? Equally how can Mrs Welton move her staff away from the group of relatively independent individuals that they have become, each doing a thorough professional job but on the whole lacking a clear sense of direction and balance in the education that they are providing for the children in their care? How can the staff group become a staff team? It is to this difficult issue that we turn in the next chapter.

Activities

1. Using the person specification for your own post, compile a list of the types of evidence you would use to identify a person who met those specifications.

2. Draw up a list of information you might send to an applicant for a post at your school.

3. Plan an initial visit for a person applying for your post at your school.

4. Plan an induction day for somebody taking over your post.

Chapter 6

MANAGING THE PRIMARY TEAM

It has been argued thus far that primary schools are now subject to a range of pressures and demands from within the education service and external to it which require certain types of response from the schools. These responses involve a gradual, almost grudging application of management techniques to institutions in which such techniques might, a decade ago, have been regarded as alien. The need deliberately and consciously to manage primary schools has found expression in a number of influential documents, in a range of courses provided for teachers at all levels in primary schools and, most recently, in the *Pay and Conditions of Service for Teachers Order* (1987). At the same time the curriculum in primary schools, and in other sectors of education, has also come under scrutiny and continues to do so. As a result new subject areas are emerging, CDT and computer technology for example, while the proposals for a national curriculum and the related proposals for testing are likely to change the relationship between the various subject areas. Prior to this the *Curriculum 5-16* documents raised questions about the breadth balance, relevance and differentiation of the curriculum. One implication of *all* these developments, not only of the proposed national curriculum, is that the decisions about the nature of teaching and learning in the primary school can no longer be taken by the individual teacher in her classroom, if they ever could.

Primary schools increasingly are being required to respond to current developments in education by making the most of the wide range of expertise available within each school. There is an obvious need for primary schools to acquire and to develop staff with clear areas of expertise. Appointments such as the one at Rosemary Lane which was discussed in the previous chapter are becoming more common: appointments, that is, based on clear statements about areas of expertise and curriculum leadership rather than on classroom experience alone. Where these appointments are being made it is no longer sufficient for the expertise which thus becomes available to the school to be allowed to remain contained within an individual classroom or to be disseminated through relatively accidental processes of osmosis, influence and the setting of good examples. The expertise has to be made available to all staff in a systematic way. This presents many primary schools with a major management problem, staffed as they are on the basis of one teacher to every 35 children with, in some LEAs, the head-teacher being expected to carry out a major teaching responsibility. There are no easy solutions to this problem, although several different strategies are possible. At Rosemary Lane, which is large enough for the headteacher not to have to carry a full teaching load, Mrs Welton deliberately uses her teaching time to free her staff so that they can work alongside their colleagues or develop materials for their colleagues to use. She is gradually clarifying the responsibilities of her staff so that they all have an area of curriculum responsibility, not just an age-related one. As the Select Committee Report on Primary Education (HMSO 1987) pointed out, all teachers in primary schools whatever their salary scale will be expected to have such a responsibility. As was suggested in Chapter Four, agreement on and clarity about roles and responsibilities of all staff is essential for effective management. One way to achieve this is through negotiated job descriptions related to school development plans.

Mrs Welton will use the discussions she has with her staff on both the school development plan and on job descriptions to explore other ways of making their expertise more available to all colleagues. She will also look at the ways in which her staff are deployed to ensure that she is making optimum use of the staff available. Norman Thomas, the architect of the Primary Survey (DES 1978) and the author of Improving Primary Schools, (ILEA, 1985) has suggested that in many primary schools the issue of staff deployment has not been grasped in a purposeful way. In this he echoes the belief of many others that in primary schools all too often an extra teacher is used only to reduce class sizes to a point where further reductions may become almost a waste of a valuable resource. His guideline is a simple one. Where the deployment of an extra teacher reduces the class size to much less than 35 (reception classes excluded) then careful consideration ought to be given to alternative uses to which that member of staff might be put. In Rosemary Lane the class sizes are such that, if the reception class is excluded and if the part-time teacher is also excluded, the average class size is 32.5. If one teacher was to be excluded from this then the average size would increase to 39 which is clearly unacceptable. If, however, Rosemary Lane ever received the extra staffing which is intimated in the Select Committee Report, then should that colleague be used merely as a class teacher? The average class size would fall to just below 28. Thomas would argue that this is not the most effective way to employ the extra teacher. Far better to use that teacher to free other teachers with specialist expertise to work alongside colleagues in their own classrooms at appropriate times.

In the absence of this extra staffing other ways have to be found to make this expertise available. Within the organisation of most primary schools there is normally little, if any provision for non-contact time to enable such work to take place. This is a fundamental weakness in the resourcing of primary education, especially if schools are expected to respond positively to current initiatives and developments. The need to respond will still exist even if the desired level of resourcing has yet to be achieved. If the staff of the school is being deployed as effectively as is possible along the lines indicated by Norman Thomas then there are only a limited number of alternative strategies available to the primary school manager, most of which will be familiar to those who have wrestled with this problem. Classes, year groups or the whole school can be combined in some purposeful activity in the care of one teacher or with a small group of teachers working together, while the rest of the staff are engaged on a joint project or on individual consultations during that period. Musical activities, PE or games, drama or even prepared projects inside or outside the school lend themselves to this form of organisation. GRIST money can sometimes be used to facilitate staff cooperation and the more effective use of expertise by buying-in supply cover, where it is available, to enable one or more teachers to be free to work with their colleagues. Such use of GRIST money has to be well-planned in advance if the most is to be made of such opportunities. GRIST can also be used to resource in-service days and, of course, schools now have five such days at their disposal.

In-service days and in-service meetings after school are valuable ways of sharing expertise through learning from and with colleagues. Such events should be related to the school´s development plan and will need to be well planned and professionally presented. Apart from the content of such in-service work however, the establishing and fostering of a common approach within the school to common areas of concern and the development of a staff group identity are vitally important. No single person can manage a staff group effectively when that group has to respond to the type of demands which now confront primary school staff. Managing schools is not an end in itself. The desire for effective management must rest on the belief that through effective management will come more effective teaching. Through more effective teaching will come more effective learning. Through more effective learning, children in primary schools will benefit, both while they are in the schools and in the future.

Collegial management is presented here as one model of management which might enable this to happen. It is a model in the sense that this form of management may not exist as a pure form in any one school although it is a state towards which many schools may want to move in their different ways. Thus in Rosemary Lane, collegiality is embryonic yet Mrs Welton is already laying the foundations on which to build a more collegial structure. She sees collegiality as a way of sharing the tasks of the school and as a way of giving responsibility based on expertise, believing that in trying to encourage her staff to work in this way they will find that their talents are being used more effectively and that, ultimately, the children will benefit from this. Collegiality here does not involve the "hard" approach to management that was discussed earlier since directing, controlling and commanding are not appropriate among groups of professional colleagues. Involvment, co-operation, participation, delegation and effective communication are more likely to enable Mrs Welton to achieve her objectives. Thus relationships will have to be established within the Rosemary Lane staff group to enable these activities to take place. The staff will have to develop good working relationships, not exactly the same as good social relationships. In short the staff need to be helped to work together as a team.

What is Team Work?

The primary school staff team will have a number of characteristics. It will have a process for discussing its aims for the school and it will seek to identify and achieve common objectives. Whatever its structure the effectiveness of the group will be increased if the importance is recognised of agreed perceptions of the task and of a shared achievement of these common objectives. Thus, shared and agreed plans for the development of the school and for the part to be played in that process by identified individuals is important. The consensus implied in this view of primary school management will not be achieved by accident. Each staff team, whether it is the whole staff group working together or a smaller group of colleagues with a shared function, will have to develop working relationships which are consistent with the overall philosophy of the school. These relationships will need to be negotiated within the group. They cannot be imposed from outside. Once they are established, they will need to be managed. Building and managing the staff team is the prime responsibility of the primary school headteacher. It is also an important responsibility of any individual teacher who happens to be leading a group of colleagues at any particular time. Thus, although professional or subject expertise may be the basis of such leadership, the leadership function can only be carried out to its maximum effect if the staff team is consciously built and effectively managed.

In any discussion of team building and managing an understanding of the nature of team work is crucial but this is seldom considered. It is generally assumed that everyone knows what teamwork is. Thus, when "staff team" is mentioned teachers are expected to have a shared perception of what that means. Most staffroom discussions of this matter will reveal just how erroneous that assumption is. For example, the prevalent notion of professional or staff development among almost any group of teachers will focus on developing the skills, knowledge and experience of individuals but the key to successful teamwork is to be found in the way in which groups of teachers relate to, and work with each other. Group development, therefore, should be seen as no less important than individual development because teamwork means individuals working together to achieve more than they could alone. The success of the primary school staff team, then, depends not only on the individual skills of its members but on the way those teachers support and work with each other. (See Table 23)

Table 23 TEAM WORK

What is team work?

A group of people working together on the basis of:

- o Shared perceptions
- o A common purpose
- o Agreed procedures
- o Commitment
- o Cooperation
- o Resolving disagreements openly by discussion

This will not happen automatically. Teamwork has to be managed if it is to be effective.

Teamwork has been described as playing from the same sheet of music. The implication of this statement is that teamwork can build upon the strengths of individuals and create confidence within the group which individuals on their own may lack. Thus teamwork, which is demanding and time consuming, can help to reduce stress and pressure through the mutual support which it can provide. Within most primary schools the individual teacher has, hitherto, been regarded as the focal point for change and innovation and the locus of expertise. It has been argued here that this emphasis is changing and that it has to change. The team, the staff group, the collection of cooperating colleagues, will increasingly be the focal point of professional activity within the primary school. Such activity, if it is well managed, may bring significant benefits to individuals, to groups and to the whole school, as Table 24 shows. Thus the collegial approach to management in primary schools, while it may be developing through force of circumstance, may bring with it some important benefits to schools. For this to happen the nature of teamwork has to be

Table 24 THE BENEFITS OF TEAMWORK IN THE PRIMARY SCHOOL

- Agreeing aims
- Clarifying roles
- Sharing expertise and skills
- Maximising use of resources
- Motivating, supporting and encouraging members of the team
- Improving relationships within the staff group
- Encouraging decision-making
- Increasing participation
- Realising individual potential
- Improving communication
- Increasing knowledge and understanding
- Reducing stress and anxiety

thoroughly understood. Effective teamwork will not happen automatically by placing groups of individuals in a room together with a task to perform. It requires a conscious and deliberate set of management strategies. These must be employed by the team leader whether she is the headteacher working with the whole staff or one teacher using her expertise in a particular area of the school's work in conjunction with, say, a group of colleagues who teach the same year group. Colleagues may be members of several teams at any one time. Some teams may be temporary with specific and limited tasks such as planning part of an in-service day or a school concert. Others may be permanent, with responsibility for a part of the curriculum. At Rosemary Lane the deputy headteacher is beginning to establish such a team for multicultural education.

The newly appointed teacher with curriculum responsibility for mathematics, Mrs Green, will need to build her own team. She may also need to work with teams of colleagues who are grouped according to the age of the children that they teach. Thus she will be a temporary team leader of a team which is relatively permanent. The headteacher may consider creating a team to help her with the major management tasks of the school. This might include her deputy head and Mrs Cass who has responsibility for the infant department. All of these groupings are teams. Furthermore, they are working or functional teams since they have a task or a series of tasks to complete. They will all consist, to a greater or lesser extent, of a number of individuals with their own skills, experience and responsibilities as well as their own levels of commitment, personal concerns, pressures and influences. They will be guided by a team leader who accepts overall responsibility for the development of the team, its aims, the standards which it sets and the results which it achieves. The leadership of any such team may not depend on factors such as position in school, experience, seniority or interest. Team leaders will tend to be those people with direct and relevant expertise. Therefore the teacher accepting responsibility for leading the work of a particular team may be a relatively junior colleague. In the team may be the headteacher or deputy head. In this instance they will be team members and not team leaders. The leadership will be provided by the teacher with the expertise. Thus it is crucial that all members of staff in primary schools understand the processes involved in managing and leading teams. This chapter will concentrate entirely on exploring a model for effective teamwork which can be applied to the whole staff room in the primary school or to working groups within that staff team. It is recognised that teams normally work through meetings and through the delegation of tasks to team members in order to maximise the use of time, skills and experience especially in situations in which, as at present in schools, there are considerable pressures for change. Delegation, organising effective and useful meetings, the optimum use of time, and responding to pressures for change will all be dealt with in subsequent chapters. This chapter will concentrate on the processes of teamwork.

If teamwork is seen as a group of individuals working together towards some common purpose and, in so doing, achieving more than they could alone, then the justification for the existence of a working team in any school would seem to be self-evident. Almost no one enjoys working in a situation in which she is isolated, alienated, criticised, overcontrolled or where she feels frustrated and dissatisfied with her own performance as a teacher or colleague. Successful teamwork can only take place, however, when the team has the facilities required to gather relevant information, to make sound and informed decisions and to implement those decisions. The absence of any of these factors can mean that the team cannot work effectively or that it will not work at all. Lack of individual commitment can have a similar effect and so can a variety of personal issues which are not brought out into the open within the team context. Individuals may have such undisclosed aims as ambition, retribution, destruction and covert support which they may intend to pursue within the working of the team. The effect of such factors can be considerable and it is the responsibility of the team leader to be able to identify such factors and bring them into the open as part of teamwork.

Colleagues will contribute to the staff team only that which they feel, as individuals, they wish to contribute. This may include their knowledge and skills but it may also include their dislikes and jealousies, their uncertainties and perceived, or real lack of ability or experience. None of these factors need present the team leader with insurmountable difficulties provided she is aware of their existence. Lack of skill may be overcome with training. Dislikes need to be aired within the team in a sympathetic and controlled way. Jealousies have to be countered by building self-esteem rather than by diminishing the worth of another individual within the team. An effective team leader will recognise that there are a number of psychological processes operating within any team through which colleagues come to identify with the team. These processes can be seen as a useful counterbalance to those factors which may make effective teamwork difficult.

Interaction between the individual and the team may take place on the basis of one or more "psychological contracts" which the individual may make, consciously or unconsciously, between herself and the team. The interaction may be based on compliance, that is on the avoidance of some form of punishment, isolation perhaps, or to gain some form of reward such as acceptance by the team. To the extent that the individual wishes to gain the reward or avoid the punishment, he or she will comply with what the team is doing. This need not result in passive conformity, especially if the ethos of the team is such that decisions are taken and actions planned on the basis of informed, open, analytical discussion. Secondly the interaction may be based on identification. That is on the need to find support for some course of action which the individual may wish to pursue and which she regards as being compatible with activities of the team. The interaction may be based on rationality: that is on the recognition that the individual does not have to like the advice for this form of contract to be effective. Even if such advice or support is contrary to the individual's normal role or set of expectations such a contract can exist provided the individual recognises that what the team is offering is logical and rational. Finally the contract may be based on internalisation, that is on the belief that what the team is doing, or how it seeks to perform its functions, is, in itself, worthy of support and participation. This, clearly, is the strongest form of contract and the one which is likely to generate the most commitment from the team members to the team itself. Nevertheless the other forms of contract should not be dismissed or disparaged provided that the team leader can identify them, recognise them for what they are, and be aware of the limitations which they imply, for it is with bricks such as these that successful working teams are built.

Team Development

Good teamwork will not just happen. It needs to be developed and managed. It also needs to be based on an understanding of the different reasons which colleagues may have for participating in a staff team in the ways in which they may do. Each individual will participate to a slightly different extent and for somewhat different reasons depending on the nature of the "psychological contract" she has made between herself and the team. The effective leader of a staff team has to be aware of these factors. Such factors constrain the extent to which colleagues are prepared to be involved in the workings of the group but they are not the only relevant factors affecting involvement. The individual factors mentioned in the previous section are also relevant and so is the way in which teachers perceive the staff team itself. The way in which it appears to operate is a crucial factor in determining the extent to which colleagues are willing to give their time to the team. People are usually more willing to commit themselves to expending their time and energy on a staff team if they understand clearly what they are doing and why they are doing it. This means that the team leader has to understand and communicate to colleagues the rationale which underpins the work of the staff team. In other words the existence, within the school, of a clear and agreed approach to primary education is a crucial element in the effectiveness of the staff team, be it the whole staff working on a project or a group of colleagues with some special responsibility.

It will be clear from the way in which the school is organised that the activities of any staff team are only one part of the total work of the school. Realistically, therefore, there are limits to what any team can do, the problems with which it can cope, and the issues which it can address. It serves no useful purpose to have an exaggerated view about what is possible within the framework of the working team. For example neither the team nor its leader can necessarily be held responsible for having the wrong people appointed to the staff. No amount of teamwork can fit a square peg into a round hole. The team can, however, attempt to develop training programmes for its members who may lack certain skills or information. These need not be as elaborate as a fully blown in-service course but might simply be the provision of an opportunity for an experienced colleague to work with a less experienced one on a particular aspect of primary school teaching. The team cannot necessarily address directly the problems created by a confused or inappropriate organisational structure in which, for example, a particular group is not functioning effectively or, conversely, is too powerful for the good of the whole organisation. The team can only try to ensure that it achieves as much as it can in the circumstances. Nor can the team deal with situations which are characterised by a lack of overall planning within the school, low morale in the school or in the wider education system, an inappropriate system of rewards and promotions or other similar problems. These are management problems which may not be capable of solution within the staff team. They may provide part of the context within which the team has to work and over which its members have little or no control. They do not make effective teamwork impossible but they may make it more difficult.

The members of any staff team working on a particular task have to recognise that they are part of a team which, in turn, is part of a larger organisation, the school. Effective teamwork on their part is only one of the factors, albeit an important one, upon which the school depends. For example effective teamwork cannot solve all the "people problems" in the school but well developed teams can go a considerable way towards improving the effectiveness of any school. What, then, is a well developed team and how is it achieved? If the team is seen as a group of individuals working together in such a way that some of what they do is independent of the other members but much of what they do depends upon and overlaps with the activities of others, and that this interaction takes place smoothly, efficiently and effectively so that the general provision of education within the school is maintained and improved, that is a well developed team. This is only achieved by a careful consideration of the four main elements of teamwork. These are the aims and objectives of the team, its procedures, its processes and the ways in which team members relate to those processes, and the ways in which the activities of the team are reviewed and monitored. All teams are concerned about the image which they have of themselves and which others may have of them. They are concerned about the standards which are set and about the results which are achieved. They are concerned with the extent to which they can improve and develop both as individuals and as members of the team. Therefore, they are concerned about the extent to which their own needs, as well as those of the team, are taken into account when activities are planned and responsibilities allocated.

All of these concerns crystalise around the nature of the tasks which the team is expected to undertake. In any staff team the members will, to a greater or lesser extent, be aware of what has to be done. Successful teamwork, however, is best achieved when the aims and objectives are clear and when all members subscribe to them. The distinction between aims and objectives in this context is a crucial one. Aims, in the context of managing a team in a primary school, are best regarded as being derived from the overall philosophy of the school and are broadly strategic in nature. To provide guidance for colleagues on developing their mathematics teaching may well be an appropriate aim for Mrs Green at Rosemary Lane. Doubtless, given the terms of her appointment and her job description, colleagues would accept this as a proper and legitimate aim for Mrs Green and the team which she may identify to work with her. In the first instance this team might include all members of staff, given the central importance of mathematics in the primary school. Alternatively initial work in this area might be done by Mrs Green, Mrs Cass and the headteacher in consultation with all other colleagues at various times. Although the activity is accepted as a proper one difficulty might arise with the objectives which have to be identified and from which the tactics to achieve those objectives are derived. These will involve decisions about who is to be involved in giving such guidance, when it is to be given and to whom, what actions are to follow the giving of that information and by whom. The objectives, then, are statements about what requires to be done, by whom, with whom, by when, to what standard of proficiency, and what should be done as a result. These are the tasks of the team. Each team member should understand exactly what is required of her, and should be informed about the scale and urgency of the task to be carried out. It should not be assumed that team members _do_ have this information. The leader of the team should accept the responsibility for providing that information, for checking that it has been assimilated and understood, and that the appropriate actions are taken. This is not an intrusion on the professional autonomy of colleagues but, rather, it is an essential part of the process of effective team management. Nothing inhibits successful team work more than the perception, whether accurate or not, that one or more members of a team is failing in her responsibilities to colleagues or pupils. It is rare indeed for any teacher to believe that she is culpable in this respect. Staff teams will respond to a situation in which the nature of the task to be undertaken is discussed, agreed and fully understood especially when outstanding disagreements about these matters are resolved before any action has to be taken.

Teams of teachers in primary schools will tend to operate in somewhat different ways according to their circumstances. The different mix of individuals who make up the teams, and the nature of the larger organisation which in this case will be the whole school, all affect the functioning of the team. It is important to recognise that teams cannot exist independently of each other, or of the school itself. Nor should they seek to do so. The team's preferred way of working should be clearly understood by all members. The options are numerous but it might be that the team is organised on an open, fully participative basis. At the other extreme the team might be firmly and directly controlled by the team leader. The preferred method of operating for many teams is somewhere between those extremes and relies on a policy of encouraging all team members to be involved in decision-making where appropriate, but set within a clear and specific policy framework based on the school´s overall philosophy, aims and objectives, and negotiated with and agreed by the team members. The extent to which it is appropriate to involve team members will depend on such factors as the nature of the immediate task. Does it require quick decisions and action? To what extent does it demand clear direction or arouse much emotion?

When clear direction is required or when the issue is emotive, too much participation can be counterproductive. Who is affected by the issue or task? Where several team members are affected by the task it is essential to involve all of them in key decisions. Who can make a useful contribution and who feels that they have a contribution to make? If several team members have knowledge, experience or even an interest in a particular task or issue then it is best to involve them in making decisions about it. The appropriate method of operating, therefore, might be on the basis of a predetermined view about who should be involved or about who should take the decision to involve other team members. A team leader who has the trust and respect of the team will be able to carry out this function effectively and to ensure that the team can adopt procedures for taking decisions and carrying out tasks. The team can then concentrate on the process of achieving results.

If the procedures adopted by the team dictate how the individuals in that team operate as a group then the processes used by the team will influence how that team sets about achieving its objectives, getting the results and attaining the standards which it has set itself. Team processes are, inevitably, related to team tasks and procedures but, unlike procedures, which are only indirectly related to achieving the task, processes are directly related to specific task achievement. In fact they are the means of achieving the objectives which make up the task. The process of task achievement should start by ensuring that all the members of the team fully understand the aims and the objectives. How this might be done has been described in the preceding paragraphs. If the overall aim is to improve the teaching of mathematics throughout the school, as it might well be at Rosemary Lane, this will need to be subdivided into a number of objectives. One of these might be to catalogue the existing mathematics equipment and other resources which are available within the school since teachers have tended to order equipment for their own rooms rather than for the school as a whole. Another might be to make recommendations for the more effective use of such equipment. These objectives now need to be further subdivided into a number of tasks. It must be decided who will check on the numbers of particular items of equipment, who will look at the text books and work sheets being used in the school and how the use of books and equipment will be monitored and by whom. Thus the team has moved from an aim, through the stage of identifying relevant objectives, to breaking objectives down into a series of tasks. Identifying and carrying out those tasks are part of the process of teamwork. The team is already into the realm of planning. Planning is simply a matter of identifying what has to be done, by whom, with what resources and to what time scale. It involves allocating tasks so that everyone within the team knows who is responsible for what. With those responsibilities should go the necessary authority to ensure that the task can be successfully completed. Resources, both human and material, must be analysed, known and allocated in order to meet the requirements of the various tasks in the most effective way possible. All too often tasks are allocated and resources deployed on the basis of tradition and common practice rather than on the basis of what is actually needed to complete the task in hand. Timing, similarly, is important. Time is always at a premium and it needs managing. One team member's deadline may be another's start time. If the deadline is not met then the next task may not be completed on time. If, for example, the review of existing equipment and the identification of existing text books and work sheets are not completed on time then it becomes very difficult for the colleague who has to monitor equipment use to carry out her responsibility. If this is not done then it will not be possible for recommendations about the future use of equipment to be considered. It is worth ensuring, therefore, that the team member responsible for achieving this particular objective knows how this task fits into the overall programme. Perhaps one member whose main function is to ensure that the various schedules are met, a timekeeper in fact, should be identified. Carrying out the plans, then, requires good communication but it also requires that team members should listen to each other, be supportive and allow ideas and suggestions to be generated and used where possible.

Once the task has been completed this process should still continue. Time should always be allocated so that the team can review what has been done.

Team review is a valuable learning and team development function. All of the team members should be involved in discussing such questions as:

> "Did we complete the task successfully?"
>
> "What went well in our process and can be repeated next time?"
>
> "What went badly and held us back?".

It is because these questions are important to the present activities as well as for the future development of the team that all team members should be present at such discussions even if their roles were only marginal to the enterprise being considered. There are other review techniques which can be applied to many team activities and there is much more that can be said about delegating, allocating responsibilities, communication and the effective management of time. These will be considered further in Chapters Seven and Eight.

The tasks of any staff team may change over time, especially if it is based on year groupings. The processes to be applied in any given situation may vary somewhat from that described above but it is important to remember that the tasks of the team form only one dimension of the teamwork. The membership of the team is of crucial significance because it transcends any single set of tasks, tends to persist over time, and because any individual team member´s commitment to the team and its tasks is determined, in large part, by the extent to which members of the team feel that they are, in fact, team members. Commitment to, or membership of, the team may vary according to the issue or the task. Colleagues will devote more energy to that which they think is important. They will also give their time if they believe that they can influence outcomes or that they have something of value to offer. Membership of the team should not, therefore, be accepted as given. It should, rather, be regarded as a variable which may need to be taken into account, reconsidered, developed and cultivated. Team members may need encouraging, reassuring and appreciating in order to establish and retain their membership of the team in an active sense. Commitment in terms of time and effort cannot always be expected of any team member as of right even if it is a part of a teacher´s professional responsibility.

The effective team leader has to be aware of

these recurring factors and, over a period of time, needs to ensure that the various members of her team do feel themselves to be a valuable part of that team. This can be done simply and informally by finding out from team members how far they feel able to relax in the team meetings; how far they have private reservations about team decisions; how far they really do accept and understand team objectives; how well the team operates as a group and to what extent influence is shared by all team members or is concentrated in the hands of a very small number of colleagues. Such questions as these need never be asked directly by the effective team leader who will be able to collect much of the information implied in these questions by observation, not by interrogation. In the same way the team leader will recognise the extent to which responsibility is really shared within the team and the degree to which differences within the team are suppressed and denied or are identified and worked through satisfactorily. Team membership can be regarded as the single most significant variable in the development of a successful team. It has to be seen for what it is, a variable rather than a constant and, therefore, it has to be kept under review if the team is to remain effective. Thus for any staff team in the primary school four elements are essential to effective team development. Objectives need to be agreed, shared, clearly understood and subdivided into a number of tasks. Procedures for decision-making and planning should involve all team members. The resulting processes for carrying out tasks should be clear to all team members. These procedures should be reviewed frequently in terms of how far they are facilitating the achievement of the objectives of the team at that time. (See Table 25)

Managing the Effective Staff Team

The development of an effective staff team is a complex business. It will not happen by accident and it can be damaged by neglect, but with sympathetic and careful management it can devise processes for fulfilling its aims and objectives and completing its tasks successfully. It can also provide considerable satisfaction for its members. In order to do this, considerable attention has to be paid to those key factors which contribute to the effectiveness of any team. These are the individual, the task, the team and its leadership (see Table 26). These elements form the framework within which the management of the staff team has to be carried out. It is the function of the team leader to ensure, by effective management, that a satisfactory balance is achieved between these elements.

Table 25 DEVELOPING THE STAFF TEAM

TEAM DEVELOPMENT	
OBJECTIVES	The objectives of the team should be clearly understood by all members
PROCEDURE	All team members should be involved in making important decisions
PROCESS	All team members should be clear about what has to be done, by whom, with what resources
REVIEW	The team should review its work regularly as part of a learning and development process

All individuals bring to the team certain strengths and needs. The combinations may vary but the categories remain the same, (Maslow, 1943). We identified four categories which influence the extent to which colleagues are committed to a team and which help to determine the nature of that commitment. Colleagues might, for example, have basic needs related to survival and existence. Such people will obviously be motivated by the need to earn money and, to the extent that they feel their rewards are just, they can be expected to function reasonably well. When, as with the 1986/87 teachers' pay dispute, a significant number of people feel that their rewards are not just, or conditions being imposed are unacceptable, then motivation may depend directly on changes related to basic rewards. Nothing much can be achieved until these needs have been satisfied. This is a fairly extreme position which is unlikely to appertain in all schools with all colleagues, many of whom may identify other forms of needs and rewards. The second category might best be understood as the need for an acceptable self-image. Team members can be helped to become valuable team members by helping them to become the people that they want to be. Thirdly, there is the need to do something useful or meaningful. Clearly this is

Table 26 MANAGING THE TEAM

TEAM MANAGEMENT	
INDIVIDUAL	The nature and extent of the individual team member´s commitment to the team has to be understood
TASK	The task has to be identified, explained and communicated to members and progress towards its achievement monitored
TEAM	The integrity of the team should be maintained by encouraging cooperation and exploring the causes of disagreement
LEADERSHIP	Team leadership has to be flexible, based on an understanding of what is to be achieved in particular situations

related to self-image but it does point out to the team leader that effective team management depends on understanding what colleagues want as much as knowing what the team objectives are. Closely related to the previous two needs is the need to belong to groups of different kinds. Few people genuinely want to exist in isolation and most people want the recognition which comes from being a valued member of a group. This can be a firm basis on which to build team membership. This is particularly true when the team can also provide the opportunity for personal development and, in so doing, meet the need to grow and develop which is experienced by most people. This need is recognised in pupils and is often expressed in terms like fully stretching them or allowing them to reach their full potential. Teachers have a similar need. A good team leader will be aware of that and manage to provide opportunities for team members to grow as part of the team´s activities.

Apart from the obvious financial rewards, therefore, it is possible to provide rewards in several different ways. Those directly related to the task in hand might include more responsibility, a more interesting activity, freedom to plan and implement, or a change in working conditions such as an office space in which to work. Perhaps more subtle than these, the second set of possibilities might include more opportunity to express a particular talent, the chance to develop or improve knowledge or skill, or the chance to exercise full control over some aspect of the team's activities. Then there are the rewards which come from team membership itself. These might include approval, co-operation, friendship. Finally, and least obvious of all, are the rewards connected to those needs which may never be articulated by the individual such as the achievement of some long-term or idealistic aim, or the desire to earn popularity, admiration or respect from others within the team. These possibilities all provide the team leader with opportunities to manage her team to obtain the best effect both for the individual and the group.

The importance of the task in effective team management has been emphasised throughout this chapter. The setting of clear and attainable objectives for the team, allocating responsibilities within the team, identifying targets and establishing ways of measuring progress of the team towards meeting those targets are all part of the duties of the person who is managing the team. Planning to ensure that the group attains the success which its members would not otherwise achieve either as individuals or without the management skills of the team leader is, therefore, a crucial part of the role of the effective staff team manager. Central to this is the ability to identify, define and communicate the nature of the tasks to the team members. The ability to explain why the team is performing the tasks which have been identified and the flexibility to redefine tasks and encourage the team to reallocate responsibilities and resources when this becomes necessary are equally important. A plan is only a good plan as long as it is relevant and as long as it is taking the team where the team wishes to go. Management, in this context, includes the ability to recognise when things are going wrong as well as knowing when they are going right.

When things are going right the essential task of the team leader is to maintain the team and ensure that it continues to work together as a co-operative, supportive entity in its own right. With encouragement this will usually happen but, at times, things do go wrong. When this happens the "commonsense" explanation frequently given for it is in terms of "conflicting personalities", that is in terms of people who are so different and difficult that hostility is endemic and conflict is inevitable. This extreme form of social determinism appears to have very little validity in real situations since, more often than not, it is possible to improve most situations. The "conflicting personality" explanation, on the other hand, would indicate exactly the reverse. It might be more useful to view any threat to team co-operation in terms of a conflict of expectations rather than a conflict of personalities. Whenever the behaviour of one person violates the expectations of another it could reasonably be anticipated that co-operation might be withdrawn and conflict result. People will then attempt to hurt or punish colleagues rather than helping or supporting them. In such a situation the team leader has to recognise what is happening and maintain the integrity of the team. This will, more often than not, have to be done by helping team members to explore their own behaviour with the intention of highlighting where the conflict in expectation is located but without attempting to attribute blame. Such team maintenance activities are the third dimension of effective team management in the primary school.

The final dimension of effective team management is the recognition that the leadership role will be different as the nature of the team's activities change (Adair 1983). For example, as has already been argued, the team may need firm and clear management when it has to complete a specific task within a limited period of time. Alternatively when the team is exploring ideas and issues the emphasis needs to be on the thinking of team members, encouraging all colleagues to contribute and drawing contributions together in order to build upon them. At some of its meetings the team might be receiving a briefing about a forthcoming activity. Here skills of exposition, checking understanding and the management of information are relevant. Persuasiveness, openness, and patience combined with the perception to recognise the importance of what is not being said as well as what is being said might be the essential characteristics required of the team leader when running a meeting to review the processes for achieving a specific objective in order to learn from what has just happened. Different management skills are required of the skilful team leader in different situations.

These four elements, the individuals, the task,

the team and the leadership role, have to be balanced by the effective manager of the staff team. This requires an understanding of the individuals in the team, an awareness of what is going on in the group and of what this might mean in the context of the group and its activities, the skills to act upon this knowledge, and the recognition that different actions might be appropriate in different circumstances. If members are strongly motivated to achieve results, if the team has shared standards and targets, if colleagues seek ways to improve their processes through co-operation and if individuals gain in confidence and ability through belonging to the team and contributing to its success, then the team leader has gone a considerable way towards ensuring that the basic elements of effective team management are all receiving attention.

It is still necessary to build on this however. The team leader may have a duty to assist colleagues in their own professional development as part of the work of the team and as an extension of the work of the team. This is related to delegation but it must also involve some consideration of the career aspirations of team members from their point of view. Do you, as team leader, know what the career aspirations of your colleagues actually are, as opposed to what you think they are? If you do, how far does the allocation of the duties within the team equip them to attain those aspirations? This is an especially difficult area for some colleagues in primary schools to cope with since the position to which team colleagues aspire may well be that of team leader within the same school or elsewhere. Nevertheless team leaders have a responsibility to broaden and expand the experience of staff in order to prepare them for their next promotion. The delegation and the organisation of work within the team ought to be structured with this in mind.

This is the very least that we should all be doing for our colleagues. We should also be aware of the other in-service training opportunities which might be available and be sure to pass that information on to team members. Those team leaders with a curriculum responsibility may be tempted to identify and defend an area of expertise so that it is exclusively their own. Alternatively they may, by working with and developing colleagues, share such areas of expertise in much the same way as Mr Jowett at Rosemary Lane planned to work with Jaswinder Gill to develop her expertise in the multicultural area. In larger primary schools such opportunities tend to occur more frequently than in smaller ones. Team leaders at every level should maximise those opportunities which do become available and which can be used to develop colleagues and to assist them in gaining valuable and necessary experience to fit them for promotion whether this is within the school or elsewhere. This concern with professional development will tend to be the province of senior members of staff but all team leaders may be involved from time to time. Such professional development of staff can only take place if the team leader sets aside time to talk to her colleagues about their own development. Some team leaders may wish to initiate regular, although possibly not frequent, and relatively formal discussions with colleagues while others may prefer to leave colleagues to take the initiative. However such discussions may come about they need to be given the same detailed attention that would be given to interviewing pupils or parents. Be sure, for example, that the purpose of the interview is clear but remember that the objective is to advise rather than tell people what they might do. Make certain that there will be no interruptions during the interview and, above all else, make sure that you are as well informed as you can be about your colleague, including her areas of interest, her aspirations, and the information which she may need from you. If you give advice only do so if you are sure that it is appropriate and accurate. If you are not certain of your facts be honest enough with your team member to say so but offer to find out whatever needs to be discovered. This is not only an indication of your efficiency as team leader but is also an indication to your team members that you are interested and concerned about them as people and about them as colleagues. The professional development of the team is the responsibility of the team leader and this can only be successfully achieved if the individual members of the team feel that the team leader is interested in them as individuals. The processes of professional development are considered more fully in Chapter Ten. Suffice it to say for the moment that such concern makes the team a more effective unit and, at the same time, makes it easier to manage. Priorities may be agreed upon more readily, responsibilities may be allocated more appropriately, communication becomes more open and meetings can be more useful to the whole team.

Activities

1. a) Identify two situations in which your staff team worked well together and completed its tasks or attained its objectives. Why was this so?

   b) Identify two situations in which your staff team failed to work well together or successfully to complete its tasks or attain its objectives. Why was this so?

   c) What are the main differences in the two sets of circumstances and what forces are working in favour of producing an effective team?

2. a) List the main tasks of your team.

   b) List the main strengths of your team members.

   c) Identify which team members can tackle the main tasks.

   d) Identify which team members need help with their professional development.

3. Collect the data to answer the questions posed in the final paragraph in the Team Development section of this chapter.

4. The chapter examines the four key elements in effective team management. Under each of the four headings, Individuals, Task, Team, Leadership:

   a) List your own strengths and weaknesses.

   b) Ask a colleague to identify your strengths and weaknesses.

   c) Identify strategies for building on your strengths.

   d) Plan a training programme for yourself to strengthen your weaknesses.

Chapter 7

THE PRIMARY SCHOOL STAFF TEAM: ITS PRIORITIES AND THEIR MANAGEMENT

The primary school staff team, whether this term is used for the whole staff or for a subgroup within the whole staff, is both a functional and a developmental grouping. It is functional in the sense that the people in the team will be united by sets of common purposes and processes. The members of the team will have as their major concern the education of the children in their care or, at least, a specific aspect of that education. This concern will result, for the effective team, in the determining of clear and attainable priorities, the appropriate allocation of responsibilities and the measuring of progress towards achieving targets which are derived from those priorities. The staff team also provides a framework within which the professional growth of each of its members may take place. This is particularly true since the advent of GRIST with its emphasis on whole-school INSET based on the identified need of teachers within those schools. Such professional development may enable a colleague to contribute more to the work of the team or it may provide the foundation for a change of professional direction. The functional and developmental balance within each staff team will be determined by the circumstances of the individuals within the team and by the situation in which the school finds itself at any particular time. Each school, and each team within each school, will have its own starting point although, as was argued in earlier chapters, the priorities in each school can be the focus of whole-school discussion and can form an integral part of the appointment and development of staff.

The priorities of each team ought to reflect the priorities of the school. These may not always be as clear as they need to be in order to be useful to teachers seeking to establish priorities for themselves and their teams. It is a vital element of the role of the headteacher to ensure that the school's priorities are both clear and clearly understood. The priorities of the primary school staff team are, then, a product of the inter-relationship between the philosophy of the school as expressed through its activities, and the management and organisation of those activities. For example, as Mrs Welton at Rosemary Lane proceeds with her plans for that school in conjunction with her staff, the teachers at that school will be searching for appropriate strategies which will enable them to bring about these developments in their school and which will enable them to meet the educational needs of their children. Thus, the priorities which they establish will find expression through the activities of individuals and groups within the school as they address themselves to their professional functions. The priorities which are established are more likely to be met effectively through staff groups acting in concert for all the reasons which have been rehearsed in the previous chapters of this book. In view of this, it should be recognised that all members may have in common two significant failings. Firstly they may have no clear idea of what they are trying to achieve, of what their targets or objectives are. Secondly they may not recognise that they should share in the responsibility for establishing those priorities, at least at the team level. As part of this process of taking responsibility for the work of the team, the team leader has to ensure that the priorities of the team are clarified and reinforced through a process of identifying those active, positive tasks which the team has to undertake. This requires that those in positions of middle management, as well as senior management, adopt a realistic approach to the allocation of available resources, including staff time. The fair and effective delegation of duties, the establishing and maintenance of communication between team members, and ensuring that all members of the team are able to make the most effective use of the time available to them, are crucial components of such a realistic approach to the work of the primary school.

It was argued in Chapter Three that management can be thought of as a combination of three distinct but related activities: getting things done, or administration; doing new things, or innovation; reacting to crisis, or salvation. The management of any organisation or part of an organisation involves all three forms of activity but the effective management of an organisation only comes through establishing the right balance between those activities. Any manager who is perpetually reacting to one crisis after another can hardly be in control of events, let alone be capable of managing an effective team of colleagues. It is not unusual, however, for those in middle and senior management positions in schools, as well as in other organisations, to argue that they only have time for crisis management and do not have time for innovation, and the planning and thinking which it involves. Alternatively the person who has allowed the routine administration to become such a burden that it occupies every available moment is equally at fault as is the permanent innovator who is always dealing with change and can never establish stability. They are all unable to manage their own time. The ability to do this is essential before a manager can seek to share the responsibility for the work of others. The leader of a team must, therefore, be capable of managing the time available for the work of that team. Before this can be achieved, however, we each need to be able to organise our own time effectively. In order to do this the manager in the primary school may find it helpful to be able to plan her work in terms of objectives or targets to be achieved.

Objectives and Targets

In Chapter Six aims were said to be broad strategic guidelines or statements of interest for the guidance of teachers in the various aspects of their professional activity. They are derived from the overall philosophy of the school. Objectives are statements about specific action. In this context, then, targets are a particular form of objective. The targets which any teacher may set herself, either as an individual or by agreement with colleagues, are those objectives to which she attributes some particular importance at that particular time in order to achieve specific outcomes. Decisions about such targets, whether they be taken at the school, team or individual level will, obviously, be related closely to what the school is trying to achieve. They will also need to take account of the results of the school profile which was suggested in Chapter Four or of similar types of analysis of school performance, some of which are discussed in Chapter Ten. At Rosemary Lane Mrs

Welton might wish her staff to identify some clear targets in the areas of multicultural education or, in conjunction with Mrs Green, in mathematics. Each member of staff should also have targets related to all the other areas of their work in the school. This is not to say that the whole of primary school teaching and its planning can be expressed in terms of specific targets to be achieved over an identified period of time. The setting of targets is a technique which can help in our planning and in teaching. Perhaps it can be employed more usefully and effectively than has hitherto been the case for, as Adair (1983) reminds us, a target is visible, tangible and concrete and, therefore, it can become a focus for activity.

Clearly defined targets can help the primary school teacher to know where she is going; to check that she is succeeding in getting there; to organise the necessary resources; and to sequence her work appropriately. The same is true of the teams to which she may belong within her school. The essence of a helpful and useful target is that it will contain within its formulation a clear statement about the acceptable criteria for success. Teachers do often use targets to help them plan their work. "I will hear each child in my class read at least twice each week" is a typical target, but such an approach is not always applied as widely as perhaps it might be. For example a further target connected with reading could be:

> At the end of the school year each child in the class will have a reading age which is at least the equivalent of his or her chronological age.

In some schools, or with some classes, this might not be a realistic target. It might seriously understate the abilities of the children or it might overstate their abilities. In such cases the target could be modified to take this into account:

> By the end of the school year at least half of the children in the class will have a reading age which is at least the equivalent of their chronological ages and no child will have a reading age which is more than one year below his or her chronological age.

or

> At the end of the school year all the children in the class will have a reading age which is the equivalent of their chronological age and at least one third of the class will have a reading age which is two years or more higher than their chronological age.

Where, as in the case of Rosemary Lane, a school is in an LEA which is moving rapidly towards integrating children with special educational needs into the main stream of primary education, teachers may wish to express a reading target as:

> By the end of the academic year each child should have a reading age at least one year in advance of the reading age recorded at the end of the previous academic year with the exception of the children specifically identified by the special educational needs co-ordinator, who will recommend individual targets for those children.

These targets are clear and specific. They should form part of a <u>written</u> work plan or forecast. They are quantitive rather than qualitative in that the extent to which success has been achieved can be measured accurately. They focus on identifiable results rather than on activity. They are, or should be, realistic to the extent that they are achievable and yet they provide a challenge. They have a time scale. Words such as "understand" and "appreciate" are not used but the intended results of achieving the target are listed in clear and simple terms. The emphasis is on the end results rather than on processes or activities. This is not to say that processes and activities are unimportant. Nor is it to deny the obvious importance of understanding and appreciation in primary education. Targets represent a way of helping individuals, teams and whole schools to be clear about what they are doing and how successful they are being in a wide range of situations. They may not be universally applicable although they can be widely applied. Where they are applied they need to be formulated carefully. Table 27 provides a checklist of factors to be included in well formulated targets.

Although targets should be measurable and attainable they should not be so rigid as to restrict or inhibit the work of the school or of

Table 27 ESTABLISHING EFFECTIVE TARGETS

- DOES THE TARGET DEFINE A REQUIRED RESULT?

  Always define results, not actions to achieve results

- Each child will complete a minimum of five mathematics cards each week and will successfully complete at least seven out of ten examples (or the equivalent) on each card

---

- DOES THE TARGET INCLUDE A TIMESCALE?

  If timing is important, it should be included in the target

---

- CAN PERFORMANCE AGAINST TARGET BE MEASURED OR ASSESSED ACCURATELY?

  Build in hard measures whenever possible
  Avoid general or woolly definitions of yardsticks

  Each child will be able to write a short computer programme in Basic NOT - group will understand computers

---

- IS THE TARGET DEFINED IN PRECISE, UNAMBIGUOUS TERMS?

  If the target is precise everyone using it will interpret it in the same way

---

- IS THE TARGET REALISTIC AND CHALLENGING?

  Do not set ideal performance levels that cannot be achieved
  Do not set slack performance levels that can be achieved very easily

---

- DOES THE FULL SET OF TARGETS PROVIDE A COMPLETE PICTURE?

  Make sure that you have included all the key targets to measure total success

individual teachers. Thus in attempting to achieve the reading targets the teacher may give detailed consideration to the various teaching strategies which she is adopting in this area with particular children in order to improve their reading performance. Should her efforts prove unsuccessful, however, in normal circumstances she should not be blamed or made to feel that she has failed professionally in any way. Targets are guidelines and not absolute criteria of success in themselves. The reasons for missing targets may well need to be explored but this must be done in a professional, co-operative and supportive manner. More will be said of this in Chapter Ten when staff appraisal is examined. Suffice it to say for the moment that if the particular target is of sufficient importance then those involved will want to achieve it and will want to know why it has not been achieved if such is the case. Targets of no real consequence should not be set in the first place.

Targets have been discussed in the context of teaching and learning but it is important to recognise that there are several different types of targets with which primary school teachers may be concerned and which they may be involved in attaining. Trethowan (1987) identifies five types of target:

- Targets concerned with teaching and learning and the fulfilling of related responsibilities and with maintaining certain standards
- Targets concerned with the individual teacher's professional development or personal development where this has a bearing on school work
- Targets which have to be attained by a group, team or department within the primary school
- Targets related to major but temporary projects which might be innovations or connected with solving specific problems
- Targets to be achieved by the school staff as a whole either acting in concert or as individuals

Taken together a complete list of such targets should relate to the objectives of the school for that particular period of time and will indicate what are the priorities. Over a sufficiently long period of time these targets may well include most, if not all, of the items contained in the school profile and will thus form part of the long-term planning of the school.

Day, et.al. (1985) suggest that such long-term planning can be facilitated by encouraging the primary school staff to identify three or four targets which they would like to attain in the course of a forthcoming school year. This might be done by individual consultations between a teacher and her team leader or headteacher in the Summer Term, followed by a team or staff discussion early in the Autumn Term. Whatever the method used, it is important to ensure that the short-term targets do relate to the objectives that have been set for that period of time and that the objectives themselves are stepping stones towards fulfilling the aims of the school. It is also important to ensure that no member of staff is attempting to achieve too many targets at any one time. Day et.al., (1985) indicate that four priority areas may be identified. Trethowan (1987) warns that no teacher should be expected to work towards more than an absolute maximum of six targets at any one time. To demand more than this is to be unrealistic and counter-productive because by expecting too much a situation will be created in which nothing is achieved. Far better to be clear about the ordering of priorities and thus specific about the identification of targets. It is impossible at school, team or individual teacher level to achieve everything immediately. A realistic approach to target setting can be a useful technique towards achieving much in a relatively short space of time. Even when the targets set, either by the individual teacher upon herself or by negotiation within the staff team, are realistic yet challenging and not likely to attract the odium of failure if they are not quite attained, the demands of teaching are such that the primary school teacher will need to organise her time and plan its use most carefully in order to ensure that as much as possible is attained in the time available. This is especially true where she is responsible for an area of the curriculum or for co-ordinating the work of colleagues within the school. We each have to be able to organise ourselves before we can even begin to consider organising others.

Organising Ourselves: The Effective Use of Time

In the final analysis the only person who can manage my time effectively is me and the only person who can manage your time effectively is you. Knowing how to use the available time effectively can separate the capable, coping teacher from the harassed colleague who is always under pressure without ever quite understanding why the pressure is there. Managing your time, and that of colleagues, in the most efficient and effective way possible is even more important now than it was before with the introduction of the 1265 hours of directed time and the possibility of an unspecified amount of "professional" time. More will be said about this, especially from the headteacher's perspective, in Chapter Eleven. Clearly, however, the effective use of the time available is a significant management issue for all teachers, for, as Waters reminds, 'One of the most precious of resources is time; one of the most valuable skills is the ability to manage it' (Waters, 1983, p.82).

Different people work best in different ways. Some people work best early in the day, while others are more effective in the evening. Some work best in a quiet, uncluttered environment but others need noise and thrive on what may appear to the outsider to be chaos. To use our time effectively each of us needs to know something about our own work patterns and preferences. Since these work patterns will be different for each of us and because they may change over time, it is not possible to prescribe a single "best" way to use time effectively. It is possible, however, to establish some guidelines for the effective use of time which can help the individual teacher and which can also be applied to the work of teams and, in many cases, to the whole staff working together. These guidelines will help to ensure that time is being used purposefully and that teams are well organised. They are based on the assumption that for time to be managed effectively its use has to be analysed and its future use has to be planned. Before this can be done, however, it is necessary to establish the priorities and targets for the individual or the team. It is only in the light of clearly established priorities that time can be managed for it is very easy to be busy doing the wrong thing or to be busy spending too much time on one task when another task should be receiving attention. A great deal of energy can be expended in such situations without achieving anything of note.

In the previous section we have discussed the importance of targets and how to set them. Even if we do this well within our school we will still be faced with the unexpected for which we have not planned and with choices about what to do first, what to do next, and what not to do at all. We all recognise that the tasks which face us every day come in different shapes and forms. They do not all deserve the same amount of attention but some often get more attention than they deserve. This may be because they <u>seem</u> important; or because that task is the first one we pick up in the morning; or because we enjoy doing it; or because we know we do it better than anyone else even if it is not a part of our job and is not helping us to achieve what we have set out to achieve. It may help to recognise that tasks tend to come in four different forms. First we have the urgent tasks which have to be done now if not before. There are, in fact, far fewer of these than might be supposed although it often takes courage and determination to admit that this is the case because it can involve saying "No" or, at least, "Not now" to people. It should be noted that urgent tasks may not also be important. They may be urgent but trivial. These will need doing immediately but will not deserve much of our time.

Important tasks, however, do deserve a significant amount of our time. These tasks may not have to be done immediately but will require some considerable attention. These can be scheduled in order that they can be given the attention they deserve. Some tasks are both urgent and important. They will require considerable attention and have to be done now. Then there are the tasks which, at first sight appear to be both urgent and important but which, in fact, are neither urgent or important. We may believe that they are urgent or important or both from the way they are presented: somebody in a state of agitation, enthusiasm or disbelief perhaps, or because the task originates from a particular source. It may be necessary to spend a little time on such tasks but, on the whole, they are best left alone because they tend to be tasks which either do not need doing at all or, if they should be done, they could wait until time becomes available for them. The acid test is the question, "What will happen if I do not do this?" These tasks should not be forgotten, however, since they just might become urgent, important, or both. Urgent and important tasks have to be given a high priority and require that a significant amount of time is spent on them. It ought to be possible to plan for most of these tasks simply because they _are_ important and urgent. If a teacher is confronted with many such tasks which she has not been able to predict and which are entirely unexpected then she should ask herself why this is the case. This is especially true in her role as manager or team leader. If a task is both important and urgent then normally we should be able to predict that it will arise. If tasks which really _have_ to be done now and which do make a significant contribution towards attaining our targets or meeting our priorities regularly confront the primary school team leader or manager without warning then either the communication within the school needs examining, or somebody has the wrong set of priorities or different targets, or tasks are being dumped, that is passed on without due consideration. Setting and agreeing targets have been discussed above. Delegation, the considerate way to pass on tasks to colleagues, and communication will be discussed later in this chapter although it is worth noting here that communication systems, even in the smallest schools, will not work unless we actually take some time to use them properly. Communication in the primary school will be considered in some detail in Chapter Eight.

Where Does the Time Go?

The extent to which any task should be described as urgent or important has to be determined entirely on the basis of a clear, unambigious answer to the question "What am I trying to achieve?" or "What is the team trying to achieve?" Once you have an answer to this question then you can establish how far any given demand on your time is important and/or urgent in terms of your objectives or targets. Most primary school teachers feel that they have more to do than they can fit into the time available. This is especially true of primary school heads and of teachers with curriculum or some other responsibility. The question "Where does all the time go to?" is often asked. To manage your time effectively you need to be able to answer that question.

One way of doing this is to keep an activity log. For at least three working days record all the things which you do by noting down each separate activity, the time you started and finished it and a

Table 28 KEEPING AN ACTIVITY LOG

Method

i. Start a new sheet for each day, and use as many sheets as you need for the day

ii. Record each separate activity in the order in which it occurs. Enter start time, finish time, a brief description of what happened and a note of the total time spent

iii. If an activity is unplanned, but requires immediate action, mark your entry with a star *

iv. Keep the log up-to-date during the day

v. If you find it inconvenient to carry separate log sheets around, use a notebook

vi. At the end of each day's entries note anything which made that day different or caused special problems (e.g.teacher off sick)

Example

TIME FROM-TO	ACTIVITY	TIME SPENT
8.15 - 8.35	Drive to School	20 "
8.35 - 9.00	Daily administration	25 "
9.00 - 9.20	Assembly	20 "
9.20 - 10.00	Interview with Parent	40 "
10.00- 10.45	Teaching	45 "

REMEMBER: An activity is anything you do, including meal breaks, driving, talking, waiting, etc.

brief description of what happened and the total time spent. Keep the log up-to-date during the day because if you try to leave it to the end of the day you will not be able to remember everything that you did and the times will not be accurate. At the end of the day note anything which made that day different or caused special problems. Remember to include travelling, meal breaks, waiting, talking to people and time spent just thinking, if any. You can now compare the actual use of your time with how you ought to be spending it in terms of what your real priorities are. In order to do this, identify all those items on your log which make little or no contribution to the achievement of your priorities; those which should be done by other people but which, for some reason you are doing (even when the reason is that you like doing, or think that you are good at, that particular activity); those activities which take up more time than they should or than you can afford to spend on them.

You are now in a position to examine more closely how you actually spend your time and to consider ways of using time more efficiently. Review the activities which you have listed on your activity log and think about how some of the activities can be reduced or eliminated. For example is waiting a problem? Do you spend too much time waiting to see colleagues, waiting for information or searching for it? Do you make unnecessary journeys to and from parts of the building or do you make journeys which are not as productive as they could be? How much time do you spend on social activities or just chatting and do you make the most of those times when everyone is together at break times? Do you allocate specific time to do necessary paperwork and do you keep the paperwork to an acceptable minimum? These are just a few of the questions which might be asked on the basis of an activity log but remember that such a log is only as useful as you allow it to be. You can benefit from repeating this exercise every term.

Once you have completed an activity log there are three more things you can do in order to plan the use of time more effectively. Firstly you can seek to reduce the number of unplanned activities with which you have to deal. Use your experience to try to spot problems before they happen. If an unplanned event seems to be urgent consider what would happen if you did not attend to it. Is it really urgent? Make sure that other members of your staff team know how to deal with those emergencies which might arise and that they can cover for each other by dealing with the problem immediately if that is necessary. As a rough guide, you should never be spending more than 20 per cent of your time dealing with unplanned activities and nor should any member of your team. If more than 20 per cent of time is being spent in this way then it is the responsibility of the team leader to try to minimise the extent to which unplanned events interfere with the smooth operation of your activities and, where appropriate, those of her colleagues.

This brings us back to priorities again. Each member of the team should be encouraged to plan her use of time for at least a week ahead and write it down. This is not the same as the weekly forecasts which teachers are often required to make. Rather it is an attempt to ensure that everyone in the team is using the available time most effectively. This plan should include a list of prearranged events such as routine meetings, teaching time and visits. Although you cannot predict which unplanned events will arise it might be possible, with foresight, to leave some time for them in your planned use of time. The plan should also include a list of those things which you have to do but, before you can write this list, you need to look again at your own priorities, those of the staff team in your particular area of responsibility, and those of the school.

Bearing in mind what the priorities are, it is possible to prepare a list of those tasks which have to be done. This list should include at the start everything which you expect to have to do in the particular time period under consideration. Once you have your list, give each task a rating of A, B or C. A tasks are those which are important and urgent for meeting your priorities. B tasks are important but not urgent and C tasks are those which you would like to do if time allows. Having done this you can then plan your time. Do not try to do all the A tasks first because, although these tasks are important and urgent, there are other considerations to take into account. For example can you start a task and then stop it easily, to return to it later? If not, then you have to ensure that there is sufficient time available to complete it. This might mean moving some routine tasks in order to provide the necessary time. Are some of your A category tasks dependent on other people providing information or resources? If that is the case then you have to allow time to obtain that information or those resources before embarking on that task. Do you need an item of equipment, say a typewriter, in order to do the work? This may need to be arranged in advance. Once you have taken into account all these considerations, then you can plan your use of time for the week. Remember that the aim is to match the time available to your priorities by doing first things first.

Once you have planned your time then put the plan into operation. No plan is perfect, however, and things will go wrong. Review your plan regularly and revise it when necessary. Check that your estimate of the time necessary for key or routine tasks was accurate and if you are wrong make a note of the actual time taken. Include in your plan time to think and plan ahead. Remember, if you are a team leader, that you are responsible for the work of your team members. You have to find time for them. You should encourage them to make the most effective use of their time. You may even find, as you carry out your own review of your activities, that you are doing work which ought or could be done by other members of your team. The work of any primary school staff team involves sharing responsibility within the team. This means that the team leader has to ensure that those responsibilities are shared equitably between people able to carry out the necessary tasks. This means more than simply allocating responsibilities to people. It means delegating.

Delegation

Delegation within the primary school is inevitable since no team leader or headteacher can possibly do all the necessary work. There are, however, some things which cannot be delegated. As Everard and Morris (1985) point out, common policies, common systems, agreed objectives and targets, and a clear view of what each individual is expected to achieve, provide a framework within which effective delegation can take place. All staff need to be involved in taking decisions about such matters but at the school level the headteacher has the ultimate responsibility for them. This responsibility cannot be delegated. At the team level setting the objectives and priorities for the team has, ultimately, to be the responsibility of the team leader and so does the organisation of team members, in so far as this responsibility is delegated to the team leader from the headteacher. It is also the team leader who has to accept responsibility for communication within the team and between the team and other parts of the school. More of that later. Monitoring the work of the team, staff development within the team and making the routine decisions should also remain the sole province of the team leader after appropriate consultations with team members. The things which should be delegated include those tasks for which the person to whom delegation is to be made is or should be responsible by virtue of the post she holds, because it is in the relevant job description, or because the person concerned can be trained to carry out the necessary tasks.

Delegation is, in a very real sense, a part of

staff development. More often than not in schools it is treated as dumping or abdicating, giving away work which a superior does not want to do, cannot do, and cannot bother to train somebody else to do properly. If tasks were delegated effectively in schools more frequently then people who gain promotion would already be able to carry out most of the essential duties attached to their new post. It is part of the duty of the team leader to ensure that tasks are delegated effectively especially as delegation involves far more than merely giving another colleague a job to do. It has more to do with the assignment of responsibility and authority than with the transfer of a task from one person to another.

In order to identify which tasks might usefully be delegated, headteachers and team leaders in primary schools might ask themselves the following questions:

- Which of my tasks can already be done by some or all members of staff?
- Which of my tasks make only a small contribution to the total success of the school?
- Which of my tasks take up more time than I can afford?
- Which of my tasks are not strictly related to my key targets?
- Which of my tasks are really the day-to-day responsibilities of a colleague?
- Which of my tasks cause problems when I am away because nobody else can take them on effectively?
- Which of my tasks would help members of staff to develop if they were given the responsibility?

It is then possible to take this one stage further by listing your answers to these questions on the left hand side of a sheet of paper and then, for each task, ask yourself which of your staff team is likely to be able to carry out that task already, or could be trained for it; which of the staff team might benefit from the experience; who is overloaded and who has a fairly light load. The answers to

Table 29 STAGES IN EFFECTIVE DELEGATION

Stage	Actions
Plan Delegation	Decide what to delegate and to whom Assess the task and the person Decide how much training and help the person requires Plan the briefing or training session Give sufficient authority to enable the task to be performed
Delegate the Task	Brief and train the member of staff Define the task and its limits clearly, making sure that your colleague knows what you want her to achieve and the limits of her authority Make sure that your colleague understands why the task is important and why she is being asked to do it Give her clear guidance Present information clearly, in a logical sequence and do not rush it Check that she understands what she has to do by getting her to rehearse the task or answer questions Do not merely assume that your instructions have been understood Build her confidence by showing that you believe she is capable of performing the task successfully and by briefing and training her properly for it Make your role after delegation clear Inform other colleagues about the delegation of task and authority
Monitor Progress	Do not interfere but give help when it is needed. Your colleague may not perform the task in the same way as you but this is not important if she achieves the desired results Check that she is succeeding by monitoring from a distance the results that she is achieving. This becomes less necessary as she gains in confidence but should never be thought to be unnecessary

questions such as these can help to identify to whom to delegate as well as what to delegate. Be sure that you delegate whole tasks, not just parts of them. These are the first stages in effective delegation (see Table 29).

Delegation should never be undertaken without some form of training. Training, in this context, does not necessarily mean that a teacher has to be sent on a long-term secondment or on an in-service course. Training needs prior to delegation can and should be met from within the resources of the school. More often than not this should be the role of the team leader or some other experienced colleague. Schools now have much more flexibility in this area since they can use GRIST funding and have available to them five "Baker Days" for in-service training each year. These resources are meant to meet much wider demands than those being discussed here. This they may or may not do. Within the context of delegating effectively, however, they do provide primary schools with some resources to enable colleagues to be prepared adequately for new and different roles. It should be remembered that training need not cost money. Explanation, coaching, demonstration, trial and error in a supervised situation and, "sitting by Nellie" are all forms of training which have been successfully applied in schools at very low cost. The point is that training should come before delegation and not the other way round. The extent and nature of the training will be determined by the experience of the teacher receiving the training, by the nature of the task being delegated since a complex task will need more training with closer supervision than a simple one, and by how much margin for error there is. If an error or misjudgement will have serious effects inside or outside the school training and close initial supervision is necessary.

It has been suggested that successful delegation depends on four factors. Defining clearly and precisely areas of responsibility to be delegated is the first. Our colleague should understand the purpose of the job to be delegated to her and what she will be responsible for. Her agreement on these points should be obtained. Here a modification to the job description may be required. Hence the importance of discussion and agreement. In any case a number of points need to be made clear. Firstly is the responsibility permanent or does it last for a specific and specified period of time? Are the limitations of the task clear in terms, say, of how much money is available, how much staff time can be used and how much secretarial and reprographic help is to be forthcoming? The second factor concerns the authority to carry out the responsibilities. Does the team member have the necessary authority to do the job? Can she sign letters or use the school office or take decisions without referring back to the team leader? Thirdly, the team member has to be clear about how her performance will be judged. Nobody can ever be expected to take on new responsibilities without making some mistakes but performance criteria should be agreed and specified at the outset. It is against these criteria that the headteacher, team leader or other person responsible for planning and implementing the process of delegation can check that her colleague is succeeding in the delegated task. Thus if Mrs Welton at Rosemary Lane decided to delegate the organisation of the parents' evening for the infant classes to Mrs Cass then a clear indication of what is required might include arranging interviews for a maximum of 76 sets of parents in three classrooms, allowing for the possibility that some parents may have more than one child in the infant years, and giving the opportunity for the parents to have a fifteen minute discussion with the class teacher and a discussion with Mrs Welton if she or they thought it necessary. Mrs Cass would thus be left to decide on the basic organisation in terms, for example, of whether the interviews would be spread over two nights or not, remembering, of course that this might be affected by Mrs Welton's decisions about directed time. Mrs Cass would also have to decide how times are to be allocated and on the most appropriate form of communication with parents. Effective delegation includes showing a colleague what is required, leaving her to do it her own way after appropriate briefing and training, and checking that she is succeeding.

A further factor, and the one which is most often neglected or carried out badly, is the direct responsibility of the person who is delegating. This is to ensure that every member of the staff or of the team has been informed about the change in role and the delegation of authority. Thus Mrs Welton will need to inform her staff that Mrs Cass has assumed responsibility for the organisation of parents' evening for the infant school children. Since this was previously part of her role, Mrs Welton should do this herself. Mrs Cass should not be left to inform her colleagues. The effective communication aspect of delegation helps the headteacher or the team leader because colleagues will no longer come to her for help and information about those tasks which have been delegated. It helps the team or staff member to whom the task has been delegated because, by telling all relevant colleagues that delegation has taken place, the head is acknowledging that, in this case, Mrs Cass has been given the authority to carry out this particular task. It also helps the rest of the staff to know who has that particular responsibility since they can now turn to the appropriate person for help and advice or with suggestions. It should be remembered, however, that although authority has been delegated, the final responsibility has not. This remains with the team leader or the headteacher. Given the demands on the staff of primary schools, effective delegation is essential. The communication to the staff team, in this case those with infant responsibilities, and to the rest of the school is vital for the success of the delegation process, for the effective management of the team, the school and to the work of the teachers and children within the school.

Activities

1. Identify four targets which you have to achieve next term. Follow the guidelines in Table 27.

2. Carry out an analysis of how you spend your time in the next full working week. Compare this with how you think you should spend your time bearing in mind what your priorities are.

3. Identify all the unplanned events which confront you in your working week. Identify ways of (a) coping with the most time consuming ones and (b) having time to deal with those that might occur next week.

4. Identify one main task which you carry out at the moment and which might be delegated to an identified member of your team. What criteria have you used? Plan a training programme which would enable you to delegate this task and, after obtaining agreement from your colleague, implement the programme.

Chapter 8

COMMUNICATION IN THE PRIMARY SCHOOL

Communication in schools, as in any other organisation, is an extremely complex topic and a thorough coverage of it would deal with everything from policy making at senior management level to individual job descriptions for each member of staff, taking in the school, departmental and team communication systems along the way. It might include formal and informal interviews with staff, pupils, parents and others and would have to look at types, patterns and the content of communication. It would certainly include a discussion of staff handbooks, handbooks for parents, reports and other communications with the wider community. Such an exhaustive analysis of the topic of communication is beyond our scope here. Instead it is proposed to examine briefly those factors which will tend to inhibit or facilitate communication within the primary school and to consider those types of communication which are especially relevant to teachers working together in teams within those schools.

Problems with Communication

In the example of communication mentioned in the context of delegation in the previous chapter the headteacher, Mrs Welton was required to inform other colleagues about a change in responsibility brought about by a process of delegation. Providing information to colleagues is one of the main reasons for communicating with other members of the team. Obtaining information from them is a second crucial reason for communicating but we also communicate regularly in order to request, to advise, to admonish, to warn and to praise. Communication is essential if we are to help pupils learn, if we are to influence or persuade, negotiate or bargain.

Almost all communication is concerned with action: with initiating action, preventing action or giving people information on which they may wish to act. We often, consciously or unconsciously, evaluate the effectiveness of our communication in terms of whether or not action has taken place. Most of our routine and not so routine activity requires us to communicate with others yet, apart from this vague assessment in terms of actions by others, we tend to be singularly unaware of how our messages are coming across, of how effective we are as communicators. We ignore, all too often, those factors which inhibit communication.

The one factor above all others that inhibits good communication by most people is the fact that we have all been doing it all our lives. Therefore we must have been relatively successful in order to have survived; but the skills which enabled us, as infants, to attract the necessary attention, as adolescents to cope with the strains of impending adulthood, and as teachers to cope with the daily routine of teaching, are not necessarily those which make us effective members or leaders of staff teams in schools. The fact that we have all been communicators for so long often leads us to forget that we may not be as effective as we or other people might like. Good communication must avoid ambiguity and the possibility of being misunderstood or misinterpreted. It should not generate suspicion or hostility since this leads to a situation in which the content of the communication is frequently ignored because of the anger which it creates. A pleasant letter is, usually, more likely to be effective and productive than an unpleasant one. In spite of our life-long practice in communicating we do need to check that we are communicating effectively. This involves transmitting the communication in the most appropriate form; providing enough information but not too much; ensuring that the intended actions occur and that it is clear who is to take them and by when.

Within a group like a staff team there is often so much that has to be communicated that the tendency is to try to communicate too much at any one time or to communicate in a style which is neither appropriate nor acceptable. As a result colleagues can find themselves being told when they should have been consulted or being asked when they needed to be instructed. The sheer size of some schools can exacerbate this situation when, for example, it has proved impossible to find a team

Table 30 ARE COMMUNICATIONS EFFECTIVE IN YOUR SCHOOL?

SIGNALS OF NEED TO IMPROVE	FOCUS OF ATTENTION
People complain about lack of communication or about not receiving information	Examine basis for complaint: it may be valid or it may be caused by frustration or lack of security
Flourishing grapevine of rumour (often inaccurate) regarding the state of the school and plans for the future	Unofficial communication channels flourish when formal ones are weak or in times of uncertainty: examine the existing channels of communication
Some confusion about responsibilities amongst colleagues	Spell out each person´s duties and authority clearly on paper as part of a job description
Sometimes people fail to bring major problems to your attention soon enough	Examine your relationship with colleagues. Do you encourage them to ask for help? Have you spelled out what they should discuss with you before taking action?
Sometimes people do not do things even though they have been told	Always follow up communications to check they are carried out
Sometimes people make silly mistakes, despite clear instructions	Are you using two-way communications? Are you checking that they understand and that they can do it? Are you following up to check that appropriate actions are taken?
People do not come forward with ideas for improvement, and show little initiative	Are you keeping colleagues fully in the picture? Are you trying to build commitment?
People appear to get the wrong message	Are you sure that you are communicating clearly, simply and in the most appropriate way?

member with whom the leader wishes to discuss a matter. The team leader may then write a short note which, because it is written in haste, is ambiguous, unclear and threatening to the reader but not intended to be so by the writer. From such stuff team problems grow. Some of these problems can be avoided or anticipated by watching for the signals listed in Table 30 and taking the appropriate action.

Team problems which have their roots in poor communication are often the product of our attitude to the process of communication. We often see this as an end in itself rather than as a means to an end. Thus the well produced notice, the apt memo or the carefully chosen phrase is regarded as the very epitome of good communication when, in fact, this is far from being the case. Effective communication should be understood as the link between thought and action or behaviour. It is the process of conveying hopes, ideas, intentions or feelings from one person to others. This is usually done in order that something can happen. Thus the sequence should be:

Thought...........COMMUNICATION...........Action

A failure in communication can arise in this process when the action or behaviour which follows the communication is inconsistent with the message contained in that communication. A simple example of this is the situation in which a team member fails to comply with a request, or fails to act upon an instruction. These situations are easy to identify and, in most cases, prove relatively easy to manage. The situations in which the disjunction between message and action is caused by the sender of the message, the team leader or headteacher, is far more difficult to identify and to handle.

Where, for example, a team leader has made it clear to her team members that certain tasks will be dealt with by one of the team rather than by her and then she is found to be dealing with one of those problems rather than referring it to the relevant colleague, how might this be interpreted? If, for example, Mrs Green as the mathematics co-ordinator at Rosemary Lane, has made it clear to the Infant staff that Mrs Butler will be responsible for evaluating new material suggested by the advisory teacher, but is seen by the staff to be doing it herself, what will they make of it? In spite of the fact that Mrs Green's intentions might have been nothing but good, helping a colleague known to have a heavy workload for example, the action of the team leader is clearly inconsistent with the message that dealing with a certain task has been delegated to a colleague. Mrs Butler may interpret Mrs Green's action as being inconsistent with her stated policy and may then be reluctant to act in accordance with that policy in the future. Further, such a situation may result in the staff team as a whole refusing to take seriously Mrs Green's stated intention to delegate responsibility in the future. Such issues as these have to be confronted as part of the communication process within the team if effective communication is to lead to desired actions and behaviour. All team members need to be aware of those factors which, unless attended to, will inhibit effective communication. In particular a team leader should be aware of the particular characteristics of those with whom communication is taking place. Any communication should be influenced by such knowledge as well as by the outcome which the communication is intended to produce.

Making Communication Work

Both the sender and the receiver of the communication, whatever form it might take, should be clear about what the objective of the communication is: whether this is to inform, request information, produce action or prevent action. The required outcome of the communication should also be quite unambiguous and incapable of being misunderstood and misinterpreted. The team leader, in sending the communication, needs to be clear about how best to gain the outcome which she is requiring from those to whom the communication is being sent. At the same time the team leader has to bear in mind how frequently communications are issued on this and other matters. The more "noise" there is in any primary school or in any staff team caused by frequent, or even too frequent communications which to the recipients seem unimportant and trivial, then the more chance there is of any one item of communication, however important, actually getting lost. For this reason Mrs Welton stopped the frequent circulation of the message book at Rosemary Lane. She found that it was seldom properly read and was often an irritating interruption. Sometimes its exact location was not known. Therefore Mrs Welton replaced it with a prominent emergency notice board in the staff room which she only used for immediate and important messages. She cleared

Table 31 MAKING COMMUNICATION WORK

Why?	The basic reason for communication is to get someone else to do something. Always bear this point in mind. It helps to keep communication to the point
What?	Spell out exactly what you want the other person to do. Making your messages precise and to the point saves you time (and money, if you are using the telephone)
Who?	When you want something done tell the person who has responsibility for it and make sure that everyone affected by it is told
When?	If you have a message for someone it is usually best to tell her now (there are not many cases in which it pays to delay communications). Putting off communications can result in forgetting, or in a build-up of work for yourself. If you want something done at a date in the future you can issue a reminder at the right time
How?	Choose the simplest and most direct method to communicate. If you are not sure whether someone will follow your spoken communication confirm it on paper
Check	When you communicate check that the other person grasps what she has to do. If you are asking her to do something outside her established routines, follow up to check that she does it

this at the end of every day by either removing notices entirely or putting them elsewhere when they were no longer urgent but still contained necessary information. In short then, effective communicating demands that the message is clear, unambiguous, short, and simple. It must be transmitted in a style that is acceptable and understandable. The actions which it may demand should be, as far as possible, easy to understand and easy to execute. The team leader, in adopting a communication style has to show concern for those team members with whom she is communicating as well as consistency in the process of communicating and the demands which are made on those with whom the communication is shared. Simple communications can be made to work by following the guidelines set out in Table 31.

Those teachers with management responsibility in the primary school have to recognise that communication is the life blood of the school. If people cannot communicate effectively then the work of the school is seriously impaired. Yet the demands of communicator and receiver of communications are constantly changing. These changes have to be understood in order that appropriate forms of communication can be used. If new staff are appointed then the communication process has to be changed in order to accommodate them. Thus the appointment of Mrs Green at Rosemary Lane will mean that staff have to communicate with her about issues related to the new mathematics work in the school and she will have to find ways of communicating with them. However this is done it will mean that the communication within that school will be different from what it was before her appointment. Communication in any organisation needs to be flexible. It must be fully understood by those within that organisation and it must allow for formal as well as informal communication between colleagues, a point often forgotten in smaller schools.

All communication will be just that little bit more effective if all the staff of the school recognise that they have a responsibility to ensure that the system works. This means that they play their part by reading notices, opening letters, checking pigeon holes and providing feedback when requested. It also means that where the system does not work or is manifestly seen to be inappropriate - not enough or too much information being received or information being received at the wrong time for example - then they draw this to the attention of the person responsible in a courteous and professional way. Mrs Welton had an item on communication on the agenda of an early staff meeting at Rosemary Lane. By asking staff to describe existing practice, she and they were able to evaluate the communication within the school and to make suggestions for upgrading it. In this way agreed routines could be established. Everyone can make communication more effective if they bear the following questions in mind:

i. What am I trying to communicate? What is the purpose of my communication?

ii. What are my objectives? What is the nature of the communication? Is the method chosen for communication appropriate for the people receiving communication?

iii. Who is it for? Do they need to know? Are they the most appropriate people to receive the communication?

iv. How should I communicate? Which method or combination of methods should I use? What style can I adopt that is best suited to my target audience?

v. When should I communicate? Is one time better than any other?

vi. Where - to what address or location - am I sending this communication?

vii. If it is written, how do I check that the message has been received?

viii. Have I established controls to get feedback on whether the message has been correctly received and acted upon?

Forms of Communication

The single most important factor in effective communication, however, is none of those listed above. It is the skill of listening. The more we are able to listen to others, the more able we will be to communicate with them and they with us. Listening can be broadly interpreted to mean a general receptivity to information which is communicated to us; but face-to-face listening, which is the result of a process of hearing which may or may not develop into listening, is the most important of all. If a team member believes that the views which she expresses to the team leader are received in a positive, receptive way then communication is likely to succeed. This does not mean that people have to agree with each other but it does mean that team leaders have to devise their own listening style. The listener should adopt a style which shows that she is concentrating on what is being said to her and which encourages the team member to talk, rather than a style which creates opportunities for the team leader to express her own views. Listening has to be an active and not a passive process which involves the listener in checking that she has understood what is being said and that there is a clear agreement at the end of the conversation on what will happen as a result of it. This should not be left to chance and should be clearly understood by both parties at the end of the discussion. Active listening, then, leads to effective communication.

This is not to say that all communication between members of the team is or should be verbal communication or individual discussions. This form of communication does have its advantages because it provides opportunity for immediate feedback and for the modification of the message if this is necessary. It also indicates if the message is as clear and unambiguous to the team members as it is to the team leader who may know much more of the background than do her colleagues. Thus it can provide the opportunity for team members to ask questions and to allow feelings to be displayed and expressed more fully, especially in a non-verbal way. Oral communication is, however, expensive on time, It should, therefore, be used when the matter under consideration is complex or emotive, unpleasant or even personal. It should also be used to give praise or where the issue is particularly important. Remember, however, that it may be necessary to record what is said in some way. This should be agreed beforehand and confirmed by sharing the record afterwards. Many team leaders feel more confident when they are communicating in writing. Letters, memos, notices, reports and other forms of written communication all have their place in the workings of the primary school team but, in order to be effective, they have to be read and understood. It is more difficult to detect errors and ambiguities in the receiving of written communications. Written communications do, however, have the virtue that they can be rewritten many times and they can be checked and rechecked. The appropriate phrase or sentence can be chosen to convey just the right idea. It is important to ensure that this is what happens and to prevent meanings from being obscured. For example the use of long words when shorter ones will do (or suffice!) may lead to ambiguity. So many employing phrases which pad out the writing such as: "in this regard" or even, "after careful consideration of all the available evidence". These and other similar phrases can usually be omitted without changing the meaning of a sentence.

Most organisations develop their own jargon and shorthand. There is nothing wrong with using this as long as the memo or letter is only going to people who understand the private language of the school or of the particular team within the school. Some phrases have almost become jargon in the sense that they are intended as a shorthand to convey meanings but, in fact, they do not do this. Phrases like "after mature reflection" which normally means "I have changed my mind", or "you were right and I was wrong", and "it is the consensus of the meeting" which may mean either "we agree" or "I am not sure what we have agreed but I am going to interpret it my way" tend to obscure meaning whether they are written or spoken. The tendency to use several words when one would be adequate, and probably much clearer, has a similar effect. Try to avoid writing phrases such as those in Table 32 if you want your written communication to be clear and unambiguous. Above all bear in mind who your reader is. Spell out very carefully why you are writing and what you want to happen as a result of your communication. You should always ask if your communication is really necessary. If it is not, then do not send it. If it is, then keep it as short as possible and make the required outcome as clear as possible.

Table 32 ONE WORD IS BETTER THAN SEVERAL

take on board	AGREE
on the hypothesis that	IF
for the purpose of	TO
during the course of	DURING
along the lines of	LIKE
in order to	TO
due to the fact that	BECAUSE
at this moment in time	NOW
in view of the fact that	BECAUSE
in my opinion it is not an unjustifiable assumption that	I THINK

Written communication, then, by its very nature provides a permanent record of that particular exchange of ideas or request for action, provided that the headteacher or team leader remembers to keep a copy and can retrieve that copy when it is wanted. The use of word processors for storing written communication on disc, for changing what has been written and for repeating standard letters can help to make our use of written communication even more effective and can help us to save time, both our own and that of other people, especially the hard-pressed school secretary. Copies of written communication can be sent in the same form to as many people as may be required. If necessary, it can be sent to different places at different times. It can, of course, be considered at length and can, therefore, be relatively complex or require a relatively complex response but the significant advantage of this form of communication is in danger of being ignored. In order to use written communications effectively the team leader has to understand that writing is not a substitute for talking. Communicating in writing is suitable for different situations and appropriate for different messages to oral communication. Where written and oral communications are treated as interchangeable alternatives, communication quickly breaks down.

It has been suggested that schools could make far more use than they do of visual forms of communication. The timetable set out on an impressively produced commercial timetabling board with a complex range of signs and symbols designating subjects, classes, rooms and teachers, tends to be as near as most of us come to such displays unless we work in a school which has produced its own video presentation. Even this is rare in all but the largest primary schools although most will have a timetable for using certain spaces, such as the hall, library or CDT area, or for access to certain equipment, such as computers, televisions, musical instruments. Some forms of visual presentations might be useful to the headteacher or team leader as an aid to planning and using time effectively. A flow diagram indicating when all the major routine tasks have to be completed can help to co-ordinate activities across the team. It can show by when certain key tasks have to be completed, indicate where chasing or checking might be required and reveal where insufficient time has been allowed or where likely hold-ups may occur. These may then be dealt with in advance in order to try to prevent them happening.

If the diagram includes a space in which to indicate when each stage has been completed it can be even more useful to the team leader. This technique can be applied to the planning and implementation of almost all routine and many non-routine activities involving primary school staff and taking place over a relatively long period of time. A microcomputer can be invaluable to store and retrieve information as part of this process.

Effective communication, then, has a vital part to play in establishing and achieving the priorities of the pastoral team and in ensuring that all team members make the most effective use of their time. It is, therefore, a worthwhile activity for the team leader to review the team's communication system regularly. She might consider how much paperwork the team generates and ask if it is all necessary or relevant. Does it always elicit the responses and actions required and if not, why not? The team leader might check with members of the team that they understand the messages that they are receiving. Indeed it is sometimes worth checking that the messages are being received at all. Where this is not happening then urgent steps need to be taken, perhaps through a team meeting, to find out why this is the case. Where this is a school problem the headteacher may need to consider it more fully and then bring it to a meeting of the whole staff for discussion.

Types of Meetings

Meetings are an extremely common form of communication in primary schools. At least, they are intended to be a form of communication although many of them singularly fail in this intent. Some meetings may be small. Year group teachers or curriculum teams may involve no more than three or four teachers. Whole staff meetings may be much larger than this. In order to run a meeting effectively, whatever its size, the person responsible for it needs to be clear about its purpose. Successful meetings are those which are productive and are not regarded by those attending them as a waste of time. Avoiding the sin of wasting time in meetings is even more important now in primary schools since some meetings take place in directed time and therefore have a precise and limited duration. Having an agreed finishing time for a meeting is no bad thing since it removes one of the uncertainties from attendance at meetings. Nothing destroys enthusiasm for meetings more quickly than the meeting which has no end. Equally nothing is more likely to undermine an important item on a staff meeting agenda than introducing it too late in the meeting so that lack of time precludes proper discussion. It is even more inept to introduce such an item and then interrupt discussion and postpone it to the next meeting. Careful agenda planning is essential. Important and regular meetings ought now to be scheduled so that everyone knows in advance when staff meetings, year meetings, curriculum team meetings and other similar meetings will be throughout the school year. This does not preclude the possibility of calling extra meetings, of cancelling meetings when there is no business, arranging different meetings. Advanced warning helps and a regular, known sequence helps to ensure that the appropriate people attend the meeting. This, in turn, minimises the possibility of somebody not knowing about decisions which have been taken or the preparation necessary for the next meeting. A minuting secretary will be necessary to record those decisions and the actions which have to be taken before the next meeting. This record will go some way to avoid the irritating processes, for those who did attend, of explaining to a non-attender what happened last time. The published schedule of meetings might indicate who is expected to attend particular meetings although in small schools this may well be self-evident. The most significant factor in encouraging colleagues to spend time in meetings is the organisation of those meetings. If the meeting is perceived to be useful then teachers will attend it.

Every fruitful meeting has to be planned. Planning starts with a decision about what the real point of the meeting is to be. What sort of meeting is it and what is to be achieved? Meetings can, of course, be defined in terms of their membership, in terms of, for example, a year group meeting or a curriculum team meeting. Alternatively a meeting might be defined in terms of its frequency as with the weekly, monthly or termly meeting. Such designations do give an indication of the timing and the membership of the meeting but they still tell us little about the purpose of the meeting, about its real function. In most cases this is because meetings tend to serve a variety of different functions and, because of this, they tend to be too long and relatively confused affairs at which miscommunication is more common than illumination because those attending do not recognise when the meeting has changed from one type to another. There is nothing wrong with holding multipurpose meetings provided that the the chairperson and the others at the meeting are clear exactly what function they are being asked to carry out at any one time. (See Table 33).

The simplest form of meeting is the one at which information is to be given, where the staff team is to be briefed about changes in school policy, brought up-to-date on current events or told about particular arrangements. These briefing or advising meetings depend heavily on the team leader, or whoever is chairing the meeting. She has to be fully informed and in control of the information which she wishes to impart as well as to be able to deal with relevant questions while, at the same time, not being sidetracked by irrelevant ones. Some thought needs to be given to providing information before the meeting since it is a waste of everyone's time to hold up a meeting while people digest material which could have been given to them well in advance. Similarly some information can best be presented on an OHP rather than by word of mouth. This is usually true of numerical data such as intake figures or class sizes.

A related form of meeting is the one called to seek information or to test opinions, although it might be asked if meetings are the most effective way of doing this. All too often people arrive at such meetings unsure about its precise purpose. They expect to be able to take a decision, rather than to provide information on which decision-making might be based. It is very easy to move from seeking information about a topic to taking decisions about it if the meeting is not chaired carefully and sensitively. It is particularly important that those organising such meetings are clear in their own mind about the nature of the meeting and that they remain so throughout the meeting, guiding its progress firmly.

A third common form of meeting is the persuading or influencing meeting. This takes place when a specific course of action has been decided upon and the team has to be convinced that this is the most appropriate way forward. A team considering a new way of recording pupils' progress where the actual decision to use this approach to recording information about pupils has already been taken but where the team leader wants agreement of the particular form of the record is an example of this type of meeting. It should not be confused with a meeting

Table 33 TYPES OF MEETINGS

Below are different types of meeting purpose - a meeting may be concerned with one of these purposes only, or the different items of the meeting agenda could have different purposes:

PUTTING INFORMATION ACROSS	You want the group to grasp information
OBTAINING INFORMATION	You want information, for yourself or for other colleagues - either hard facts or opinions
PERSUADING	You want to negotiate a deal with the group
SOLVING A PROBLEM	You want to generate and examine a number of possible solutions to a problem
MAKING A DECISION	You want the group to reach a conclusion on a particular issue
INSTRUCTING	You want the group to grasp and be able to apply certain skills or knowledge
MOTIVATING	You want the group to be committed to a particular course of action
AD HOC	You want a group to examine a particular issue and make recommendations

at which decisions are to be argued through. In this type of meeting the onus is again on the team leader to be fully informed and to be able to present information concisely and clearly. More is required, however, than a simple summary of information. The team leader may need, for example, to outline the present situation and indicate what the problems are and then to show how the new proposal will meet those deficiencies before asking team members to comment on the proposals. She may also need to negotiate some conditions or compromises, such as over the length of time allowed for implementation. These meetings can often become debates although their main purpose is to influence.

Some meetings are called specifically to solve problems. They may use a technique similar to brainstorming or simply use general discussion to generate a number of alternative solutions to the problem under consideration. At least, it is to be hoped that a number of solutions will be examined, since there is never any guarantee that the first solution will be the best or that it will be acceptable to all concerned, as we argued above. Recommendations do, however, need to be made although it is quite proper for a problem-solving meeting to suggest a small number of possible alternatives and to give advice about the advantages and disadvantages of the various possibilities. At the start of the meeting the team leader needs to present the problem clearly. She then has to structure the discussion in such a way as to allow everyone to make contributions since it is not necessarily those who shout loudest who can offer the most appropriate solutions or the best ideas.

At other meetings the main aim is to reach a decision on a particular matter. Often decision-making meetings are confused with other types of meetings in such a way that those who attend the meeting are not at all sure about the extent to which they are being informed about a decision after it has been taken, consulted about it before it is made, or are, in fact, being asked to make the decision during that meeting. Where a meeting has to reach a decision the team leader should make this clear from the very beginning of the meeting. It should also be made clear how any decision will be made. This may be done by a majority vote of all those present at the meeting or, at the other extreme, it may be done entirely by the team leader after "getting a feel of the meeting". Ideally, of course, the team leader should seek to obtain a consensus of all team members. When the decision is finally reached it should also be announced in such a way as to leave no doubt in the minds of those present about what has been decided.

Two other types of meeting can also be identified among the plethora of those commonly held in primary schools or provided for primary school teachers. The first is the meeting whose main purpose is to instruct. This usually occurs in the staff development or in-service training context where a group of teachers is being shown how to use an item of equipment or a new curriculum package. This is a meeting, just like any other, and it will need similar preparation if it is to be successful. Motivating meetings are, perhaps, less common although they do take place. They are intended to obtain commitment from a group of staff to a particular course of action and to generate enthusiasm for it rather than the mere acceptance of it which may be the outcome of the persuading meeting. They are similar in kind but differ in degree.

The last type of meeting to be considered is the *ad hoc* meeting. This is often used by schools but is much neglected since, by its very nature, it may involve those who are not practised in running meetings. *Ad hoc* meetings tend to be working parties or study groups set up to study particular areas of concern or to bring about specific changes. They usually have a limited duration and a fairly small membership. Often their brief is unclear. Are they information gathering, problem-solving, decision-making, persuading or recommending bodies? To whom do they report, how and when? The chairperson of such a group needs to be aware of the answers to these questions especially as the setting up of an *ad hoc* meeting is often an indication that the formal structure of the school has encountered something with which it cannot cope or which cannot be encompassed within its routine processes.

Managing Meetings

Knowing how any meeting is to proceed is helped by understanding what type of meeting it is and by being aware of the intended outcome. Such awareness leads to more effective meetings and can help to avoid much confusion about what is happening, and what has happened at any single meeting. Recognising that meetings are different can also help in communicating to team members about these meetings. They need to know in advance whether it is a briefing meeting or a problem-solving meeting. Similarly they ought to have relevant papers prior to the meeting in order that the information can be digested. Much time can be saved by ensuring that the objectives of the meeting are clear, and by distributing fairly brief, relevant papers well before the meeting is due to take place. By reading and discussing such papers before the meeting many ambiguities and misunderstandings can be sorted out in advance. This helps to prevent valuable time being wasted during the meeting clarifying points which could just as easily have been sorted out beforehand. The team leader, headteacher or chairperson of the meeting may also wish to spend some time before the meeting discussing each item with colleagues, exploring alternatives, consolidating a point of view and ensuring that those who are leading on any particular item are prepared for it. Communication about the business of the meeting to those who need such information in advance is a vital part of planning an effective meeting, not least because it enables the team leader to inform everybody about the objective of the meeting before it takes place. It also enables the team leader to know who may be attending and to have some idea of the size of the group.

The size of the group is important because the number of people in a meeting is an important factor in determining how far it is possible to gain the maximum benefit from using meetings as a form of communication. The benefits of using meetings as a form of communication are assumed but not often made explicit. Once we understand what the advantages of it are then we can begin to ensure that our meetings are conducted in such a way as to ensure that the maximum benefit is obtained from them. In a meeting everyone attending receives more or less the same message at the same time. It is possible, in fairly small meetings, to check everyone's grasp of that message immediately. Reactions can be heard and observed, and queries or difficulties may be resolved during the meeting. Often problems can be solved and decisions made collectively. These processes, taken together, can contribute towards building a team identity and encouraging the staff group to work together.

Group size is also important because there is a limit to how far it is possible to communicate with a large number of people. It is very difficult to take decisions in groups of more than seven although up to ten might be tolerable in some circumstances. It is fairly easy however, to brief groups much larger than this. It is also necessary to have the furniture for the meeting set out in an appropriate way. It is, for example, no accident that in the House of Commons the opposing groups sit opposite each other and that the business is conducted on the basis of advocacy and debate with very little agreement actually being reached. If a meeting is arranged in a similar way, perhaps with potential adversaries facing each other across a table, then it is likely that conflict will ensue. It is far more difficult to have an heated argument with the person sitting at your side. Apart from that, some consideration has to be given to how the communication is to flow during the meeting. A circle helps to ensure a free exchange of ideas between members of the group but it also makes the task of chairing the meeting more difficult because there is no natural focus. If the team leader sits at the head of a table with colleagues equally spaced around it, chairing the meeting becomes easier and discussion will still take place. Alternatively, by chairing the meeting from a position in front of a semi-circle, discussion is more likely to flow to and from the chairperson and not between members of the team. This might, for example, be appropriate for a briefing meeting while the group round the table might be more effective if decisions have to be taken.

At Rosemary Lane Mrs Welton deliberately moved her business staff meetings from the staff room to the library. She found that the easy chairs and casual atmosphere in the staff room did not always suit the purpose of the meeting. She preferred to work with a circle of tables so that colleagues had a surface on which to write and a clear view of everyone else at the meeting. The room could also be prepared well before the meeting, an essential factor whatever the setting. Visual aids and equipment have to be set up and checked. Nothing destroys the atmosphere of a meeting more quickly than an overhead projector which fails to project, a screen which collapses or invisible visual aids. For a well conducted meeting it is best to have all this ready before colleagues start arriving. Remember that, just as some children tend to lose pencils, some colleagues may well regularly turn up without paper and pencils. Business-like meetings may require colleagues to take notes so writing materials should be available. In some meetings points of agreement can often be displayed to advantage on a flip chart. The paper can then be displayed in the room or returned to in subsequent discussions. This is especially useful in problem-solving or decision-making meetings. Flip charts are relatively expensive but can easily be created with the help of a blackboard and easel, two big bulldog clips and some large paper. Remember that you will need something with which to stick the paper on the walls and that thick felt-tip pens are more easy to see than thin ones.

This preparation should take place well in advance of the meeting. It, too, requires a clear view of the meeting's purpose. This is equally true of other pre-meeting preparation. An agenda should be published giving the starting time, place and finishing time as well as a list of the topics to be covered and the order in which they will be taken. The agenda ought also to state the purpose of the meeting clearly, indicate who is to introduce each topic and which papers relate to each topic. If a meeting includes a number of items with different purposes, giving information, seeking opinion and making a decision for example, then these purposes should be indicated on the agenda to avoid confusion and to save time. An item of information might be listed as:

> To receive information on LEA arrangements for allocating the five in-service days. Mrs Welton.

An opinion-seeking item might be worded as follows:

> To consider three mathematics schemes for Rosemary Lane School. Mrs Green.

A decision-making item could be introduced as:

> To decide on the content of the first in-service day on multicultural eduction. Mr Jowett and Ms Gill.

Even if the agenda does not show who will introduce a particular topic, the person chairing the meeting should know this and should have checked with each person in advance that she is ready for the meeting. The sequence of items on the agenda also required some thought. It might be appropriate always to start the meeting by looking at the minutes from the previous meeting to give team members an opportunity under "matters arising" to comment or to ask about decisions and actions taken as a result of the last meeting. Informational or briefing items should come before items for discussion or decision in order that the situation can be avoided in which discussion depends on information which the group has not yet been given. Items of business not included on the formal agenda should either come at the end as "Any Other Business" or there should be an agreed procedure for including such items on the agenda. If colleagues are to prepare in advance for meetings, items of other business should be strictly limited. Perhaps such items might be restricted to information giving and early warnings of information to be provided. Mrs Welton always uses this opportunity to remind colleagues of the date, time and place of the next meeting or to arrange this if it is necessary. She also requests that items for the agenda be submitted at least a week before the next meeting together with an indication of whether they are short items or major business items so that sufficient time can be allocated when planning the meeting.

Such an agenda goes a long way towards providing clear ground rules and an appropriate structure for meetings although this approach may seem unnecessarily formal, especially in small schools. It can, however, be a great help in distinguishing between the informal chat and the formal business meeting in the smallest of staff groups. Even if the agenda does not quite go this far the person chairing the meeting will need to know what is to be achieved, who is to introduce a topic and who may wish to speak. If meetings are to contribute to the development of the staff team, especially in a collegiate environment, then it is important that the business is not all conducted by the chairperson or by the most experienced member of staff present. In order to prevent this, team members can and should prepare themselves in advance for the meetings which they are to attend. At the very least this should mean that they have read all the papers and have at their disposal any information which may be required. If they are to make a formal contribution to an agenda item then this needs to be prepared carefully. The argument should be clear, simple but accurate and complete. Visual aids often help to get across a complex argument like the significant differences between three mathematics schemes which can more easily be presented as a diagram than as a speech. All colleagues should be clear from the outset about the aims of the meeting and what is has to achieve. If they are not, then they should ask. The aims must be kept in mind throughout the meeting and all contributions should move towards them. In short everyone attending the meeting should accept part of the responsibility for making the meeting work.

The heaviest burden of responsibility for making the meeting work falls on the person in the chair. She has to prepare well in advance, especially to ensure that she has a precise understanding of what outcomes are wanted. She may also wish to identify outcomes or conditions which should be built into certain outcomes. She may wish to ensure that certain alternatives are, at least, considered if not accepted and may need to prepare her arguments in order to make this happen. Above all the chairperson must allow the discussion to flow. She can encourage this by prompting and asking questions or by injecting ideas. She can bring in the quieter members of the team. She should insist that all remarks are addressed through the chairperson and that members do not interrupt each other but wait until called upon to speak. The chairperson can encourage participation by posing questions to the group as a whole, which is less threatening than asking unprepared individuals. This can be supplemented by approaching specific individuals if they have been warned before the meeting that this might happen. Open questions to which there are no simple short answers produce more discussion than closed questions with simple answers. As the meeting progresses the team leader in the chair should summarise and record decisions taken and actions agreed. Where a particular matter appears unclear to the chairperson it should not be ignored or left in the hope that all will become clearer at a later stage. Invariably this will not happen and more time will be required to sort out the mess later. If you do not understand what has happened then it is a safe bet that most other people are also confused. The team leader must accept the risk of looking silly, if risk there is, and ask for clarification. The point should not be left until all are clear and all have agreed that they understand. Summarising misunderstandings, seeking further information and indication what has been decided are all important factors in the successful chairing of meetings. Above all, each item must be concluded clearly and agreements or actions restated and the person responsible for them named. A minuting secretary may be needed to do this.

The combination of a well-structured agenda, control from the chair and team members committed to

Table 34 THE ORGANISATION OF A MEETING

PLAN	o Know the objectives of the meeting and what is to be achieved
COMMUNICATE	o Inform other team members what is to be discussed at the meeting and why
PREPARE	o Prepare room and resources o Put agenda in a sequence and allot appropriate time to each item o Arrange your papers in agenda order o Plan results for each meeting item - know what is to be achieved o Decide membership, location, time, duration and notify all those involved o Prepare yourself and brief those who are to lead discussion o Arrange cover for self and own staff
RAISE POINTS	o Declare aims and agenda at outset o Work to agenda sequence o Put across information clearly and confidently
MANAGE DISCUSSION	o Encourage constructive discussion o Keep discussion directed toward aims o Remain in charge throughout: resist any challenges to your authority o Control the pace of the meeting to a time schedule o Keep the mood of the meeting good-tempered and objective
CONCLUDE	o At the end of each agenda item present sharp, clear conclusions o Check understanding and acceptance of conclusions
REPORT	o Prepare a report on all important meetings o Make report short, concise, listing conclusions against each agenda item o If there are agreed follow-up actions, state who does what and when, and who will check
FOLLOW UP	o Send out the minutes with decisions and actions to be taken, by whom, by when, listed o Check that any agreed actions are successfully carried out

making the meeting work well should ensure that those agenda items which are really important for the work of the team are the items which receive the detailed attention, while the items which might generate lots of discussion but which are really not all that important are dealt with speedily and effectively. The team might also wish to have a rule about the length of time which must elapse before a decision which it has taken can be reconsidered. This is useful in those situations where strong opinion prevails on a matter which can be tackled in a number of ways, like teaching reading or classroom organisation. It is also the duty of the team leader, when conducting the meeting, to avoid the repetition of argument either by the same person or by different people saying the same things. A well-chaired meeting with a good agenda can help with this as well as being an invaluable aid in keeping colleagues on the point.

The secretary and/or the chairperson together should be responsible for recording what happens at the meeting. All that really needs to be recorded is what was decided. If absolutely necessary this can include voting figures but voting should only be used as a last resort. Where an action has been agreed upon, this should also be recorded together with the name of the person responsible for taking the action and the deadline set for the completion of the task. So it might be recorded that Mrs Green agreed to obtain from three publishers the detailed costs involved in introducing mathematics schemes throughout the school and that she would present these costings to the next full staff meeting. This type of information should be included in the minutes. All meetings should have minutes. These should be kept by the secretary or by the chairperson if there is no secretary for that particular meeting. They should be circulated to all members including those who were unable to attend the meeting, as soon as possible after the meeting has taken place. Minutes are simply a record of what was decided at a meeting. They are not a detailed account of who said what to whom about which topic. Hansard may be a necessary part of Parliamentary procedure but most schools have neither the time nor the resources to reproduce their own versions of Hansard. Anyway it is just not necessary.

When the minutes are circulated they should not just go into pigeon holes to be forgotten. Team leaders should remind each colleague who has something to do exactly what has been agreed and what the deadline is by attaching a note to the individual's agenda or by highlighting with a coloured pen the tasks which that person has agreed to perform. Depending on when the next meeting is due to take place or what the deadline for any particular action is, it may be worthwhile for the team leader to make a note on her own copy of the agenda to follow up some of the points at a later date but before difficulties might arise from the non-completion of any specific task. Others might also need to be informed of the outcomes of the meeting. The head or the deputy may wish to have the minutes as a matter of course and so, in Rosemary Lane, may Mrs Cass in view of her responsibility for the infant age range. Other colleagues in the school might find them helpful: and, if some items involve or affect other colleagues, then they ought to receive the minutes as a matter of course. A circulation list for both the agenda and the minutes is always useful. It saves the bother of writing a list or checking that you have included everybody this time. If you keep some spare copies of the minutes you can then always pass a copy to anyone who has been forgotten for some reason. Smaller schools, with limited secretarial resources, may find that a minute book kept by a member of staff, and then placed in the staff room, is all that is required. The essential factor is to keep an accurate record of what has been decided and what has to be done, by whom and by when.

Finally it is worth evaluating the meeting itself. Everard and Morris suggest that we ask the following questions after each meeting and take appropriate action if we are not satisfied with the answer:

- Was the purpose of the meeting clear to all those who attended?
- Was the attendance correct for the subject under discussion? (Who else should have been there? Who was not really needed?)
- Were the participants adequately prepared for the meeting?
- Was time well used?
- How high was the commitment of the participants?

- o Did the meeting achieve its purpose?
- o What was the quality of the outcome?
- o Was there a clear definition of:
  - (a) action to be taken following the meeting?
  - (b) responsibility for taking the action?
  - (c) a mechanism for review of the action?

(Everard & Morris 1985, p.52)

Effective meetings are not difficult to organise if they are well planned and if thought is given to the whole process of meetings, from deciding what is to be achieved to circulating an accurate record of what was decided and what actions are to be taken. A team which has its meetings conducted in this way is making good use of its time in team meetings. It is also more likely to be clear about its overall priorities and how it must set about achieving them. Achieving the priorities of the staff team depends on the effective use of all the time available. This requires that people know how they actually use it. Effective use of time means that how time is being used more and more closely approximates to how time should be used. This has to be determined in the light of the team's own priorities and of those of the school. Ensuring that the total time available to the team is used to greatest effect might mean that tasks are delegated to other members of the team by the team leader or the headteacher. This has to be a careful process involving training and supervision as well as the transfer of the appropriate authority to accompany the new responsibilities. Such changes have to be communicated with all staff members. The communication within the team should not be taken for granted. Team leaders especially should be aware of those factors which inhibit or facilitate good communication as well as knowing which forms of communication are appropriate in which circumstances. Taken together these skills will enable the team leader to manage her team in such a way as to ensure that the members can make the maximum contribution to the activities of the primary school in which they work.

Activities

1. Examine the communication process in your school. Can you identify any of the signals listed in Table 30? What can *you* do about them?

2. Over a period of one week analyse all the forms of communication which come to you and leave you. Consider how appropriate and effective each is for its purposes. What changes will you make?

3. Review a representative sample of the meetings you have attended this month. How might the organisation of those meetings be improved in order to make better use of the time you spent attending them? How might your own team meetings be improved?

4. Draw up a full agenda for your next team or staff meeting, then work through the stages in Table 34 to plan and conduct the meeting.

Chapter 9

MANAGING CHANGE IN THE PRIMARY SCHOOL

Decisions and Problems

Change in any organisation generally takes place as a response to a problem or "performance gap", or to the perception of an individual or group who believe that such a problem exists. It may be that the school is not performing as well in a particular area as it might reasonably be expected to do or that approaches which were once readily acceptable are now no longer justifiable. Sometimes this perception is external to the school. External groups such as parents, HMI or LEA representatives may create pressure for change. Sometimes a change is required as a result of policy made by the LEA: a school merger or adopting a first/middle school form of organisation for example. Policy made by the DES can also require changes. The introduction of a national curriculum may have this effect. Wherever the pressure for change originates, the process of managing change tends to be associated with problem-solving.

In many cases, however, problem-solving tends to be confused with decision-making. The terms are often used synonymously, yet they require different types of management action and should take place in different circumstances. Waters, for example, discusses a logical approach to _decision-making_. His first two headings are "Define the Problem" and "Analyse the Problem" (Waters, 1979, p.247). His advice on problem-solving is sound but he has forgotten that managers should be clear about precisely what it is they are doing. They should always make a distinction between a problem and a decision because each should be tackled in a different way. A decision is required in situations where some management action or choice is necessary, such as deciding how to cover for an absent colleague or whether to cancel sports day because of the drizzle. Decisions require some form of autonomous action by the headteacher, team leader or the team, although this may take place after consultations and discussions if that is appropriate. The most significant element of decision-making is that the decision is made when the cause of that particular situation is known and understood. The decision is often based on established priorities and agreed criteria. These will affect the way in which the decision is made.

Many decisions made by headteachers and team leaders are quick day-to-day tactical decisions that must be made in a short space of time. They usually involve a change in plan, caused by work taking longer than expected; unplanned events; changes in weather conditions; staff illness or similar circumstances. The aim must be to modify plans in such a way that disruption and risk are minimised. Once it is established that a decision has to be taken four steps can be followed:

1. Check the situation. Is it your job to deal with the situation? Should anyone else be involved? Is it something you must deal with now?

2. Keep your aim in mind. Remind yourself of your priorities, and criteria. What you are trying to achieve.

3. Decide your options. Often the situation or something similar will have occurred previously and you can select a line of action from past experience. If the situation has not occurred before, think through the options that are available to you. Avoid using the first you think of.

4. Make your choice. Weigh up the advantages and disadvantages of each option and judge the potential success of each. Bear in mind any difficulties you may encounter in implementing the decision and consider the implications of your decision. Will the decision have implications for staff or the remainder of your work plan?

Problem-solving is much more complex than this.

A problem arises when there is a change or deviation from the normal or expected sequence of events, standards of performance or patterns of behaviour. It might be that the staff in the school may cease to work together as well as they used to do, or that pupil performance across the school or, perhaps, in one curriculum area has declined sharply. These are problems. Before any action can be taken the cause must be established. Unlike taking a decision, where cause and criteria are known, problem-solving begins in a situation of uncertainty about or ignorance of the real facts.

Both decision-making and problem-solving are part of the process of managing change but neither activity encapsulates the total process even in the smallest primary school. This is especially true where the whole or a significant part of the school is to be changed or will be affected by a change, as would be the case if a particular curriculum area was to be rethought throughout the school. Such changes may require modifications of both teacher and pupil behaviour, new departures in modes of teaching and learning. They may demand that the teacher develops an entirely new approach to professional activity based on different perceptions and assumptions. These changes have to be managed and it is often the responsibility of the head-teacher or team leader to manage those changes which affect her staff team. Thus at Rosemary Lane Mrs Welton had quickly recognised that the mathematics work was unsatisfactory. Despite an official policy that the Nuffield Scheme would be followed in the Infant department, at least one teacher was ignoring this. Much of the work of the department failed to give the children a good grounding in practical experience. There was no evidence of progression into the Junior classes and no system of record keeping. Work throughout the school was fragmented and lacked direction. Mrs Welton had already decided before Mrs Green's appointment that this situation needed to be changed, but how best might this be achieved? How should Mrs Welton, working with Mrs Green, approach this task? How can it be done as smoothly as possible?

Resistance to Change

George Bernard Shaw once remarked that, "Reformers have the idea that change can be achieved by brute sanity", but change cannot be introduced successfully simply by defining an end or a desired state of affairs and letting other people achieve it by following your plan. The introduction of any change will involve stress, anxiety and conflict. It will be muddled and will require carefully formulated plans to be modified and even abandoned. The change process is often presented as a simple, cyclical model (see Table 35). Such a model does help us to understand the stages in the process but only at the risk of a gross simplification of what actually happens. In reality it may be necessary to return to some stages several times and it may be necessary to deal with several stages simultaneously rather than sequentially. Change, therefore, is a complex and messy process, not least because it is a process of intensive interaction even within the smallest

Table 35 THE PROCESS OF MANAGING CHANGE

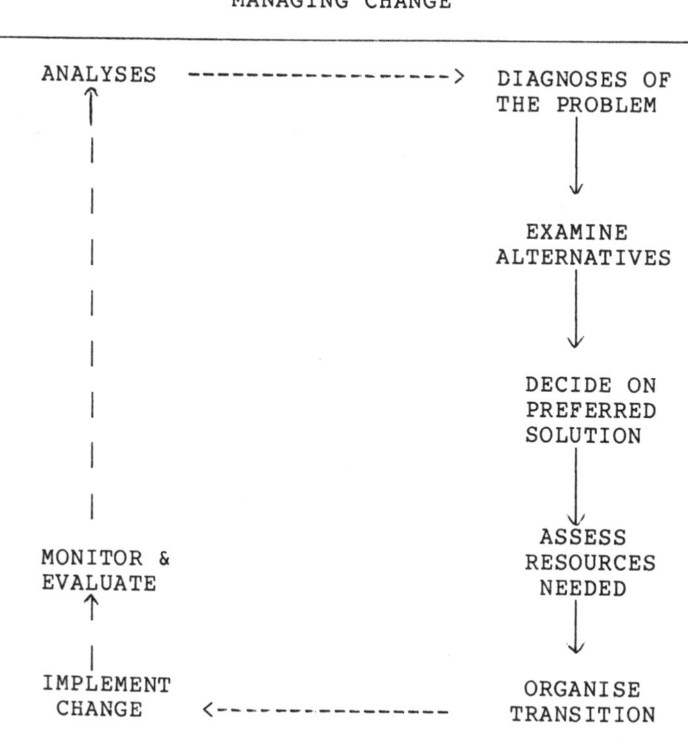

staff team.

Since change involves interaction between colleagues, this interaction forms part of the context of the change. People react to change and its challenges in different ways. This cannot be managed by intuition alone for, as Heller (1985) reminds us, some people will support the change while others will oppose it. The supporters of change may be "evolutionary" in their approach to the extent that they are prepared to spend much time building firm foundations on which the change may rest. Others may be much less patient and more aggressive in their approach. Of those who oppose the change some may actively fight against it while others may passively or truculently resist it. These attitudes become part of the context within which change takes place. A school full of "fighters" and "truculent resisters" is unlikely to change much, if at all. Time must be spent on sensitising colleagues to the need for change since even an aggressive, active leader cannot lead the unwilling. Colleagues must first be made aware of the need for change, of the reasons for it even before the process itself begins. People must be encouraged not driven.

Any change, however much it is needed and welcomed by most of those involved, will meet with resistance. Where the change affects the work of the team it is the responsibility of the team leader to attempt to manage the change in such a way as to minimise the resistance, the conflict and the hostility that will, almost inevitably, be generated. The extent to which the change is resisted will, to some extent, depend on what the change is. A move from one mathematics scheme to another produces resistance which is different from that encountered with the introduction of new forms of team work, for example. On the other hand resistance can be increased by the nature of the change situation and by the use of poor change techniques by team leaders. Where the reasons for the change are not made clear or are presented in such a way as to be unacceptable to those people most likely to be affected by the change, resistance is more likely to be encountered. It is far better to ensure that team members participate fully in exploring the need for change before any decision about the nature and the extent of the proposed change is taken. Agreeing on the need for change is the first stage in minimising conflict and resistance and it has to be done independently of the management of the specific change.

The second stage is having a specific set of objectives for the change which are fully understood by those involved and ensuring that these are communicated in a form in which they can be used to monitor and evaluate the change. In this way all team members can check on the progress and direction of the change for themselves. This is important because any change generates anxiety and apprehension among those people who are affected by it and among those people who think that they will be affected by it. Thus all the members of the staff team which is involved in any type of change are likely to be concerned about the way in which the proposed change is going to affect them. They may worry about how a structural change will influence their promotion prospects or about whether they have the necessary skills to cope with it. These concerns are often made worse by a lack of understanding about the present and future situations and by a feeling, on the part of the individual team member, that he or she has no ownership of the change which is taking place and cannot, therefore, exert any influence over it. Resistance can also be brought about by pressure of work since, when people feel overworked, having to cope with the introduction of a change is the last thing that they will want, especially if they already feel that their status, security, or position is likely to be adversely affected.

The team leader may contribute to the resistance by failing to involve other members of the team in the change process and by not demonstrating to her colleagues precisely why the change is needed and what it will involve. Such lack of specificity on the part of team leaders and others in similar positions is often a significant contributory factor in causing resistance to the very changes which they wish to introduce. Where team leaders do not take into account the existing work patterns and the ways in which pressure in any team will fluctuate, affecting different members at different times, they can increase the problems caused by pressure of work during the change, thus making the change process more difficult than it may otherwise be. Such problems emerge when those responsible for the change fail to consider how that change might best be planned.

Planning and Change

The decision to plan any change can be seen as an

attempt to impose direction and purpose on anticipated future events. Planning usually requires the identification of objectives to be achieved in the medium- or long-term rather than the attempt to match a set of immediate and unco-ordinated responses to a perceived situation. Embodied in these objectives may be an attempt to improve an undesirable situation. Planning also requires that the various parts of the school integrate their efforts to meet the overall objectives. This frequently leads to a situation in which people working in different parts of an institution need to learn more about its total function and about their role and that of others in its functioning. Previously held assumptions and modes of operation may need to be questioned and, perhaps, changed if the objectives are to be achieved. Thus the Infant and Junior departments at Rosemary Lane need to understand each other's requirements with reference to selecting a new mathematics scheme. It has been said that if you do not know where you are going, any road will get you there, although it might be asked how you will know that you have arrived. From the point of view of any school, planning is deciding where to go, how to get there and how to know when you have arrived. As Dror puts it:

> Planning is the process of preparing a set of decisions for action in the future directed at achieving goals by optimum means. (Dror 1963, p.51)

He suggests that planning is a continuous activity by which an organisation changes and is thus different from a plan which is merely a set of decisions for action in the future. The continuous nature of this process is frequently overlooked. Planning is also preparatory to action. Analytically at least, planning must be separated from implementation so that the major policy decisions can be taken and their implications understood prior to action. Unfortunately this can lead to a situation in which vital revisions are not made because the planning process, mistakenly, is thought to be not only preparatory to action but to conclude once implementation commences. As a result the required resources may not be mobilised at the appropriate times to ensure successful implementation. This can often lead to agreements about ends but disagreements about means. Interlocking, interdependent and often sequential sets of decisions need to be made in order to reproduce an activity which is broader than decision-making. The action which stems from these sets of decisions is central to the process since planning is directed towards achieving action in certain areas rather than, say, acquiring pure knowledge.

The links between planning, decision-making, problem-solving and action may, however, be less direct than Dror appears to imply. Since planning is both future- and goal-orientated it cannot ignore ways of minimising the uncertainty which the future holds. Nor can it ignore a consideration of the extent to which the means chosen are appropriate for that particular situation. These means are basic to the planning process since they are the way by which desired ends are achieved. The purpose of planning is to choose the most appropriate means after the alternatives have been identified. This, then, for Dror, (1968) is what planning should be. He fails, however, to make explicit two crucial factors which are embodied in his definition and which can lead to some confusion. The first of these is the extent to which planning contains developmental or adaptive elements: (Friedland, 1967) that is, whether there exists a high degree of autonomy over the choice of means and ends (developmental) or whether planning is heavily dependent on the actions of others (adaptive). It may be that in one area of choice, say ends, the developmental dimension is stronger whilst, over means, adaptive factors may be crucial. The second is the extent to which the outcome of the planning is innovative or allocative. Innovative planning seeks to introduce new social and technical objectives and to create new arrangements and activities. Allocative planning tends to use more gradual change processes although this may vary according to the influence of such factors on, say, external constraints. At Rosemary Lane the planning will be developmental since the staff do have a choice over both means and ends, at least until the national curriculum is implemented. It is also innovative since a new mathematics scheme will be adopted and it will be done over a relatively short time span. This will have to be born in mind as Mrs Welton, Mrs Green and their colleagues embark on the process of change.

The Process of Change

With careful planning, then, resistance to change can be minimised but never eliminated: by involvement, by communication, by awareness, and by the nature of the process itself. Involving all the people who are going to be affected by the change provides them with a basis for understanding what is going on and provides an opportunity for them to influence the change which, in turn, can generate ownership of it and commitment to it. Involvement also enables team members to have access to information about the change. Once people are informed then rumour and misunderstanding can be confronted and overcome. Sharing information allows discussion to take place. This, in turn, creates an awareness of what the problems, opportunities and intentions are. This, in itself, is helpful to the change process in any primary school staff team. A team which is characterised by openness in its relationships and by a ready flow of communication not just from the team leader to members but between the team members themselves and from the team to its leader, and by a supportive environment in which problems and differences can be shared, is likely to be able to cope with the difficult process of changing. Resistance to change will be lowered when people know why a change is being introduced and what advantages are likely to result from it.

If the leader of the primary school staff team is to be able to manage change effectively then she has to recognise that the process of change management demands the ability to predict what the likely outcomes of the change are; to prepare for the change as team leader and also to prepare others; to identify potential problem areas and the action required to deal with them; to implement the change itself; and to recognise and exploit the opportunities which the change process may produce. These abilities must be seen in the light of two most basic questions. Firstly, is the change really needed? Secondly, are the likely outcomes worth all the effort and upheaval which the change will produce? If the answer to both of these questions is positive then the change must be managed. Both Mrs Welton and Mrs Green were convinced of the need to change mathematics teaching at Rosemary Lane.

To do this, two alternative types of process are available. One is based on a minimum of consultation and involvement and is, on the whole, carried through almost entirely by the team leader alone. Where there is considerable pressure to change rapidly in the face of severe problems with a minimum of resources available, then the leader-based change may be appropriate. The process which will be considered in detail here, however, is the second alternative, a participative approach to planned change. In the discussion of this approach, however, there will be much that is relevant to the leader-based approach to change since any approach to change is more likely to be successful if it is well prepared and the plans are properly implemented. This particular approach to change is based on the assumption that the team is changing as a response to a problem which it has identified or which has been identified for it. It also assumes that the most effective way of bringing about change in the primary school is to begin by changing practices and activities rather than by worrying about attitudes. This is not to say that attitudes are unimportant. They are very important. It might be helpful for team leaders and headteachers to recognise, however, that an explicit assumption of this approach to change is that attitudes are more likely to change after, rather than before the introduction to the school of new ways of doing things provided that care and commonsense are exercised during the pro-ess of change. Care must be taken, however, to sensitise colleagues to the need for change and to prepare them for it in advance of the change taking place. The approach, then, contains a number of stages each of which will be discussed in turn. This should not, however, be taken to imply that every part of each stage will have been successfully and fully completed before the next one begins. As has already been pointed out, change is a process which will not follow simple linear guidelines. The team and its leader must be able to demonstrate one of the cardinal virtues necessary for the successful management of change, that is flexibility.

Analysis

The first stage in the management of the change process is that of analysis. Change will always be easier to manage if, within the team, there is general agreement on aims, division of responsibilities, fair distribution of work, effective arrangements for delegation and a reasonably efficient communication system. The importance of these factors has been discussed in previous chapters but, before embarking on any planned change, time spent by the team leader in reviewing them is time well spent because change in any organisation is likely to cause tension and conflict. In order to minimise the possible adverse effects of change, careful analysis is a prerequisite to any approach to managing change. If the analysis of the situation indicates a difficulty in any of these areas then it should be dealt with. Ideally this should be done before any change is introduced but, at the very least, the weakness should be remedied as part of the process of change.

Following this, it is also often worth considering the present situation in another way. If the team is in a position to be clear about the demands which are currently being placed upon it, or which are likely to emerge in the immediate future, then it is possible to develop a more realistic view about the feasibility of the planned change than if this were not the case. Therefore analyse the present in terms of the demands being made; in terms of where the team is now in relation to where it wants to be in the future; and in terms of what factors are helping and what are hindering the team in its efforts to achieve the desired change.

As Plant (1987) points out, a force field map can help us with this. It also helps us to understand why a change is being resisted. The very process of trying to understand by listening actively will begin to minimise resistance to the change. Such an analysis of the factors involved in a proposed change must include a consideration of potential problem areas. These factors may be grouped into those likely to promote and those likely to inhibit the change. The analysis was first described by Kurt Lewin (1947), and is based on the premise that a change situation is a balance between two sets of forces. Table 36 suggests the process of bringing changes about. The process is worked through a series of nine developing steps:

STEP ONE: Identify and describe the change including methods to be used to sensitise others to it. Note that the description is required in writing.

STEP TWO: Define the change in terms of:
(a) current situation including staff attitudes to change
(b) desired situation including a definition of an "acceptable state".

STEP THREE: List driving and restraining forces. Note that these forces are anything that can hinder or help the change and could be technology, material, methods, people, time, money. What is important is the requirement to be specific. It can help to draw a diagram of forces.

STEP FOUR: Highlight those forces considered to be most important.

STEP FIVE: Against restraining forces highlighted, list actions which could reduce or eliminate them.

STEP SIX: For driving forces highlighted, list actions which could possibly increase the force.

STEP SEVEN: Determine the most promising steps which could now be taken and identify the available resources.

STEP EIGHT: Reexamine the steps and place them in sequence, omitting any that do not seem to "fit". Who else needs to be involved?

STEP NINE: Implement and evaluate.

The management of change must, therefore, be firmly based on a rational approach which has defined what the change is to be, has planned how to bring it about, and has identified ways of coping with the difficulties which must, inevitably, arise during the process of change.

Having done this it is now possible to think about the future. What does the team leader and/or the team want to happen, or what is the desired future state towards which the planned change is moving the team? What will be the consequences of doing nothing? The answer to that question is, at this stage, the most crucial of all because it determines just how necessary it is to change anything at the present time. The whole of the team should be involved in, and take responsibility for, this analysis since such involvement is vital in order to get the commitment necessary from the team members to enable the change to be managed successfully. As a result of her own analysis, which was confirmed by Mrs Green and by Mr Jowett and Mrs Cass, Ann Welton was able to pinpoint the fundamental problem about the mathematics work in the school. No one person was responsible and, therefore, there was a resulting lack of general agreement. Teachers all went their own way. There was no planned progression between stages, no evaluation of effectiveness. Communication was casual, or limited to largely unread comments on the end-of-year record cards, many of which were incomplete in any case. This analysis led Mrs Welton quickly to the next stage: diagnosis.

Table 36 A FORCE FIELD MODEL

Present Situation

DRIVING FORCES	RESTRAINING FORCES
	Short staffed in key subject areas
School's desire to do well for their pupils	Low morale among teachers
Wish to improve public image of teachers	Shortage of equipment and resources
LEA support	Low self esteem among key staff
Possibility of new equipment	Lack of awareness of problem
Promotion prospects	Pessimism about future career

Diagnosis of the Problem

After the analysis comes the diagnosis of the problem. Even where a change is clearly the result of a perceived problem, team leaders should ensure that the problem is understood fully by all members of the team and, perhaps even more important, the team as a whole should agree that the proposed change will, in fact, provide the necessary solution to the problem as identified. It is easy for problems and solutions to become loosely attached to each other in such a way that the solution proposed, while it may be acceptable to many people on educational, philosophical or even practical grounds, may not actually provide a solution to the real problem. For example, giving colleagues more time in which to write record cards may not be the solution to the problem of incompleted record cards if the cards are too complex or if they require information which teachers are not easily able to provide. Whatever the initial diagnosis of the problem, the team leader should seek to confirm it from a number of sources before embarking on any action. This is not a licence for inactivity but merely a suggestion that if the initial diagnosis is wrong then everything which follows from it will be wrong. Therefore it is wise to collect as much data about the situation as possible by talking to team members and others with relevant knowledge and information, by observation, by looking at facts such as test scores, attendances and all the other quantitative data that exists in schools. In the last analysis it can be worth asking colleagues for their opinions about the present situation and what might be wrong with it.

This step is perhaps the simplest and yet the most important. It is relatively easy to recognise that there is a problem of some kind or to say that we in this school are not doing as well as we should. Recognition of a problem only indicates that there is a problem. It does not necessarily identify what that problem is and it certainly does not suggest any solutions. Knowing that a problem exists is only the very first element in its identification. It is necessary, therefore, to seek answers to questions such as:

- What is wrong?
- Where, within the school organisation is the problem? Where does it have no effect?
- Who or what is affected and not affected?
- When is the problem evident and when is it not evident?

Table 37 WAYS OF COLLECTING INFORMATION

1. Interviews - A simple, straightforward but subjective way of obtaining information but one which will usually serve as a good starting point from which to gather more detailed information

- decide what information is wanted and from whom
- interview only a small number of people
- have a set of no more than six specific questions
- encourage open ended responses

2. Observations - Structured observation can often clarify issues related to a particular problem area

- should be carried out by more than one person looking at the same thing
- observations and impressions should be recorded together with the evidence for them
- observers should review their information together

3. Opinion Surveys - These are often helpful in establishing opinions about priorities and performance held by different people in school

- can cope with fairly large population and also be quantified and compared
- can be used as a basis for small group discussions between people involved in the problem area

4. Quantitive Information - This is an often neglected area of information for those involved in the management of change in primary schools

- can compare individual or class groups
- can illustrate changes over time
- is best visually displayed (e.g. histograms or graphs)

Table 37 (cont´d)

5. <u>Group Discussions</u> -	Small group discussions between people most involved with the problem area can be held. These create opportunities for real involvement on the part of all those connected with the problem area

- can focus on opinion differences revealed by surveys
- must give everybody an opportunity to comment on the nature of the problem and suggest possible solutions to it
- discussion group may attempt to place possible causes and suggested solutions in rank order. Can link to next stage in process, looking for alternative solutions

o Why?

o What is the extent of the problem?

Accuracy and, as far as possible, objectivity are essential at this stage. Incorrect identification of the problem may cause severe difficulties at a later stage. An initial identification of a problem should only be accepted after it has been confirmed from a range of sources.

On the basis of a thorough analysis of the present situation and careful diagnosis of the potential problem it ought now to be possible to explore possible solutions and the changes that will be necessary in order to move the team towards an agreed solution. Just as it was important to explore the problem in some detail and to avoid making assumptions too rapidly about the nature of the problem, so the same is true about identifying a solution. The team leader has to ensure that all alternative possibilities are considered and that the first solution which is offered is not accepted simply because it is the first, or the most likely at a glance, or because there is some considerable support for it initially. Remember that there is no guarantee that the first choice is the best, or that the one which has the most support in the early stages will, after due consideration, be the final choice. Team leaders should, at the very least, ensure that as many ideas as possible are considered in the early stages of examining alternatves. This, contrary to how it might at first appear, is time well spent.

Mrs Welton has decided that the basic problem is a lack of clear and informed leadership in mathematics throughout the school. She has already decided that such leadership should not be provided by either herself or Mr Jowett who does have a background in mathematics. She has, therefore, appointed Mrs Green to provide this leadership and to be the change agent. (See Havelock, 1970). Ann Welton made it clear to her staff that they would all have opportunities to be involved in discussions about mathematics and in the formulation of new policies. Mrs Green and Mrs Welton could, if they wished, use all of the approaches to Diagnosis listed in Table 37. This would, in Rosemary Lane, be far too complex and unnecessary. Mrs Welton has already drawn her own conclusions. Mrs Green will talk to colleagues, observe and look at how children have performed in mathematics in recent years.

In the case of Rosemary Lane, much of this work was done by Mrs Green after her appointment. This resulted in some delay, but had the distinct advantage that she was bringing a fresh mind to the problem and was uninfluenced by any of the internal group dynamics within the staffroom. Had she been a long-serving member of staff, she would have needed careful counselling from Mrs Welton on how to approach some of her colleagues who would have felt very threatened by the implication of criticism and the prospect of change.

Examining Alternatives

Once a diagnosis has been illuminated by a range of information the problem can be clarified and appropriate action initiated. This is often best done by considering a wide range of possible alternatives. All too often the action taken is the one the manager thinks of first. Often this is successful but it is not necessarily the best solution to the problem. As Whitfield (1975) shows it is far better to adopt a simple technique such as brain-storming to generate in a very short time a large number of possible alternative courses of action from within a team. A well-run brainstorm session will produce a vast quantity of ideas although these will range from the totally wild and silly to the brilliant and perceptive. All ideas, however, are acceptable. The brilliant ones are obviously acceptable but those ideas which prove to be wild and silly serve several functions. They generate laughter which, in itself, is an excellent catalyst and prevents uneasy silences which are the very death to effective brainstorming. They also stimulate thought and this can lead the team to throw up ideas which are far from wild or silly. A brainstorm is easy to arrange if a few simple rules are followed. The initial preparation has to be carried out and shared with the team. This means that the present situation and the nature of the problem has to be analysed as described above. The problem has to be stated to the team at the start of the brainstorm and accepted so that the session concentrates on generating solutions, not debating the nature of the problem. Team members need to have had time to think around the problem before the session but, by involving them in the process of analysis, the team leader will already have ensured that this has happened (see Table 38).

When all this has been done and the team are ready, the brainstorming session itself can begin. The team leader may choose to record all the ideas as they are shouted out on a number of large sheets of newsprint displayed in such a way that they can be easily seen by the whole group. This role does not prevent the leader from joining in. The team is asked to give as many solutions to the stated problem as is possible. While this is going on, while the ideas are being shouted out, it is important that all judgement is suspended. No evaluation

Table 38 THE BRAINSTORMING TECHNIQUE

HOW TO BRAINSTORM
1. Write up short topics
2. Ask for short, one or two word contributions
3. Brief group not to challenge any idea
4. Do not question whatever is called out, just write it up
5. Write up as fast as you can
6. Give encouragement
7. Refocus the process by picking on particular words already written up
8. Stop when you feel you have enough material
9. Copy list for group members
10. Review

should be allowed of any of the ideas by, for example, making asides such as "That's a silly idea." The team leader may need to enforce this strictly in the early stages but soon the team members will, themselves, do so. Suggestions must free wheel to allow all sorts of ideas to emerge and be recorded. What is important is the quantity of the ideas obtained, not the quality. It should be made clear to the team that they can use, develop and extend any idea which emerges. Such cross-fertilisation allows ostensibly useless ideas to be refined into good ideas as the brainstorm progresses although no evaluation of any idea must be made until the session is over. The brainstorm finishes when no more ideas are forthcoming. The session, itself, is not yet over. On fresh newsprint the team leader asks the team to select the wildest ideas from the brainstormed list. These are written on the newsprint or other large sheets of paper. The team is then asked to turn them into a sensible idea by modifying them. When this process is completed the session ends. There has still been no evaluation. This comes later when the team is fresh again.

Evaluation should take place a day or two later and may be done in one or both of two ways. The whole team may assemble, consider the stated problem, and be given a typed list of all the ideas numbered in sequence. Each team member is then asked to examine the list and without discussion to select about 10 per cent which he or she thinks are worthy of further consideration. The leader collects the lists and identifies which ideas have the most support. These can then be considered in more detail, perhaps by a smaller group. Alternatively a smaller group selected from the whole team can be used to carry out a similar process. This group can examine the original newsprint and select the ideas which are potential winners. Each group member may then be given an idea or a group of similar ideas, together with agreed criteria against which to evaluate them. For example, the solutions may have to be implemented within a certain time, or within a specific budget, or in a certain building. After an agreed period of time the group reassembles to consider the evaluations. This discussion can then produce a list of best ideas for more detailed analysis. If both processes are used then the best ideas from the whole team and the best ideas from the evaluation group can be examined side by side. This can be a time-consuming exercise but, where a major change is going to be made, it is far better to spend time on getting it right than to have leisure in which to repent that it all went wrong.

Decide Upon the Preferred Solution

Out of this long and exhaustive stage, a series of alternative solutions refine themselves into the preferred choice. This should be subjected to further discussion. A series of questions might be asked about the chosen solution. In what ways can this idea go wrong?, or Who needs to be involved in or consulted about this?, What skills and knowledge does the team need in order to implement the change and are they available?

A more limited brainstorming technique can then be applied to generate answers which can be taken into account at a later stage. The fourth stage in the management of change process, that of identifying a preferred solution which will both be acceptable to the members of the team and effectively cope with the future situation, is now complete. The preferred solution to the problems of lack of progression in the mathematics teaching at Rosemary Lane, the discontinuity in provision and the failure to provide pupils with sufficient practical experience, is to introduce a new mathematics scheme rather than to impose the existing one, which in any case is not used throughout the school. The very process of selecting a new scheme may help to ensure that it is used by the whole staff because they will all be involved in choosing it. On this basis, and with the intention of selecting a mathematics scheme which is acceptable to the staff and which will help to remedy the deficiencies in teaching in that area, plans can be prepared to implement the change, bearing in mind that the planning will be developmental and innovative. These plans should state clearly what the objectives are and how those objectives are to be achieved. The identification of objectives, setting targets and establishing priorities have been discussed in previous chapters. This approach to managing change rests on the premise that the objectives identified are associated with one aspect of a school´s work; are relatively limited in their horizons; and are closely associated with the existing work of the school. These objectives are translated into a series of priorities which are, in turn, translated into direct action by specific individuals. The objectives are, simply, those changes which have to be made within the school in order to solve the problem or to improve the situation. They should state simply what has to be done and should specify exactly what the objectives are in terms of the actions to be carried out, by whom and in what sequence. These actions become the key tasks which combine to make up the action programme for implementation. The programme should also indicate how well an activity or task must be done and what resources are necessary, how many different inspection copies of books examined, how many other schools visited, how many advisers consulted, how long the report to the next meeting should be. Ensure that all the actions in the programme relate to the diagnosis of the problem and check that they do lead in the desired direction by repeated monitoring and evaluation. To help with this it is often useful to set out the action programme in the form of an Action Grid, or a series of Action Grids for more complex changes. The actions here should be stated in positive terms, the outcomes of which can be identified. To plan, to list, to design, to read, to convene, to identify, can all be seen to have practical outcomes but this may not be so of actions expressed in terms of to understand, to consider, to know or to appreciate. Resources should be clearly stated together with any additional help which will be required. All of the tasks in the action programme can be summarised in this way and put on the Action Grid. Mrs Green has produced her own grid for part of the change programme at Rosemary Lane (Table 39).

The planning of the change process should be formulated in such a way as to include those steps which are necessary in order to move from the present state to the desired future state. The plans should also recognise that there is an intermediate stage between the present and the future. This has been called the transition state. Team leaders and their teams should appreciate a fact that appears to have been largely ignored in the educational world, perhaps because of the way in which education uses time as a discrete barrier through which pupils pass at the end of the academic year. Change involves the passing of time. As time passes, a variety of tasks associated the management of the change have to be accomplished. While this is going on, the day-to-day running of the school and the part played in it by the team has to continue. Routine does not cease in order that change can be brought about, ideal though this state of affairs might be. Therefore, after the diagnosis of the problem which leads to the identification of the solution that is to be

Table 39 ACTION GRID

TASKS	PERSON RESPONSIBLE	RESOURCES REQUIRED	OUTCOME	DEADLINE	PERFORMANCE LEVEL	FURTHER ACTION
To collect a number of examples of maths schemes suitable for primary aged children	Jenny Green	Current catalogues Secretarial assistance for ordering Display area in staffroom	Completed delivery from publishers by half-term	Planning meeting: 14th November	At least 4 schemes, including all three recommended in County Maths Guide	All members of planning team to have seen copies before 14th November Item on staff meeting 18th November: to introduce staff-room display Staffroom display 18–30 November December 1 & 2: Feedback meet-ings from Infant and Junior Depts

implemented, the effective manager of change will devote some attention to the fifth stage in the process, the management of the transition.

Managing the Transition

The secret of successful transition management is to create a structure staffed by people whose main responsibility is to ensure that the change is successful and that it takes place as smoothly as possible. They should not necessarily be those people who will be responsible for running the changed situation. Transition management structures are temporary and should be disbanded when the change is complete. The team leader may wish to choose a small group from within the team to do this. Such a group might include the natural leaders in the team or those with special and relevant skills. The team leader should be associated with this group but not necessarily part of it since the rest of the work of the team has to continue and this will require much of the team leader's attention. The transition management group will have the special responsibility of making those organisational arrangements which are necessary for bringing about the change. This has to start with a plan. At Rosemary Lane Mrs Green, Mrs Cass, Mr Jowett and Mrs Welton formed the team but all the staff were involved in discussions, as they can be in a relatively small school. Planning may be handled by the transition management team alone although it is more likely that the team leader will be fully involved and that the rest of the team will participate in the process, for it is at this fifth stage that rumour often begins to fly, anxieties to develop and misunderstandings occur. Effective communication is vital and a wide understanding of what is afoot is important. By involving team members in the planning of the change these things can all be achieved, at least in part. A plan, in this context, contains detailed statements about who is to do what and by when. It should state exactly and specifically what has to be done and how those activities are related to achieving the desired change. Responsibility for carrying out the action should be clearly and unambiguously stated, remembering that a responsibility shared merely provides two people with an excuse for not doing something. Tasks should have to be carried out by a specified time according to identified performance criteria which will be monitored by a member of the transition management group. The discrete activities need to be linked to show where the performance of one task depends on the completion of another. Sequencing of this kind can often prevent bottlenecks and delays.

The plan should, however, be adaptable so that it can cope with those unforeseen problems which will arise and those tasks which will not, in spite of everyone's best endeavours, be completed on time. The plan should be seen to be cost-effective in terms of time and people. It must be remembered that everyone involved within a team in the management of change, including the transition management group, will have normal teaching duties to fulfil and that the change is imposing additional work. This may be enriching or rewarding. It may be regarded by the team leader or her colleagues as a vital and necessary part of staff development, but it still means that plans have to be realistic.

Implementation

Once the plans are formulated the change process can move, at last, to the sixth stage which is the one at which those many inexperienced managers of change in our schools want to start. That is the implementation stage. By identifying tasks and fixing responsibilities, by specifying deadlines and performance criteria, the team and its transition management group now has an action plan which can be implemented. But wait a minute! No change can be implemented successfully unless it has the commitment of a number of significant individuals, and unless it is more or less acceptable to all those likely to be affected by it. The team leader has to be sure that this is the case before the implementation process starts. Commitment and acceptance are integral parts of the same set of attitudes. Acceptance implies a willingness to let something happen without opposing, while commitment implies a willingness to play a positive role in bringing about the change. Significant individuals have to be committed to the change while all of those affected have to accept it. The most effective way of gaining acceptance and commitment is to ensure that there is general agreement about the nature and importance of the problem together with an understanding of how the proposed change will alleviate the situation. Beyond that it may be necessary for the team leader or the transition management group to cope with a number of barriers to change. These are often expressed in verbal form such as: "I can't see that working here"; or "We have tried all that before." There are effective retorts to the usual snipers and these have their uses but such statements are often an indication of hurt and anxiety. These hurts and anxieties have to be talked through and dealt with as part of the process of managing the change. They should not be ignored nor should they be allowed to assume more importance than they deserve. By involving colleagues from the outset, such problems can be seen early and can be minimised. Sharing information tends to minimise anxiety and reduce the effect of rumour. Nevertheless, by using meetings, individual discussion, seminars and brainstorming sessions, difficulties can be confronted and overcome. All of these techniques can be used to influence, persuade and negotiate with colleagues involved in the change process.

Successful implementation depends on effective planning and it also depends on ensuring that the benefits of the change are recognised by those who are doing the work. Where team members are spending their time and energy on a project they should see, if not benefit from, the results of their efforts. This may mean that they have to be told about what is going on, about how well the plans are working, as well as where the problems are. The team leader has to ensure that team members have the training and support necessary to implement the change. The implementation stage of managing a change requires as much time and effort as the other stages but, by this time, team members are often running out of energy or having their attention diverted elsewhere by tasks to which they should give some attention. The team leader must ensure that the implementation is followed through according to the plan, reminding those who have accepted responsibilities where necessary and helping the transition management group through the implementation stage. It is helpful if one member of the group, possibly the same person who is monitoring progress, also ensures that communication is effective at this stage. Are those people who have to give approval for actions being consulted? Are those people who should be informed of actions being involved? Are the appropriate and promised resources forthcoming? Above all, perhaps, are the changes which are taking place still moving the team in the direction in which it originally wished to go, and is this still the right direction? This, above all else, must be constantly monitored especially in the later stages when some of the changes already made may create situations which

Table 40 IMPLEMENTING CHANGE

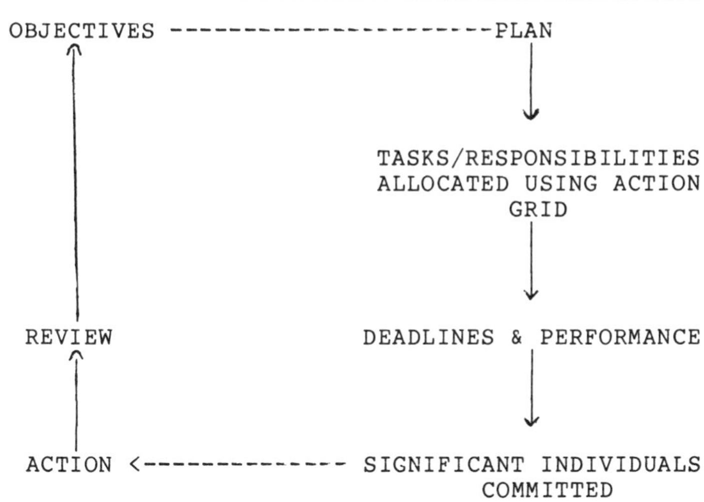

were not foreseen in the original plan. Therefore each of the different tasks in the programme must be expressed in terms which contain an element of evaluation such as a deadline and a statement about levels of performance. Throughout the implementation stage, the person or group with overall responsibility for managing the change should make periodic checks on the effectiveness of what is being done. In this case Mrs Green acted in that capacity. She recognised that it might be necessary to make modifications and adjustments to the overall programme in order to ensure that the whole staff could be involved both as a group and as individuals. In the event the time scale was too short. When she checked on possible delivery dates for the mathematics schemes with publishers she found that none of the schemes could be delivered within two months. She therefore extended that period of consultation into January and suggested criteria that her colleagues might use to evaluate the schemes. She derived these from the work of Lumb and his colleagues (1984) which she recommended all the staff at Rosemary Lane to read. She asked them to look at the content of the material and to consider:

- the range of material available such as text books, worksheets, workcards, cassette tapes, computer programs, together with additional resources required

- the target population in terms of age and ability range, modes of use with individuals, groups, class

- the aims of the material

- the forms of answering and recording whether anything is missing

She also asked them to look at the factors which might affect the way in which the material would be used in terms of:

- is it attractive, robust, easy to handle, easy to store and equally appropriate for boys and girls, and for children of different ethnic backgrounds?

- is the presentation of mathematical ideas clear and logical and does it encourage the understanding of skills in investigation and of mathematical ordering and patterning?

- is it enjoyable and linked to pupils' experience?

- does it require the pupils to select a range of strategies and techniques, exercise analysis and judgement, innovation and creativity?

- are there opportunities for practising practical, written and mental skills and for discussion?

- is the assessment material useful in diagnosing pupils' difficulties and planning programmes of work?

- is the teacher's material useful, clear and comprehensive?

- is it appropriate for the reading ability of pupils, in suitable print, logically presented, well organised and interestingly illustrated?

Such an analysis will have to be monitored by Mrs Green. It is part of the monitoring of all the tasks involved in the change process which, in turn, is necessary to ensure that implementation is taking place in the way in which it was designed and to enable implementation procedures to be changed as the need arises. It prevents the pattern which occurs all too frequently of evaluating a response to a problem only after a task is completed or a change fully implemented. Monitoring during the implementation stage increases the likelihood that difficulties can be identified and corrected. It also serves as a useful reminder that flexibility at this stage is of crucial importance, and that such flexibility must be based on the evidence produced by monitoring in the light of the objectives agreed in the earlier stages.

Monitoring and Evaluating

Monitoring of the change is the final stage in the process of change management but, as has been shown above, this does not only take place at the end of the process. It is an essential and integral part of the process of change throughout that process. It should play a formative part in planning and implementing actions designed to solve problems which confront schools from time to time. Such monitoring should be given absolute priority, since many promising innovations have come to grief because headteachers and staff have tended to shift their attention to other matters once it appears that the solution to a particular problem is in sight. Continual monitoring will prevent this from happening.

Monitoring has to be done on the basis of the original agreed definition of the problem, the identification of the preferred solution, the plan of action which was designed in order to bring about this desired future state and the implementation of that plan. Furthermore, monitoring and evaluation can be used as a trigger to help sustain energy and motivation for the change as well as to examine the progress of all or part of the change process. Evaluation during the change should be focused on the relationship between the priorities, the direction of the change, and the intended desired state. The team leader, above all others involved in managing the process of change within the team, has to be sure that the change is taking the team in the desired direction and that the priorities remain the same after the process of change has begun. It may be that the monitoring and evaluation will raise some questions about the change. In this case the team leader, working with those responsible for transition management, has to establish what else it is that they need to know, why they need to know it and what they are prepared to accept as evidence. Everyone who has been involved in the change process will need to be kept informed about the results of monitoring and evaluation especially where this leads to some modification of the original plans for action. By keeping people informed and involved, the team leader can minimise anxiety and, therefore, reduce the possibility that resistance to the change will develop as the process of change progresses.

The evaluation of the results of the change after the process is thought to be completed may need to take place over an extended period of time. This, of course, will depend on the nature of the change and the intention behind it. The ultimate test may simply be: "How far has the teaching of mathematics improved at Rosemary Lane? and to what extent have the children benefited?" To answer these questions Mrs Welton, Mrs Green and their colleagues may have to go back to the original problem, the evidence which was produced to form the basis for the decision to change, and the facts and opinions that formed part of that evidence. The evaluation will have to examine, on the basis of comparing the new state with the old, how far the change was successful in that it achieved what was intended. The criteria for evaluating the change need to be derived explicitly from the stated objectives for the change as established at the start of the change process or as modified while the change was implemented. A simple set of questions asked of colleagues might also help. Are the children learning more effectively? Are the records more useful? Did we move far enough in the agreed direction? Did the priorities remain the same? Answers to these questions will give an indication of the extent to which the problem was solved. More information may be required but it is important not to collect information simply for the sake of collecting it. The collection of further information should be preceded by establishing what it is that should be known, why it needs to be known, and how it will be used.

There is a limit to the amount of time, resources and staff effort that can be expended on any problem. Summative evaluation may have two key elements. The first will be to look at the success of the change with reference to, for example, items in the following list derived from Pountney (1985):

- Formal testing through end of year examinations, standardised tests and weekly quizzes, or tests
- Pupil profiles written by children and teachers
- Observation of children in the classroom and around the school
- Progress records kept by teachers
- Comparisons with other schools and national or local statistics
- Advice from other colleagues, outside agencies, parents and others in the community
- General impressions of classrooms, displays, teacher/pupil relationships and children's attitudes

The second will consist of an attempt to establish whether or not further expenditure of resources on a particular problem is worth the effort. This is a realistic rather than a cynical approach to evaluation since it recognises that schools have to operate with limited or reducing resources in the light of which it is often necessary to ask: "Have we done the best we can with this problem, and is it time to concentrate on something else?"

Leaders of primary school teams are, almost inevitably, going to be faced with situations in which they are required to bring about changes in their teams or where their teams are going to be involved in changes within the school. Managing change is difficult because change itself generates tension, conflict and anxiety within teams. By adopting a planned approach to change based on the assumption that change should be an activity which is shared by all those who are likely to be affected by it and which should be managed by a few for the benefit of the whole team, team leaders and headteachers can formulate an approach to change similar to the one outlined here that will enable their staff and themselves to cope with the process of managing change effectively and efficiently. If team leaders are prepared, with their teams, to devote the time and effort to the management of change, then it can be done successfully, especially in a collegiate framework where each teacher is able and willing to take responsibility for her own area within the work of the whole primary school.

Activities

1. Identify one possible change which you expect your staff team to have to make in the next two years. What is the worst thing that could go wrong in this situation? What would be your desired future state?

2. Using the change which you identified in Activity 1, list those factors which may prevent the change being successful, and those which the team has working in its favour as it manages the change. How can you minimise the effect of the former and maximise the benefits of the latter? Can you reach a situation in which the forces for, or advantages coming from, the change outweigh those factors inhibiting the change?

3. For the same change or another of your choice, draw up an action plan for implementing the change, stating what has to be done, when, by whom, and to what standard. Have you the necessary resources to carry through this plan?

4. For the same change draw up a list of criteria which you would want to take into account in order to monitor the success of the change (a) while it was taking place and (b) after the process had been completed.

Chapter 10

EVALUATION, APPRAISAL AND DEVELOPMENT IN PRIMARY SCHOOLS

In the previous chapter we saw how important the process of evaluation is to the management of effective change in the primary school. In the particular context of introducing a new mathematics scheme a number of evaluative questions were suggested which could contribute towards the monitoring of the change process. In Chapter Four we also saw how a school and a staff profile, linked closely with job descriptions and specifications, can contribute to the education of the school and how the evidence collected by these processes provided a foundation from which staff development could take place. In one sense the approach outlined in Chapter Four is one of review since it is a retrospective activity based on the collection and examination of information about the past performance of the school (DES 1985b). It is essentially school-based and school-focused although the general principles can be applied to any school at any time since the headings used on the profiles can be altered to suit the circumstances which prevail at that particular time.

None of the areas in the school profile relate directly to the work of the children in the classroom since the profile does not seek to establish in detail how well the children are performing. It is more concerned with the extent to which the school and the teachers are achieving their own objectives. The assumption is clearly being made that children will benefit in a school which has a clear idea of what it is trying to achieve, a set of strategies for achieving, and a process for evaluating progress in the desired direction. This is not to say that the progress of individual children or of groups of children is unimportant or that it should be subsumed in the school profile. Indeed the work of pupils forms a vital part in the evaluative process described in the previous chapter. Equally good class teaching and effective sequencing of learning throughout the school depend on keeping a careful record of pupils' progress. As Shipman points out:

> Observing teachers at work suggests that they use a realistic, coherent, if implicit and sometimes casual approach to evaluation as a basis for action.
> (Shipman, 1983, p.xi)

He goes on to discuss in a practical and realistic way how teachers can devise and adopt strategies for more consistent forms of pupil evaluation. Such a discussion is, however, beyond the scope of this book. The focus here will be on the evaluation of the school and its staff as a means of fostering staff development.

School Evaluation

The profiling process adopted by Mrs Welton at Rosemary Lane is but one method of evaluating the work of the school. It took as its point of reference a set of criteria based on a view of what the school ought to be doing and related these to past performance. In effect it asked how well the school had been performing in a number of areas which Mrs Welton and her staff believed to be important. Clearly the curriculum areas and the organisational functions are central to the working of the school. In the light of the proposals for the national curriculum the staff at Rosemary Lane may wish to consider revising some of the curriculum areas to reflect more closely the emphasis of the national curriculum on the core subjects, English, mathematics and science, and to take into account the foundation subjects.

In some LEAs the evaluation of schools has not proceeded along such a self-determined path. The pressures from a variety of quarters for teachers, schools and LEAs to be accountable to parents and pupils for the curriculum and teaching methods which they adopted produced a rash of LEA-based school-evaluation documents. The sequence of events which led up to the production of these documents tended to follow a similar pattern. LEA inspectors or advisers would bring together groups of teachers to identify those areas of school life which needed to be evaluated as part of the process of managing the school effectively. A working document might be produced and used in a small number of schools. This would be revised and a final document would be issued to all schools for their own use.

One of the very early documents in this field was Keeping the School Under Review which was produced by ILEA. This booklet contains a series of questions to be discussed by teachers as a step towards improving the work of their school. It was intended to enable staff to evaluate their own work in terms of their own aims for the school by looking critically at their procedures as well as at the performance of the children. The main headings in the booklet are:

- The children, their parents, the governors and the community
- Teaching organisation, school staff, responsibility structure, non-teaching staff, staff development
- The curriculum, continuity, assessment, extending the curriculum
- Organisation and management
- The building and the environment
- Questions for the individual teacher to ask himself or herself
- Questions for the headteacher to ask
- The future
- The acid test (Would I recommend a colleague to apply for a post at this school? Would I recommend this school to a friend for their children?)

As Day et. al. (1985) point out, checklists of this kind can be daunting for the teacher. This one contains one hundred questions which have to be read, digested and interpreted. They are also value-laden. For example, it has been suggested that this document is overwhelmingly concerned with institutional procedures rather than with what actually happens (Clift, 1982). Rather than actual learning it concentrates on preconditions for learning and on the adequacy of procedures, not on outcomes. The use of the booklet, however, has been left to schools and is essentially a voluntary and internal activity.

Starting Points in Self Evaluation (Oxfordshire County Council, 1979) was intended to initiate a regular and relatively formal evaluation process on a four-yearly cycle. There are ninety-three questions, many with a series of sub-questions grouped under three headings:

The Teacher's Role
- work in the classroom
- knowledge of the children
- general

The Headteacher's Role
- time
- objectives and organisation
- staffing

Basic Facts and General School Arrangements
- basic facts
- subjective assessment of general arrangements
- arrangements for staffing and resources
- the children
- arrangements for school organisation
- syllabus
- attainment and records
- final general questions

These questions are used to write a report on the school which is provided both to governors and to the LEA for discussion and follow-up. This development is an interesting contrast to the ILEA approach where the document was clearly intended to be for use in schools in any way deemed appropriate by the school concerned. Although the follow-up took the form of an external validation of internally assessed standards there was no real promise of remedial activity or related resources, where these were identified as being necessary. Perhaps for that reason as much as for anything to do with the external and open nature of the process itself, it was found that:

> ...the initially open-hearted approach to self-portrayal was transformed over time to one of caution characterized by the almost total absence from the final report of the 'evaluative comment' sought by the Authority. (Clift, 1982, p. 264)

Defining the nature, purpose and scope of the evaluative exercise has not only to be realistic. It also has to be clearly understood and accepted by all those involved in it from the outset. It should concentrate on those areas in which positive outcomes are likely to be achieved in a reasonable period of time. Guidelines for Review and Internal Development of Schools (GRIDS), which is a result of a project established by the Schools Council, does have these parameters built into its process since its starting point is to get the staff of the school to identify one or two priority areas for review and development (McMahon et. al., 1984). This is preceded by a broad rather than detailed look at the school. The aim of the GRIDS process is to produce internal school development rather than to provide a mechanism for external accountability. It demands the identification of a co-ordinator who should ensure that consultation with staff is genuine and that they feel involved; explain processes clearly from the outset; help teachers draw up a realistic timetable and ensure that deadlines are met; provide advice and keep a check on what is happening at each stage; contact people outside the school who might be brought in to help; try to ensure that the review and the development are rigorous and systematic; and make some evaluation of the effectiveness of the GRIDS method after about twelve months (McMahon et. al., 1984). This scheme emphasises that the starting point must be staff consultation and that reviewing the school´s current position as well as the specific areas for attention are crucial early stages. This approach has much in common with the management of change process suggested in Chapter Nine. Its main concern is the development and improvement of the school and one of its main features is the continous feedback to the staff of the evidence from evaluation. This approach to evaluation may, as Shipman points out, be based on a relatively simplistic view of how schools actually work (Shipman, 1983). It seems to assume that schools operate with a synchronisation, an inter-relationship between teachers, the headteacher, non-teaching staff, pupils and LEAs that may, in reality, not be the case. Thus more is required than the continuous circulation of information to ensure that change and development takes place although the GRIDS´s stress on feed-back does increase the chances that the evaluation will lead to improvement and development. One way of reinforcing the developmental aspects of GRIDS or of any of the other approaches to school evaluation, including the ones devised by and for specific schools, is to consider staff appraisal as part of the overall process of school and staff development.

Staff Appraisal

Staff appraisal can be approached in many different

ways and a number of pilot projects exist to determine what processes might be most appropriate for particular schools. It is certain, however, that the formal appraisal of performance will become a far more significant management activity in primary schools than it has been hitherto if only because it is now included as part of headteachers' conditions of service (DES, 1987a, Schedule 1, para. 21a) and also as part of the conditions of service for all teachers (DES, 1987a, Schedule 3, para. 4). To the extent that appraisal will take place within directed time, these paragraphs have considerable resource implications although it is not intended to explore them here. This section is concerned with the nature of staff appraisal and how best to implement it within the context of the primary school.

As Fearon suggested, writing a preface to Delaney's (1986) description of the introduction of appraisal into a primary school in Salford, appraisal of teachers is not new since all promotions depend on some form of appraisal. What is new is the government's intention to ensure that the performance of teachers is regularly appraised and to enshrine this determination in legislation. No definition or description of appraisal is given in this legislation. It might simply take the form of an individual teacher asking herself questions and, perhaps, discussing her answers with a colleague. The questions could be:

- What are the tangible results of your job being well done?
- What happens when your job is not well done?
- In order to improve your performance, on what should you spend more time/effort/imagination?
- How can you best be helped to improve your performance in these areas?
- What will the tangible results be of such an improvement in performance?

These questions are relatively non-threatening in themselves. They will help all teachers to fulfil what has been called the fundamental principle of staff appraisal in primary schools, that of improving the education of children in those schools (Thomas, 1987). They will also serve Thomas's two dependent purposes; the professional development of teachers and the effective management of teachers within the schools. In spite of a recognition on the part of many teachers that:

> ...all teachers need help in assessing their own professional performance and in building on their strengths and working on limitations identified (DES, 1985a, p.13).

The context within which much of the discussion of staff appraisal has taken place has helped to make its introduction into any school a potentially hazardous exercise because teachers perceive a range of meanings which can be attached to the process and which may be either the justification for its introduction or the hidden agenda behind its implementation. These have been discussed extensively elsewhere (Bell, 1988), although it is worth pointing out here that one of the most damaging of the justifications was its proposed use to identify incompetent teachers. This was based on the view that the teaching force needed to be cleansed of teachers who were in some way incompetent and who were probably responsible for the ills of the education system. The most oustanding example of this position can be found in Sir Keith Joseph´s speech at the North of England Education Conference in January 1984 in which he argued that it was vital for incompetent teachers in our schools to be identified and removed. He pressed this view further in 1985 by asking students to comment on the comparative quality of teachers during private meetings on several visits to schools over a two year period. This belief in the existence of a substantial number of incompetent teachers has proved difficult to sustain but, nevertheless, it is still implicit in a number of statements on appraisal contained in DES publications. In particular it can be found embodied in Better Schools (DES, 1985a) and in Quality Schools: Evaluation and Appraisal (DES, 1985c).

A similar set of justifications attached to appraisal and based on the view that there is a significant number of weak teachers who need to be removed from the system in order to restore public credibility in education has been developed by Eric Midwinter, in the Times Educational Supplement, (8 Feb. 1985). He justifies his support for teacher appraisal by arguing that "surrogate consumers", that is parents, should have more say in teacher appraisal. This would, he argues, allay their anxiety about "bullies, mental now more than physical" and the "no hopers and nincompoops" as well as the "idlers" who now teach in schools and who were recruited during the late 1950s and early 1960s when it is argued standards of entry were dropped at a time of acute shortage. Midwinter places considerable faith in the power of parents to assess who the "good" and "bad" teachers are, he goes on to argue that "the lore of the launderette is unerringly accurate."

These two sets of meanings share the view that there is considerable room for improvement within the teaching profession. Their point of departure is over how such an improvement might be best brought about. The search for incompetent teachers as envisaged by the DES would be carried out according to the criteria set out in DES publications and would presumably use those staff appraisal procedures which LEAs would establish. From Midwinter´s perspective appraisal would be carried out by groups of parents acting as vigilante representatives of all of the parents for a particular school. Quite how this process would work was never spelled out. Strangely enough, a similar perspective emerges when the views expressed by head-teachers and LEA representatives are considered although, in this case, incompetence is replaced by demoralisation and the appraisal process would be carried out by teachers themselves within their own schools. The use of staff appraisal for motivational purposes is well documented in industrial circles. The extent to which this deliberate provision of a Hawthorn Effect will work is not clear but the assumption that it will is certainly built in to a number of management courses and has also been made by HMI who argue that in many cases appraisal procedures "lead to a better working climate and to improved performance by the school and by individual teachers". (DES, 1985c, para. 141).

If appraisal can be used for motivation in this way then it has been argued the linking of appraisal to salary can reward and motivate more directly. This has been described as the identification of the "super teacher" and is based on the assumption that better teachers deserve higher pay and that the appropriate process for identifying who the high quality teachers are is that of staff appraisal. How far this is true remains to be seen. The assimilation of teachers on to the new main professional salary grade and the allocation of allowances may be seen to be rewarding outstanding classroom teaching. It seems unlikely, however, that the use of appraisal as the process by which assimilation might take place will do anything other than alienate teachers since it will be regarded by them as a punitive measure if it is related to salary and merit pay. The NUT makes this quite clear (NUT, 1985, p.45.) where it is argued that the union is opposed to assessment of teachers being linked directly to financial awards.

If this set of meanings which links motivation, reward and appraisal is perceived as hostile and threatening by teachers and their representatives then the argument that appraisal might be justified in terms of the needs which LEAs have to plan the staffing of their educational intitutions could, at first sight, be regarded as more neutral. Again, Sir Keith Joseph has argued (1985) that LEAs can only be satisfied that each of their schools is properly staffed if they know enough about the skills and competence of individual teachers and that such knowledge can only come from some form of systematic appraisal. This view was reasserted in Those Having Torches..., (Suffolk Education Department, 1985) which drew attention to the needs LEAs have for more information upon which to base their planning as well as the need for resources to establish schemes of staff appraisal and to train relevant staff. It is possible, however, that teachers might in some circumstances regard this as an attempt to introduce, redefine, or reinforce redeployment practices.

Perhaps the least threatening of all the inherent sets of meanings as far as teachers are concerned is that which links staff appraisal to the professional development of teachers. This view emerges both in the documents produced by LEAs such as Northamptonshire and Croydon and also in DES publications. In Teaching Quality (DES, 1983) it was argued that those managing the school teacher force have a clear responsibility to establish policy for staff development and training based on a systematic assessment of every teacher's performance. Staff appraisal schemes which are geared primarily to identifying in-service needs or other kinds of experience that might enhance career development appear to be, at least in part, acceptable to many teachers if the views expressed in the publications of teacher unions are to be accepted as a guide. This view of appraisal is certainly the one adopted throughout this chapter. The assumption is made here, therefore, that the rationale behind the introduction of any staff appraisal system into a primary school is that its main intention is to provide opportunities for professional development for the teachers in that school. It is also assumed that appraisal will, in due course, be introduced into schools, and that it would be sensible for schools to develop processes which suit their own ethos rather than to try to cope with an imposed system.

The major difficulties associated with the introduction of staff appraisal tend to focus on the natural suspicion that many teachers have of such a change in their working conditions. This suspicion has manifested itself in two forms. Any form of staff appraisal could be regarded by teachers as a direct attack on their own professional autonomy. Teachers have, in the past, exercised this autonomy within their classrooms almost to the exclusion of all other forms of influence. A staff appraisal process which impinged on the right of teachers solely and entirely to make professional judgements about activities within the confines of the classroom would threaten that jealously guarded privilege. Suspicion is also expressed by some teachers about the ability of their colleagues in middle or senior management to carry out an effective appraisal process or to implement such a process impartially because of past problems or past professional relationship difficulties. These two basic suspicions lead to a natural reluctance to accept this change.

The second difficulty which many teachers express is the extent to which they would be placing themselves in a highly vulnerable position if a staff appraisal process required them to indicate those areas in their professional life where they were experiencing difficulties or were requiring help or further training. It is felt that such information might prejudice promotion prospects or lead to a general diminution of their esteem within their school. It is also argued that staff appraisal, if carried out badly, would increase the level of cynicism within the schools and lead to a lowering of teacher morale. The major barrier to implementing staff appraisal effectively is believed to be the extent to which those training needs or staff development needs identified by the process could or would be met by the school or the LEA. Clearly in order to overcome the suspicions and concerns, any staff appraisal process needs to be introduced into a school carefully and effectively. This will mean that all of those to be involved in such a process will require training before the system can be introduced and the extent to which such training is required and the time that it would take is also identified as a difficulty when introducing an appraisal system. Concern is expressed about the extent to which LEAs and schools could provide the necessary training and the extent to which those people who are to be in the position of appraisers would recognise that such training was necessary.

None of these difficulties associated with staff appraisal can be resolved easily. It is incumbent on those who wish to introduce such a system into schools to take account of these difficulties and to seek to overcome them in a variety of different ways. This can be done even in the smallest primary school (Bell, 1988). There is no doubt, however, that the major disadvantage of introducing staff appraisal into schools is the fact that it will require a significant amount of scarce resources devoted to it in terms of time and money. It is unrealistic to expect an appraisal process to be carried out outside normal working hours. Therefore the resources have to be provided in order to free those people who are involved in the process so that they can meet, prepare for, and conduct appraisal interviews and also so that they can follow up the interviews effectively. Resources will also be required in order to meet the training needs which such a process undoubtedly will identify. On the assumption that the introduction of a systematic appraisal system into all schools will require:

- central administration
- release time for all teachers
- training for heads, deputies and heads of departments
- secretarial costs

one LEA has calculated that the process itself will cost over £900,000 in one year (Wilcox, 1986). These costs do not include the subsequent training needs either in school or from the resources of the LEA. These additional costs are too complicated to be able to compute with any degree of accuracy given that the funding of in-service training is undergoing a radical change. Thus, there seems to be a strong argument for a school-initiated and school-based approach to staff appraisal which can be linked closely to the professional development needs in that school.

Apart from the cost in resource terms the other major disadvantage associated with the introduction of staff appraisal into schools is the cost in personal terms. An effective process requires honesty and courage in the application of the process to all colleagues. It requires objectivity and the ability to separate personal relationships from professional relationships. It also requires those involved to recognise that appraisal can provoke conflict and controversy, but that it need not do so if they are well trained and are committed to carrying out the process effectively.

In order to see how this might be done we need to consider the question, "What is staff appraisal?" in the context of primary schools. Simply stated appraisal is an opportunity for both the appraisee and the appraiser to stand back and take stock of performance over, say, the last year, to examine how far targets which were agreed at the last appraisal have been realised, and to identify new targets for the next year. Appraisal is not an opportunity to criticise any individual´s personality or opinions, or to discuss other colleagues. It should focus specifically on the individual teacher´s own performance within the school. It provides an opportunity to explore with that teacher:

- How well she is performing
- Whether she can improve in any areas
- Actions to improve her performance
- Ambitions and aspirations
- Potential for taking on more demanding jobs
- Actions to develop new skills
- Views and feelings about the job and the school or department.

If such an appraisal were to be carried out by Mrs Welton at Rosemary Lane then a number of benefits would accrue to the staff of the school, to Mrs Welton and to the school overall (see Table 41).

As Delaney (1986) reminds us, appraisal is a sensitive issue in most primary schools so its introduction has to be carried with diplomacy and with the full co-operation of the staff. It is important from the outset to involve all members of staff in the discussion about the proposed process and to respond openly to their natural fears and reservations. Since primary schools have tended to be organised around the single class teacher who is responsible for the planning, preparation, teaching and evaluation of the curriculum for each individual child in her class it is not surprising that many teachers approach the idea of performance evaluation with some anxiety even in an environment which, as was argued in earlier chapters, may now be characterised by a shift towards a more collegiate style of co-operation. With this in mind Mrs Welton recognised that the introduction of teacher staff appraisal needed to be a natural and logical consequence of the development of the school's activities.

Table 41 THE BENEFITS OF STAFF APPRAISAL IN PRIMARY SCHOOLS

BENEFITS FOR THE INDIVIDUAL	BENEFITS FOR THE HEAD AND THE SCHOOL
o Knowledge of where she stands regarding the rating of her performance	o A better understanding of how staff see their jobs, and how satisfied they are
o Knowledge of where she is going in terms of improvement and development plans	o The opportunity to plan for improvements in performance
o Obtaining help to improve and develop	o The opportunity to plan the best use of ability and potential
o Gaining a greater sense of belonging through realising the value of her contribution to the school	o An insight into the effectiveness of the management of the school

There is a better chance of getting these benefits through appraisal, rather than through daily contact, because the appraisal interview is a chance to stand back from day-to-day work pressures.

In order to bring this about she spent some considerable time working in each classroom with each teacher, following these sessions with a private discusssion with her colleague to identify those areas in which the needs of the children were being successfully met and to explore the various teaching strategies being employed. These discussions soon led to the consideration of wider issues such as resourcing, school and classroom organisation and staff development needs. As we have seen with her analysis of the mathematics in the school, she was also concerned with continuity and progression throughout the school, the assessment of pupils' work and, related to that, the expectations which each teacher had of her pupils. Thus, gradually, Mrs Welton was creating a situation in which teaching was no longer a private act carried out by qualified adults alone in the presence of children.

One of her early tasks was also to introduce job descriptions. This process has been described in Chapter Four. The effect of the introduction of such job descriptions, in consultation with her colleagues, was to give Mrs Welton and her staff a clear, formal, written record of the allocation of responsibilities throughout the school. Mrs Welton was then able to introduce the idea of regular performance appraisal to her staff for discussion at a staff meeting. She stressed that it would be objective and fair, open and job-related and that it would be used as a basis for staff development. Once her staff had accepted the proposal she drew up a standard structure and content for all their appraisal interviews, recognising the importance of treating everyone in the same way. Her questions were arranged in the following sequence:

- o What are the most important areas of the teacher's job?
- o What are her strengths - the things she has done well?
- o What are the main problems she has encountered?
- o Can these problems be avoided in future?
- o What are her staff training and development needs?
- o What is the best way to achieve each improvement?

The above points deal with performance of teachers in their present job but Mrs Welton wanted to cover future opportunities as well. She explored the following areas with each of her colleagues:

- o What abilities, if any, are not being fully used in her present job?

- What new jobs could she take on in the coming year?
- Does she want to take on more demanding jobs?
- What is the best way to develop each new skill?

Finally, if she wanted to check job satisfaction during the interview, she could include the following:

- What aspects of the job give her most satisfaction?
- What things, if any, cause dissatisfaction?

She then drew up some guidelines for preparing the interview (Table 42) and briefed her colleagues about them. She planned to hold the interviews in her office but arranged that she would not be interrupted while they were taking place.

Mrs Welton gave her staff the following six questions set out on paper equally spaced to allow room for written comments:

1. PERFORMANCE: Consider your performance and comment on your most important achievements. Itemise particular results and successes with which you were involved. (In subsequent interviews this question would refer to the period of time since the last appraisal interview).

2. Consider your present performance and comment on your disappointments with respect to your own responsibilities. (In subsequent interviews this question would refer to the period of time since the last appraisal interview).

3. OBSTACLES: What factors outside your control hindered you in achieving a better performance?

4. TRAINING AND NEW EXPERIENCES LAST YEAR:
   (a) What training or new planned experiences did you undergo last year?
   (b) In what ways have they helped?

5. INCREASED SKILL OR KNOWLEDGE:
   What part of your present job could benefit if you received additional training or new planned experiences?

Table 42 PREPARATION FOR STAFF APPRAISAL

MAKE ARRANGEMENTS

- o Set a date, time and place for the appraisal interview.
- o Allow at least 60 minutes for the interview. You will need this amount of time for a thorough interview.
- o Give at least two weeks´ notice of the interview to your member of staff, to allow her time to prepare.
- o Brief her on how to prepare, running through the interview questions. It is a good idea to give her a copy of the interview questions, to help preparation.

HEAD´S PREPARATION	COLLEAGUE´S PREPARATION
o Before the interview go through each interview question, noting important points	o Before the interview, go through each interview question to decide responses
o Concentrate on training and development needs, and ways to satisfy these needs	o Concentrate on: - things that have gone well - problems - training and development - aims for the next year
o Provisionally decide realistic training and/or development aims for the next year	o Think of realistic training and/or development aims for the next year
o Consider whether any problems might arise during the interview and plan how to handle them	o Think of ways to achieve improvement aims with guidance or support

Asking your member of staff to prepare is an important stage in appraisal. You are seeking to gain commitment, so that both of you treat the appraisal as a genuine opportunity for improvement.

6. LIST OF TRAINING NEEDS:
As a result of completing the whole form, list the areas of training or planned experiences you need in order to further develop your professional expertise.

Mrs Welton asked for a copy of the answers to these questions in advance of the interview. She was then able to:

- Read carefully through the appraisee´s responses and decide the areas of agreement and omission
- Concentrate on things that have gone well and improvement needs
- Think of realistic improvement or development targets for next year
- Think about ways in which she could help or support the member of staff to achieve her targets

Mrs Welton planned each interview in detail, basing her approach on two principles. Firstly she asked her colleague to comment on each issue and then commented on that response, adding additional points where necessary. Secondly she planned to move from her colleague´s strengths to any weakness that may exist, finishing on a set of agreed actions to improve the situation and to foster the professional development of her colleague. These agreed actions are to be written down and a copy provided for Mrs Welton and her colleague showing clearly what has been agreed, what has to be done, by whom, by when and, where relevant, to what standard or criteria. This agreed set of actions could then be placed in the context of the school and staff profiles and seen against a background of the information which Mrs Welton had at her disposal as a result of her work with her colleagues in the classrooms and the subsequent discussions.

The whole staff reviewed the process after the first round of interviews. They recognised that relatively brief follow-up interviews might be necessary to check on progress towards agreed targets and that they might take the initiative for arranging these within the timetable agreed between each individual and Mrs Welton. The question also came up about Mrs Welton´s own appraisal. She decided to adopt the approach to this advocated by Moore (1988) and invited her pastoral inspector to appraise her after familiarising him with the key features of the appraisal process which had been adopted at Rosemary Lane. At the same time, to give an internal perspective on her work, Mr Jowett also conducted an appraisal of Mrs Welton. In this instance the school's pastoral inspector had been the headteacher of a school similar to Rosemary Lane and Mr Jowett was a deputy headteacher of some experience. Both brought relevant expertise, experience and knowledge of the school to the process. In other circumstances other combinations of people might be chosen with those qualities in mind. In Mrs Welton's case, just as with that of her staff, the emphasis of performance appraisal should be on her professional development. Therefore this process, including its preparation and organisation, is an integral part of staff development.

Staff Development

Even when closely linked to staff development, staff appraisal is not "the alchemy for turning base metal teachers into golden ones" (Bunnell and Stephens, 1984, p.291) nor should it be. If it has anything to offer in the context of the primary school this must be the contribution which it can make to the professional development of the staff of the school. The approach adopted by Mrs Welton enabled her staff to explore their individual professional development needs as part of an open discussion of their performance within the school. As Mrs Welton found, her involvement in the appraisal of her staff required her to fulfil a number of different roles. First she was confidante or counsellor to her staff during the process of appraisal. She was then, as Mason (1987) has pointed out, to find herself taking on three other related and equally demanding roles. She became, perhaps always was, the exemplar of good practice, appropriate attitudes, acceptable behaviour and commitment to her pupils and staff. She also had to be the initiator of many of the individual programmes of staff development and more general in-service training which was generated by the review of staff performance. At the same time she had also to become the facilitator in order to make the staff development happen. GRIST will help her to do this more effectively but it will also demand that the staff becomes involved in a more general discussion of school development needs over and above those related to the appraisal of staff performance. Such discussions must be carried out within the framework of what the school is trying to achieve. Thus staff appraisal has to be linked to both individual and school development needs in such a way as to ensure that the maximum individual professional development can take place while still ensuring that the aims and objectives of the school, expressed, perhaps, in terms of projections based on the school profile, can be achieved.

How, then, can staff appraisal and whole school development be linked in such a way as to emphasise the formative and developmental aspects of both processes? One possible approach, based on a detailed discussion by the whole staff, of the aims and objectives of the school, its various needs, and the staff development requirements of the staff, is illustrated in Table 43. Here full consideration of the needs of the school take place in parallel with the introduction of staff appraisal so that discussions in one area can inform those in another. This is similar to what took place at Rosemary Lane although there the school profile was produced in advance of the introduction of performance appraisal and Mrs Welton took the lead in that process rather than delegating it to a staff development co-ordinator. Simply described, the process in Table 43 might begin with a whole staff consultation out of which a group responsible for managing the process would be identified. Most schools, as a result of GRIST, already have a staff development co-ordinator who should be involved in the process. In primary schools this responsibility often falls upon the headteacher. If a supporting group of colleagues can be identified the ownership of the process can be more widely shared and, when appraisal interviews are being considered, a number of this group might be involved where appropriate. As a result of discussion at school, department, year, or other functional group level, the main priorities for the school might be identified and agreed upon before appraisal interviews start. In this way the action plans, which will result from the appraisal interviews can be informed by the discussions on the school's immediate needs. The professional development of individual teachers can, in this way, be more closely linked to the priorities of the school. In turn this will make it more likely that those needs can and will be met. The meeting of individual staff development needs as they emerge from the appraisal process is perhaps the single most important factor in ensuring that staff appraisal is successful in so far as it is understood and accepted

Table 43 STAFF APPRAISAL AND SCHOOL DEVELOPMENT

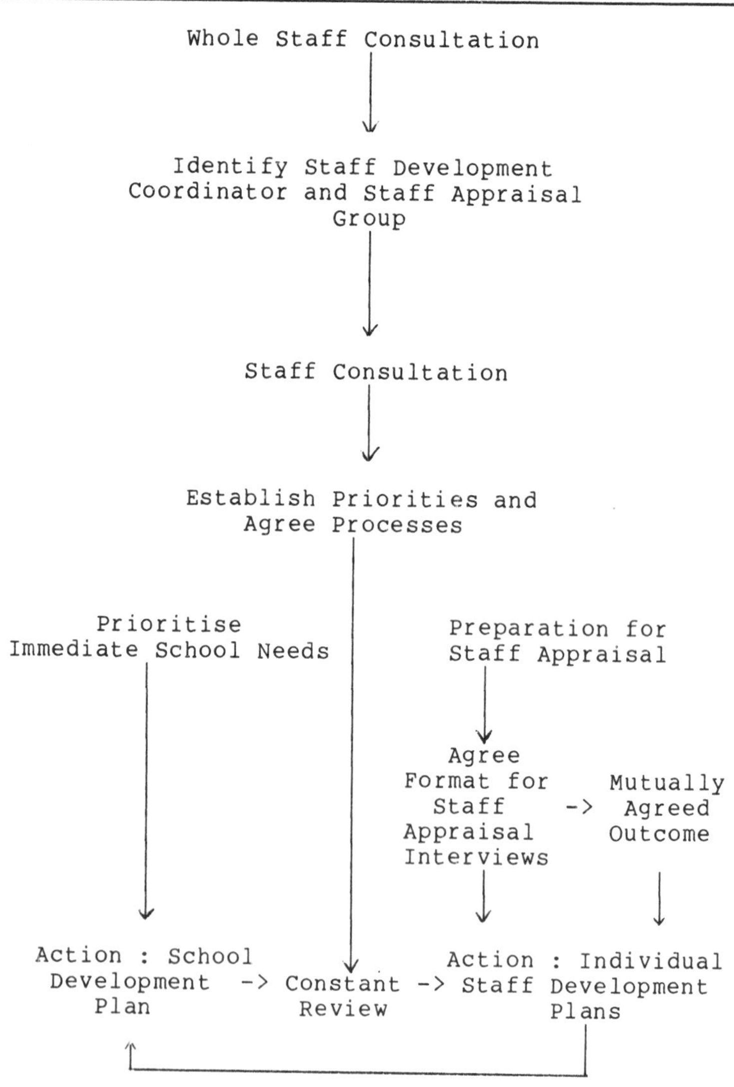

by teachers and it produces the desired outcomes for their pupils, that is an improvement in the quality of the education which they receive. It must always be recognised that the principle aim of teacher appraisal should be the improvement of children's education by improving the effectiveness of the school and the professional capabilities of the teachers. This may well be achieved, at least in part, through a staff development programme which is a planned sequence of experiences designed to enhance the knowledge and expertise of teachers.

Producing a staff development programme for a primary school needs, therefore, to be based on a clear understanding of what it is that the school is trying to achieve as well as on a knowledge of the professional development needs of its teachers. Such a programme may also take into account two further sets of factors. It may include specific steps to remedy situations in which the work of the school does not always proceed quite as smoothly as might be wished, especially where such situations are a result of a lack of knowledge, skill or expertise on the part of the staff. It might also be necessary to take into account the changes which are likely to affect the school over the next few years. Included here are those changes which a headteacher like Mrs Welton actually wants to bring about, the development of multicultural education for example, as well as those changes which may happen for reasons beyond her direct control, like a member of staff leaving or the introduction of the national curriculum. Wherever possible such factors should be part of the information used to identify a staff development programme because they help to ensure that the school is as well prepared as it can be to respond to changes in a positive fashion rather than to have to react to them hastily.

Once the content of the staff development programme has been identified some thought has to be given to implementing it. This is obviously an integral part of the programme but all too often externally provided courses or in-service days are seen as the two main, indeed desirable, alternatives without real thought being given to the choice between them and without consideration being given to other alternatives. If the two main options are to hold in-service sessions in school or to go elsewhere for INSET, what should influence the decision? Table 44 shows how this decision might be taken in a considered way in order that the strategy chosen for that particular part of the in-service programme is most beneficial for the school and for the teacher or teachers concerned. The message is clear. Do not use a course just because it is there but do not base everything on the school simply because in so doing resources can be stretched to the very limit. Make the choice on the basis of what is possible at any given time.

If, after careful consideration it is decided that the most effective form of staff development is to use an externally provided course then the implementation of this process ought to be carried out as thoughtfully as would be the planning of a school-based programme. The following guidelines can help to ensure that this is done:

Before the course:

- Give as much notice as possible.
- Be sure the person knows where the course is and what she has to take with her.
- Discuss what you expect her to gain from the course - check your staff development plan and the training results you are seeking to achieve.
- Inform the course organiser what you want your colleague to achieve.

After the course:

- Discuss the course, arrangements, people attending and the quality of presentation.
- Identify what your colleague felt she gained from the course.
- Agree job actions that will be taken as a result of the course, when and how the effect can be measured.
- Do not forget to check that agreed actions are taken, and the results achieved. Give further help yourself if necessary.

Within the primary school there is a range of other options available for implementing staff development. At the very simplest level these might include briefing a colleague in a planned and formal way on a new task; coaching a colleague on the performance of a new task; and embarking on a programme of development for an individual or group over a period of time when the skills or tasks to be understood are complex and require practice. If the leader of a team in a primary school undertakes staff development at any of these levels she should ensure that she discusses the following points with

Table 44 CHOOSING A STRATEGY FOR IMPLEMENTING STAFF DEVELOPMENT

For each part of the staff development programme there are two options

SCHOOL-BASED INSET One of the staff or a consultant will provide in-service training	AWAY FROM SCHOOL Sending to a course run by the LEA or other provider
WHEN YOU CHOOSE SCHOOL-BASED INSET	WHEN YOU CHOOSE AWAY FROM SCHOOL TRAINING
o When a member of staff has the skills and time required to give instruction or a suitable consultant is available	o When there is a course which is appropriate in timing, in achieving the results you require and for the level of person requiring training
o When you can provide INSET in the most cost-effective way	o When such a course will be cost-effective
o When you are sure you use the best method for doing the job	o When you require attitude changes which are best achieved by mixing with others in similar jobs
o When the skill and method are specific to your school/ department and no courses are available	o When staff have neither the skills nor the time to give the instruction
	o When you have the re-sources to meet the costs and to provide cover for the colleague on the course

the colleague involved:

THE REASON Explain:
- why you have selected your colleague for the particular training
- why you are planning it at this time

THE TASK	Explain and agree: - precisely what you want doing - targets or standards of performance
CONTROL	Discuss: - your availability to confer on any problems - how you will keep informed about progress - whether there is a need to delegate some of her less important duties after training
ATTITUDE	Check: - that she is keen to take on the training - that she has enough confidence to tackle it

The team leader should ensure that all other members of staff who are likely to be affected know about this part of the staff development programme.

There is a range of related activities which can be incorporated into different kinds of staff development programmes to suit individual colleagues or to meet the needs of all or part of the staff group. Some of them have been touched upon elsewhere in this book but all require careful preparation based on a clear and explicit understanding of what is to be achieved by the exercise. Targets need to be set at each stage. Table 45 provides a summary of some useful activities and an indication of when they might be used.

For each type of strategy adopted to implement part of a staff development programme, whether it is for the whole school, a group or an individual, the basic principles to be followed are the same:

1. Plan the programme thoroughly on the basis of what is to be achieved.

2. Carry out an initial briefing with those involved in that part of the programme and ensure that outcomes, expectations and targets are understood.

3. Monitor progress while the programme is being implemented and make any modifications.

4. Follow up the programme by taking the necessary steps to ensure that the agreed actions are carried out since this is the only way that the school can benefit from the in-service training of its teachers.

Planning a staff development programme requires detailed preparation whether it is for an individual, a group of colleagues or the whole staff. The following points refer to an individual colleague in the example which follows but they are also useful for planning whole school in-service days:

DEFINE RESULT	It will help you and your staff if you: - identify what you want her to do - decide on performance standards
DECIDE METHODS	How can necessary skills and attitudes be developed to achieve the result? Stages may include: - watching or helping you - doing jobs under your supervision - attending training sessions
AGREE PROGRAMME	Gain agreement and commitment on: - the stages in the programme - the timing of each stage and resources required - dates when progress will be reviewed by all those involved
USE PROGRAMME	While the development is going on: - check progress at each stage - offer help, advice and encouragement if needed - modify the programme to cope with delays or difficulties

One final step remains. That is to review the planning, implementation and follow-up to ensure that it was as effective as possible and that future parts of the programme are well planned and carried out. This review should focus on the questions listed in Table 46. These can be asked of all forms of staff development activity for different numbers of teachers. The essential features remain the same.

Table 45 SOME FURTHER STRATEGIES FOR STAFF DEVELOPMENT IN PRIMARY SCHOOLS

ACTIVITY	APPLICATION
PROJECT WORK	You may be able to match individual (or group) development needs with a project providing a focus. Useful if you want your colleague to stand back from day-to-day activities, or if you are seeking to encourage initiative
INFORMATION COLLECTION	An initial activity may be to establish a basis of hard fact. Also useful for developing organising and fact-finding skills, and attention to detail
INFORMATION ANALYSIS	A follow-up to information collection. Also useful for developing skills in interpretation, evaluation and decision-making
PLANNING	Contribution to planning the programme with you, or planning required by the nature of the task. Helps to develop the practice of thinking before acting
PROBLEM SOLVING	The total plan may be built on a problem-solving project, or it could include activities to solve problems. Helps to develop objectivity, reasoning and decision-making skills
WRITTEN REPORT PREPARATION	Useful for improving written communications, and ability to think logically and reason things out

Table 45 (cont´d)

ORAL REPORT PRESENTATION	Making formal presentations to you at stages of the plan (reporting back), or to a group. A particularly good activity for developing the skill of communication with other people
OBSERVING SOMEONE ELSE	Arranging first-hand experience of you, or someone else, performing a task - possibly assessing the performance against a checklist of key requirements. A useful step in delegating, or in trying to overcome a weakness, by providing a model of required performance
STANDING IN FOR YOU	A practical way to obtain experience in a management or other task, through temporary delegation
UNDERTAKING A DIFFERENT ROLE	Doing part of someone else´s job, on a temporary basis. Useful for broadening experience, or to realise effect of own performance shortfalls on others
PLANNED VISITING	Finding out more about other schools. Useful for gaining better insights into alternative ways of doing things provided key observational points are agreed in advance
SELF-STUDY	Directed study of relevant books, or other materials with a specific brief to report back on a particular aspect

Much of the above discussion on staff development, staff appraisal and school evaluation has sought to show that all the staff of the school have a role to play in each of these processes although these roles may vary according to the position or responsibilities held in the school. These functions, like the more general management of the school, are not the sole responsibility of the headteacher but of the whole staff team, each of whom will make a contribution according to her qualifications, expertise and experience. Such contributions will also be determined by the opportunities offered to her or created by and for her. Team leaders of whatever kind have a vital role to play in this regard in primary schools for they are often in a position to initiate and develop such opportunities. However skilful a primary school team leader may be in doing this there is no doubt that such activities require, at the very least, the tacit approval of the headteacher. More often, as Mrs Welton has at Rosemary Lane, the headteacher plays a more proactive role in initiating and implementing change and staff development. The extent to which this is true of any individual headteacher will depend on her view of her own role within the school, her assessment of the school and its requirements, her skills and abilities and, perhaps above all at this present time, on her perceptions of the internal and external changes which face primary schools at the end of the twentieth century.

Table 46 REVIEWING STAFF DEVELOPMENT STRATEGIES IN PRIMARY SCHOOL

STAFF DEVELOPMENT	COLLEAGUE DEVELOPMENT
Check whether you can improve in any aspects of your staff development performance:	These are the checks to make:
PLANNING	
o Was the target clearly defined, and realistic? If not, what further actions are required?	o Has the target been achieved?
o Was your choice of activities sufficiently imaginative?	o Can your colleague now perform the task or fulfil the new role without further staff development? Or will further actions be needed?
o Did the sequence of actions and timing prove sound?	
o Did you gain your colleague´s involvement and commitment?	
CARRYING OUT	
o Did you check progress frequently enough?	o How has your colleague reacted to the staff development experience? Is there a favourable attitude to further coaching in other tasks?
o Did you let your colleague know how well she was progressing?	
o Were you successful in overcoming problems?	o What is your colleague´s next development need? Should you start on it immediately or hold off for a while?
STAFF DEVELOPMENT SESSIONS	
o Did you prepare sufficiently?	o How have the rest of the staff responded to this process?
o Did you work to clear aims?	
o Did you involve your colleagues fully?	
o Was your manner encouraging?	

Activities

1. If your LEA has a primary school review document, explore with colleagues how you might use this as a basis for initiating a review in your own school. If there is no such document in your LEA, then use one from another LEA.

2. Identify the steps you would need to take in order to implement staff appraisal in your school. Prepare your own answers to the six questions suggested on page 240 or the six questions on page 241. Discuss them with a colleague. What personal professional development needs can you identify?

3. Follow the steps outlined in the section on staff development to draw up a staff development plan for your school. Involve colleagues as far as you can.

4. Plan and implement one of the strategies for staff development and then carry out a review of the process using the questions in Table 46.

Chapter 11

MANAGING HEADSHIP IN THE PRIMARY SCHOOL

Throughout this book it has been argued that the whole staff of the primary school has a collective responsibility for its management and that individual teachers have specific responsibility for particular parts of the work of the school. Some of the considerations which have produced this situation have been discussed and much space has been devoted to exploring the implications of such developments for the organisation, administration and management of primary schools and the role of teachers within them. It has been argued that primary schools can be managed much more effectively if all staff are involved in the processes of management. It has been suggested that, in some circumstances, responding to change for example, most of the staff must participate if the enterprise is to succeed. What emerges, then, is a view of management processes which is relevant to primary schools. The essence of these processes is, as Tomlinson has suggested, that the primary school staff team should be able to ensure that:

> o Aims and objectives are clarified.
>
> o Methods for teaching and learning are chosen and applied.
>
> o Evaluations and assessments of the results are made.
>
> o What is learnt from the judgments is fed back to improve the aims and the methods.
>
> (Tomlinson, 1987, p. 9)

These processes should be continuous and natural. They should involve the whole staff as well as parents, governors and others who co-operate with the teachers. Thus the assumption which underpins the management processes which have been explored in the preceding chapters is that authority within the school should be shared. Indeed it has been suggested in the early chapters that if the school is to be managed effectively, for the maximisation of staff expertise to ensure the optimum long-term benefit for all the children, then such sharing is a necessity.

Managing Directed Time

The overall day-to-day responsibility for the running of the school rests with the headteacher but this responsibility cannot be effectively discharged without the close involvement of all her colleagues within the school. Many of the management skills discussed in this book are designed to help headteachers and primary school team leaders achieve such involvement. It must be recognised, however, that colleagues will bring to their participation in the work of the school their own sets of ideas, their own agendas and their own aims, objectives and targets. These cannot be disregarded or dismissed. Disagreements about policy are a normal part of the process of policy formulation and not simply an indication of awkwardness. Issues such as the organisation of pupils, the distribution of teaching duties and the allocation of resources may well cause disputes within the staff team. These have to be resolved by negotiation. This has not always been thought to be the most appropriate way to approach certain matters in the past.

For example, Mrs Welton consulted several of her colleagues before deciding to use her responsibility allowance in the way she did. Similarly she involved all her staff in taking decisions about lunch-time supervision. More importantly she consulted everybody about the allocation of the 1265 hours of directed time before she arrived at a time budget which she then shared with her staff who commented on it. This was a new departure for Mrs Welton and her staff since the School Teachers' Pay and Conditions of Employment Order (DES 1987a) was the first occasion when the length of a teacher's working year was defined in terms of actual hours. Mrs Welton and her colleagues had to recognise that there are three different expressions related to time. These are:

1. Directed time which means time spent on duties required by the head. It can include time spent before or after the teaching day and may be spent away from the school.

2. Self directed time which is time which a teacher voluntarily spends after the teaching day on school-related work.

3. Additional contracted obligations which refers to time spent by the teacher in discharging her professional duties including marking, preparation and writing reports.

The staff at Rosemary Lane were usually to be found in their classrooms long after the "official" end of school. Most lunchtimes were used for staff consultation and lesson preparation, and there were several well run after-school activities. However, Mrs Welton knew that she and the staff had to have a clear definition as to what constituted directed time, and that the agreed pattern would need to be reviewed and changed according to circumstances. She therefore proposed an annual review and produced a framework in which the allocation of hours could be placed:

School hours a.m. : 0900-1200 = 3.00 hours
School hours p.m. : 1300-1530 = 2.30 hours

After staff consultation, she then added the agreed "directed" times when teaching staff should be on site before school, how long they should be on site after 1530, and at lunch times:

Staff on site	: 0850	=	0.10 mins
School hours a.m.	: 0900-1200	=	3.00 hours
Staff on site	: 1200-1205	=	0.05 mins
Staff on site	: 1255-1300	=	0.05 mins
School hours p.m.	: 1300-1530	=	2.30 hours
Staff on site	: 1530-1545	=	0.15 mins

The agreed "directed" length of the teachers day was therefore six hours and five minutes. This, multiplied by the 190 child contact days, gave an annual total of 1146 hours 15 minutes. To this figure had to be added the five staff training days at six hours each, a figure fixed by the LEA, leaving a balance to be negotiated and assigned to parents' evenings, staff meetings and other activities. The final agreed programme looked as follows:

Teachers contract ....1265 hrs. 00 mins

190 child contact days		1146.15
5 staff training days		30.00
Parental consultation	say	9.00
Staff meetings	say	30.00

TOTAL...........1215 hrs. 15 mins

Balance at discretion ....49 hrs. 45 mins

Two safeguards were built into the discussions. There had to be sufficient discretionary time to cater for the unexpected, and there needed to be an annual review to take into account any special circumstances or to reflect lessons learned in the previous twelve months.

It was important that all the staff understood what was required of them. A casual remark by Mrs Welton that the library ought to be ready for use by the children as soon as possible might be seen by the teacher concerned as a "direction" and that, therefore, the three extra hours she puts in after school the following two nights should count against her contract hours. Similarly, Tom Jowett must be clear that if his field trip to the Country Park means a late return, the time he is with his class in excess of the six hours five minutes is not "directed" unless Mrs Welton has so agreed.

In arriving at this allocation of time Mrs Welton took account of the LEA advice to draw up a programme of planned activities for the year such that it did not exceed 1265 hours and that it did not depart in any substantial way from the current practice at Rosemary Lane. This was the working definition of "reasonable" which the staff agreed to adopt for the time being. Mrs Welton was happy with this. In her LEA the length of school day was not specified although in other authorities this has now become the practice. While having a standard length of school day is helpful to headteachers for plan-ing purposes it can also limit their scope for flexibility. For example another headteacher in the same LEA arrived at the following budget for directed time:

	Hours
Teaching Day : 5½ hours x 190	1045
Supervision : 1 hour each week	38
Parent Consultations : 3 evenings x 3 hrs.....	9
Staff and team meetings : 1½ hours per week...	57
School clubs & pastoral work : 1 hr per week..	38
INSET days : 6 hours x 5 days	30
Emergencies : 1 hour per week	38
Ad hoc meetings throughout the year	10
TOTAL:	1265

The final outcome of this process depends on the advice given by the LEA and on the negotiation with colleagues, but the important part of the process is the planning of the time so that its use enables everyone to help the school to move towards achieving what is best for the children. This process has clear implications for the management of time in a general sense as was considered in Chapter Seven and for other aspects of work such as staff development and appraisal. Arrangements have to be made for these although they may come out of non-directed time in some cases.

Although the Conditions of Service Order (DES 1978a) prescribes a number of hours of directed time which has never been done before, it also contains a significantly developmental element which often goes unnoticed in the reaction to the prescription of the directed hours. It is clear that teachers have a right, as well as a duty, to participate in programmes of staff development. The Order also requires headteachers to ensure that:

> all staff have access to advice and training appropriate to their needs...
> (Teachers´ Pay and Conditions Order 1987a, Section b)

Two further factors help to make staff development more available for all teachers. The identification of five "Baker" days, in addition to the 190 days in school with pupils, which are to be set aside for staff development activities provide a basic minimum provision for all teachers although it remains to be seen how effectively these days are used by LEAs and by schools. GRIST funding is, at the same time, moving the emphasis of in-service training from LEAs and other providers to schools as consumers of the training. The more effective schools become in being able to identify the specific staff development needs of their staff and then using the resources available progressively to meet those needs, the more schools and the teachers within them will be able to own their own processes of staff development. Some of the current policy initiatives are helping to make this possible. Other areas of primary education which are about to become the subject of policy-making may lead to further developments along these lines or, alternatively, may require some aspects of the management of primary schools to be reconsidered. Undoubtedly the new proposals for a national curriculum, for example, will have far-reaching implications for the primary headteacher and her staff, as will the changing responsibilities of governing bodies and the devolution of more financial responsibility to schools.

The National Curriculum 5-16

On the 24th July 1987, the Secretary of State for Education and Science published a consultation document on the national curriculum (DES Welsh Office, 1987). The intention of the proposals in this document is to ensure that all pupils study a broad, balanced range of subjects throughout their schooling and to raise standards by setting clear objectives for children's performance for all subjects over the full ability range. Progress towards these objectives will be checked at various stages in the pupil's school career. These proposals will enable schools to be more accountable for the education they offer to their pupils, individually and collectively. The governing body, headteacher, and the teachers of every school will be better able to undertake the essential process of regular evaluation because they will be able to consider their school, taking account of its particular circumstances, against the local and national picture as a whole. It will help to alert teachers to problems experienced by individual children so that they can be given special attention. Parents will be able to judge their children's progress against agreed national targets for attainment and will also be able to judge the effectiveness of their school. LEAs will be better placed to assess the strengths and weaknesses of the schools they maintain by considering their performance in relation to each other and to the country at large, taking due account of relevant socio-economic factors; and the Secretaries of State will be better able to undertake a similar process nationally.

Employers, too, will have a better idea of what school-leavers will have studied and learnt at school, irrespective of where they went to school.

The proposed curriculum will consist of foundation subjects. Mathematics, English and science will form the core of the curriculum and first priority will be given to these subjects. In addition to the core subjects, the foundation subjects should comprise a modern foreign language, technology, history, geography, art, music and physical education. It is not proposed that a modern foreign language should be included in the foundation subjects for primary school children. The majority of curriculum time at primary level should be devoted to core subjects.

Attainment targets will be set for all three core subjects of mathematics, English and science. These will establish what children should normally be expected to know, understand and be able to do at the ages of 7, 11, 14 and 16. These will enable the progress of each child to be measured against established standards. The Consultative Document argues that the range of attainment targets should cater for the full ability range and be sufficiently challenging at all levels to raise expectations, particularly of pupils of middling achievement who frequently are not challenged enough, as well as stretching and stimulating the most able. Targets must be sufficiently specific for pupils, teachers, parents and others to have a clear idea of what is expected, and to provide a sound basis for assessment. There will also be attainment targets for other foundation subjects where appropriate, in Wales for the study of Welsh, and for the other themes and skills taught through each of the foundation subjects. For art, music and physical education, there will be guidelines rather than specific attainment targets. These targets will provide standards against which pupil´s progress and performance can be assessed. The main purpose of such assessment will be to show what a pupil has learnt and mastered and to enable teachers and parents to ensure that he or she is making adequate progress. Where such progress is not made, it will be up to schools to make suitable arrangements to help the pupil.

Within the framework of the national curriculum as currently proposed there are some significant issues for all those concerned with the management of primary schools. Campbell, Ridley and Saunders (1987) suggest seven such issues which include the following:

- Entitlement

  The national curriculum is based on the assumption that pupils are entitled to a curriculum which draws upon their individual talents and which challenges them. At the same time parents are entitled to know what schools seek to teach and how well.

  It is not clear, however, whether this entitlement will eventually be to a restricted minimum curriculum or to a rich and varied set of offerings, since the consultation document gives no indication of how those responsible for implementing the curriculum in primary schools are to find the necessary resources to provide it. This will be a major concern for headteachers who may be under pressure to provide a national curriculum irrespective of the resources available.

- Consensus

  The national curriculum will be introduced progressively,

  > as broad agreement is achieved on attainment targets and programmes of study for each foundation subject.
  > (DES Welsh Office, 1987, p. 14)

  It may be possible to achieve a consensus on the content of programmes but at primary level such a consensus on attainment targets, or even upon the basic need for them at age seven, does not appear to exist. The effect of such targets on processes of teaching and learning in the primary school will concern many people as will the effect on individual schools if the results of such tests are published in a raw form in order that:

  > parents will be able to judge their children's progress against agreed national targets for attainment and...also... judge the effectiveness of their school.
  > (DES Welsh Office, 1987, p.5)

- Curriculum Content and Attainment Targets

  Curriculum content is expressed in subject terms. While the analysis of the content in subject terms may be appropriate, its delivery at primary school level is not. Nor does it cover the many areas of importance which are normally found in good primary schools. At the same time the restrictions which may be imposed by the attainment targets could further restrict curriculum provision while creating an early sense of failure among many young children. The whole of the primary school staff team have to combine to meet these challenges in order that the best provision is preserved and that testing is used for diagnostic rather than evaluative and judgmental purposes.

- Professionalism

  If it is accepted that the new conditions of service are an attempt to establish extended professionalism throughout primary education (see Chapter Three) then the failure to accord to teachers a high degree of professional control over decisions to be made about relevant professional matters in the national curriculum seems to militate against this development. The imposition of such a curriculum and the implicit view of teachers which it appears to embody may shift the emphasis in primary schools from processes of teaching and learning and related strategies of staff development to testing, assessing and delivering a predetermined set of packages.

- Responsiveness

  If schools are to respond to their individual circumstances it is difficult to see how this can still be done within the context of the national curriculum proposals since it has long been held as axiomatic in primary education that the curriculum must start from where the children are. Parents need to be partners in this, rather than scrutineers of the outcomes of the process.

These proposals threaten to move the decision-making about crucial aspects of the education of children away from schools and locate it with the

DES. This may not be the intention but it is the impression given by the presentation of the proposals. Teachers may no longer be involved in the making of relevant professional choices about the content of the primary curriculum or, at worst, about the related pedagogy. They may be restricted to concerns related to the delivery of the agreed national curriculum. The criteria against which schools may come to be judged may be derived from the extent to which they appear to be successful deliverers of that curriculum as determined by the attainment tests. These developments are taking place at the same time as the Secretary of State is proposing a policy of open access to schools which is intended to ensure that parents can move their children from one school to another in relative freedom in search of the "best" education. Such open access, based on admissions procedures related to entry targets derived from a notional maximum capacity of each school's building, is intended to allow popular schools to expand and less popular ones to contract.

At the same time the availability of grant-maintained status may offer parents and children another set of choices although only the largest primary schools, those with more than 350 pupils on roll, will be eligible to apply for this. Nevertheless the existence of such proposals helps to create a climate of expectation which headteachers in smaller primary schools have to take into account in their approach to the management of their own schools. In particular it moves the locus of decision-making about the whole direction and purposes of a specific school away from the professionals who work in it to the parents of the children who attend it and to the governing body to such a degree that teachers have no control at all over how decisions might be made or what the outcomes will be. The teaching staff do however have influence which they can bring to bear on the decision-making process. Schools, therefore, are becoming much more open in the sense that those areas of activity which have, until now, been regarded as the legitimate province of the professional teacher are now open to control or, at the very least, significant influence from parents, governors and others in the wider community. The organisation and management of every primary school has to take into account these changes since this will have a far-reaching effect on the management role of the headteacher and her colleagues. This is especially true in relation to school governors.

School Governors : a changing body

The duties of school governors are derived from the 1944 Education Act where it is stated that boards of governors have responsibility for overseeing all aspects of work of schools including the curriculum. By the 1970s, however, many of these responsibilities were being ignored or had passed by default to other groups including teachers themselves. Furthermore the arrangement of governing bodies made it impossible for them to fulfil their duties. Schools sometimes had to share a board of governors with a dozen or more other institutions within the LEA. The governors would deal with business related to many schools at one meeting. Some governors belonged to scores of governing bodies and, not surprisingly, failed to attend meetings regularly. Governing bodies often retained no more than a rubber stamping function for decisions made elsewhere or else they concerned themselves with the state of the drains and the upkeep of the buildings. The school's organisation, its curriculum and its finances were rarely if ever considered. People with a real interest in the school, parents and teachers for example, had no voice. School governors were largely irrelevant to the education of children in schools. This situation is changing.

The changes began with the 1980 Education Act which sought to broaden representation on governing bodies and to encourage them to accept the wider responsibilities contained in the 1944 Act. The 1980 Act was vague about what these responsibilities were and about the precise mechanisms for achieving this broader representation. The 1986 Act is more precise. This Act provides for a parental representation on all governing bodies equal to that of the LEA. This will vary from two for governing bodies of schools with fewer than 100 pupils to five for schools of more than 600 pupils. Provision is also made for teacher representation on governing bodies. The processes for electing both teacher and parent governors and the conditions which determine eligibility are outlined. Similarly the arrangements for co-option are clearly stated since all boards of governors are required to represent the local community (Sallis, 1988).

The duties of governing bodies are also made explicit. The Act makes it clear that the whole of a school's work comes under the direction of the governors except where the Act assigns specific functions to others. Concern for the curriculum is a central part of these duties. Here the Act states that:

- The LEA must have a written policy on the school curriculum which must be kept up-to-date.

- Governors must study and understand this policy as it applies to their school. They must decide how it might need to be modified to be appropriate for their school and must prepare a written statement of the curricular aims for their schools.

- The headteacher is responsible for the determination and organisation of the curriculum.

- All governors and parents have a right to see curriculum statements, syllabuses and schemes of work.

(DES 1986, Annex 1)

At the same time the 1986 Act makes explicit the role of governors in staff appointments and in the processes of dismissals and suspensions. For example governors must have equal representation with the LEA on panels for appointing headteachers. Both the LEA and the governors now have the right to add up to two names to the short list. Governors must now produce an annual written report on all aspects of their work to be circulated to all parents and to be presented to an annual meeting of parents at which the report will be discussed. In the matter of school finance governing bodies will now receive an annual statement from the LEA on the expenditure incurred by the LEA in meeting the running costs of the school and on any capital costs that there may be. There must also be made known to governors the sums that they are entitled to spend on books, equipment, stationery and similar items necessary for the running of the school. Powers in this respect may be delegated by the governors to the headteacher. Thus in a number of significant areas of school life the role of governors is being made clearer and is becoming more central to the management of the school.

Financial Delegation to Schools

Governing bodies are now being encouraged to play a more central role in all aspects of the education of children within schools. This trend will continue as new proposals become law. Local financial management and the possibility of grant maintained status (opting-out) for schools will increase both the power of governing bodies and their capacity to influence strategic areas in the life of schools. Much will depend, therefore, on the extent to which volunteers can be found to serve on the governing bodies of schools both from the ranks of parents and from representatives of the wider community. Much also depends on the ways in which headteachers are able to relate to their boards of governors. This relationship is important in many respects but it will be especially so in areas which are new both to the head and to her governors. Although attention is now drawn to the role of the governors in determining curriculum policy this has long been regarded as the province of the headteacher and, in most cases, is likely to remain so even though there may be more frequent and, perhaps, more open and better informed discussion of curriculum matters by the governors. Where schools are moving into other areas such as local financial management the governors/headteacher spheres of influence are not already finely drawn. Here there may be areas of negotiation between the distribution of duties and responsibilities.

The proposals delegating financial responsibility to schools apply only to schools with 200 or more pupils. This is, in itself, a rather odd figure since in most circumstances a one form entry infant school would have 105 pupils and a two form entry school would have 210 pupils, while a one form entry infant and junior school may have up to 245 pupils. Financial delegation related to junior or infant schools of two or more forms of entry and to combined infant and junior schools of one or more forms of entry would be a less confusing approach. Nevertheless, as with the grant maintained status proposals, it is not simply the substance of the proposals that is important but the climate of expectation which they help to create.

The government's proposals for financial delegation to schools have two main objectives. These are:

- to ensure that parents and the community know on what basis the available resources are distributed in their area and how much is being spent on each school;

- to give the governors of all county and voluntary secondary schools and of the larger primary schools the freedom to take expenditure decisions which match their own priorities, and the guarantee that their school will benefit if they achieve efficiency savings.

(DES 1987b, p 1)

The objectives say nothing directly about the educational arguments for financial delegation although the implied message is clear. It is that the parents and the governors are best placed to be the guardians of the expenditure in each school since they will play the major role in identifying the educational priorities for that school. Therefore they will wish to ensure that expenditure is allocated so as to meet the objectives which they have established. Again areas which have previously been the province of the teachers in the school are being opened up to both scrutiny and participation by parents and governors. The consultation document makes this quite clear when it states that:

> Governors would be free to spend the delegated budget at their discretion, provided that their own, and the LEA´s statutory duties were met.
>
> (DES 1987b, p. 3)

This view is reinforced by the changes in the staffing provision which the Secretary of State intends to make, namely that the selection of headteachers, teachers and other staff would be delegated to the governing bodies (DES 1987b, p. 5) although the LEAs would continue to have the main responsibility for the professional development of their teachers including appraisal, statutory probation and in-service training.

It is in precisely this area of staff appointment and development that pilot schemes on school financial autonomy appear to have had their greatest impact, given that the room for manoeuvre in the budget of any school is likely to be very small, in the order of 2 per cent to 6 per cent of the total budget (Humphrey and Thomas 1986). In the pilot schemes the principal aim of financial autonomy was to make more efficient use of scarce resources by placing the control of the school budget in the hands of the headteacher who would then be able to have total management control over her institution. The main issue in at least one pilot scheme was to identify who should benefit from such increased efficiency remembering that efficiency can mean either achieving the same with fewer resources or doing more with the same level of resourcing (Humphrey and Thomas 1983). In this particular scheme heads were allowed the power of virement between the main financial headings which were: staffing; premises costs; establishment costs; part of grounds and building maintenance; capitation and furniture. This scheme began as a cost-saving exercise but the ethos soon changed to that of making best use of scarce resources by management at the point of delivery. Just how far the current proposals will enable effective and efficient use of resource management to take place at the point of delivery when the responsibility for setting priorities and managing the resources rests with a part-time set of governors remains to be seen. What is likely to happen is that the delegation of financial autonomy to schools will serve to highlight the differences between schools based on the range of different decisions which have to be taken about the use of resources.

Policy Changes and the Role of the Headteacher

The current changes in the policy concerning the education system in England and Wales have formed a major part of this final chapter for two reasons. Firstly they will play a significant part in shaping the context within which the approach to primary school management advocated here will need to be applied. Thus the collegiate management of the internal aspects of the primary school will be influenced by a similar approach to the external management of the school which will involve the governors and parents. Furthermore the internal strength which, it has been argued throughout this book, can come from collegiality may be necessary in order to meet the new challenges with which policy changes may confront all schools. The second reason for dwelling on the proposed new policies for education is the likely effect that those policies may have on the headteacher and on those with areas of responsibility in the school. As the new policies are implemented, the responsibility for managing the school will, in many cases, move from those inside the school to a position of shared responsibility with those outside the school. Thus the headteacher may find herself more closely involved in matters which have, hitherto, been considered as either peripheral to the school or external to it. This may mean that the team leaders inside the school have to play a more active part in the internal organisation of the primary school than perhaps has always been the case up to now.

These policy changes, which are being justified on the grounds of raising the overall standard of educational provision for the children in our schools, are based on the application of the principles of the social market economy to education. This approach to the ordering of social life makes the assumption that the aggregate of individual decisions is better for making and implementing policy than corporate or state planning. Provision is regulated through the market place which gives the consumer control by allowing consumer choices to be made. In order for this to happen the consumer has to be able to choose and, therefore, has to have a range of options from which to select. In educational terms, therefore, parents have to be able to move their children easily from one school to another and there have to be clear differences between schools and recognised ways of perceiving and understanding them. In this context the provision of City Technical Colleges, the availability of grant-maintained status and the delegation of financial autonomy to the school combine to provide a range of alternatives since these policies will serve to accentuate differences between schools. The insistence on "open access" to schools based on their maximum capacity is part of a process of making movement between schools easier. The national curriculum with its universal, nationally agreed standards which are to be tested at regular and prescribed intervals in a pupil´s school life not only help to make such movement easier but also provide criteria against which the performance of schools might be judged. The provision of information about school spending and its internal allocation is also intended to enable parents who may wish to send their child to a particular school to form a view about the relationship between a school´s priorities and its expenditure.

Much of this is based on a further assumption that, in the context of the provision of education for children, the parents are more able to make judgements about what is appropriate for their children than are the teachers. Thus professional knowledge has little or no place in this process. There is emerging, therefore, a new definition of professionalism. This is not based on the ability to make choices about what should be taught; how it should be taught; when it should be taught; to whom it should be taught; and why it should be taught. It is based on the development of a partnership between different groups within the wider educational enterprise including parents and governors. As a result of this, new ways of working have to be established and ways of managing have to be clearly identified. The management skills discussed in the middle six chapters of this book lend themselves to this new situation. The new ways of working will mean that teams within the primary school may need to be even clearer about what they are doing and why they are doing it and even more able to explain their particular use of resources. All primary school colleagues, and headteachers in particular, will need to be able to communicate more effectively and conduct meetings well for different sets of audiences.

As long ago as 1977 it was recognised that a good headteacher needed to be a diplomat, a negotiator, a public relations officer and a personnel manager (DES 1977a). These were not roles which were traditionally associated with headship, especially in primary schools. In 1979 a group of headteachers in Salford identified the framework in Table 47 which would help to define the managerial role of the primary headteacher. Much of it is still applicable to the internal management of primary schools today and many of the managerial skills considered above would be appropriate for enabling those headteachers to carry out their responsibilities as they saw them. There is a recognisable emphasis on the need to develop teams and to establish well founded working relationships. The fourfold differentiation of the headteacher's role mirrors that which Mrs Welton at Rosemary Lane was working out in practice for herself. What is missing, however, is the external dimension that present policies are thrusting upon heads. The elements of headship in Table 47 would also be recognisable to a group of newly appointed primary headteachers in a shire county in the Midlands who were asked to identify

Table 47 THE PRIMARY HEAD AS MANAGER

ROLES

- o Academic
- o Managerial
- o Professional
- o Organisational

REQUIREMENTS

A good head needs
to be a visionary;
to build teams;
to establish a wide
range of good relationships

SKILLS

- o Teaching
- o Changing
- o Consulting
- o Innovating
- o Participating
- o Facilitating
- o Supporting
- o Evaluating
- o Leading

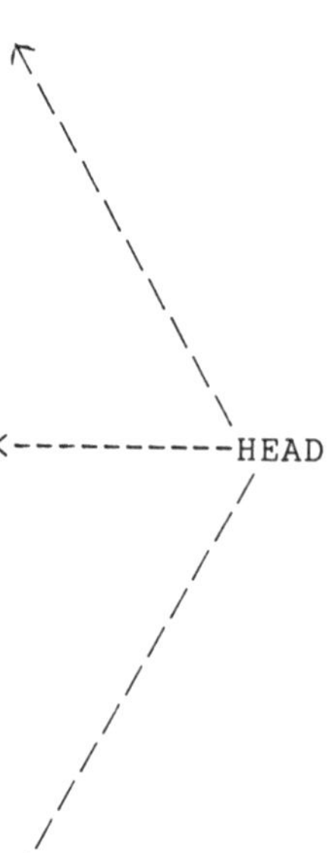

(Derived from Salford Education Department (1979) _The Role of the Headteacher_)

their expectations about the main roles that they would have to play as heads. They listed five different roles within the overall context of caring for the welfare and education of the children. These were:

i. teaching and providing professional leadership;

ii. managing colleagues and helping to develop and deploy their expertise;

iii. setting educational priorities for their schools;

iv. building good working relationships inside school and including parents and governors in many cases;

v. basic administration.

When the same group of headteachers was asked to indicate how they saw their role changing over the next few years they suggested that the emphasis of what they did would change from being one of caring for the education of the children to that of serving and maintaining the system within which they worked. Their main functions would become:

- testing and assessing children and colleagues;

- directing and controlling the professional activities of teachers;

- managing resources on the basis of priorities which were set elsewhere;

- public relations to various audiences;

- basic administration including the financial management of the school.

It is certain, however, that those policies which are at present under consideration by the government will add some of the functions in the second list to those in the first. Headteachers in primary schools may well have to be more actively involved in the managing of the professional activities of their staff. They may also find themselves in a situation where they have actively to promote the school and themselves and to recruit pupils by influencing parents. At the same time establishing and retaining the confidence of both governors and parents may have a higher priority for heads than it does at the moment. If financial delegation to schools is implemented then the managing of the finances, or the managing of the person who manages the finances, will be an added responsibility for headteachers. At the same time schools will still need to respond to the inevitable changes in society, especially as perceived by groups outside school. All of this may fall on the shoulders of the headteacher who will perhaps need to spend more time on the external aspects of her role while delegating much of its internal aspects to her deputy and to her team leaders. Thus the present policies have implications for all those in primary schools with curriculum or organisational responsibilities, not just for the headteacher.

Whether we like the present developments in educational policy or not they will provide a context in which primary schools have to be managed in the future. With this in mind Brunt has argued that headteachers ought to give serious consideration to the application of a marketing strategy to schools. He argues that:

> Marketing a school involves balancing society's needs for a cultured population against the immediate demands of parents, providers and consumers so as to maximise the school's contribution to society at large.
>
> (Brunt, 1987, p. 211)

He suggests that this would require a school to identify its potential customers and define their essential characteristics and the criteria which different subgroups may adopt when choosing a school. A school can then take a conscious decision about how it approaches those potential customers. At the same time marketing would lead the school to look at potential competitors, other schools both state funded and private, in order to decide how best to compete by emphasising similarities or by accentuating differences. Resource acquisition may also be an important part of this process and so may the active promotion of the school in its locality. All of this is a far cry from the internal focus on teaching and learning which is one of the great strengths of primary education. The internal life of the school must not be forgotten since it is that which directly affects the children in our schools at any given time.

Just as the primary school team leader may have to negotiate with the headteacher over matters of resources or priorities, so the head may have to negotiate with the governors. Negotiation may not always mean obtaining what you want. It may mean having the flexibility to achieve the best that you can and revising your plans in the light of what is possible. As Scott (1981) has pointed out, effective negotiation has five phases. These are: Purpose, Preparation, Plan, Pace and People.

The purpose is why the negotiation is taking place. It will focus on a broad issue but in order to be as successful as possible it is necessary to be clear about what the actual purpose of the negotiating meeting itself is. We have to be clear on what is to be agreed. We also have to be precise about what, ideally, we want and what, realistically we may accept. This clarity of purpose enables us to recognise an agreement when we have one. Preparation means collecting evidence to support our case; collecting information about possible alternative cases and evaluating it; understanding the position of those with whom we are to negotiate both in terms of what they will want to achieve and the reasons for their position. This will enable us to move towards identifying a position of mutual accommodation rather than outright victory or defeat, since the latter is always a possibility for both parties. Planning is the ordering of strategies, the structuring of the agenda items of the meeting, the decisions about who will lead on which topics and which evidence will be deployed and when during the process of negotiation. Pace is the speed with which it will be desirable to proceed. If, for example, negotiations are to take place about the allocation of resources between identified curriculum areas it might be necessary to spend some time exploring the essential features of each of those areas in advance of the actual discussion on resource allocation. If, on the other hand, the complexities of the issues are well understood by both parties then the position can be stated briefly. In either case the opening statement of a negotiation is often crucial in determining a successful outcome. So is an understanding of the people involved, the ideas they may bring to the negotiation, the outcomes they may most like to see and the strategies they are most likely to adopt to achieve those outcomes. Using this broad approach it is possible to negotiate successfully especially if we remember that it can often help to give satisfaction to the other party and that listening, rather than arguing, is the basis for skilful negotiation.

The main role of the primary headteacher may well then become that of negotiator of the external framework within which the internal work of the school takes place in terms of establishing priorities and the appropriate allocation of resources. Coulson (1987) in his analysis of the managerial role of primary headteachers uses concepts derived from Mintzberg who stresses that in many organisations maintaining an active network of outside contacts, monitoring, disseminating and transmitting information, searching the wider environment for opportunities and negotiating on behalf of the organisation are all vital functions. This may be the way in which primary headship will develop. In this case primary headteachers may need to become far more familiar with the skills of negotiating than they are at present.

Throughout this book it has been argued that the management of primary schools is a collective endeavour. In the main the focus has been on staff teams and their management and on ways of establishing the necessary partnerships based on shared responsibilities which effective teamwork in the primary school requires. In the final chapter the scope has been widened to encompass the new policy changes which now face us as we enter the 1990s. These, it is argued, will mean that the management of our primary schools will have to be even more purposeful than it has been hitherto. Our objectives and targets will have to be more precise and our rationale for adopting them more explicit. The processes of appointing and developing staff, of identifying the different responsibilities of staff and of monitoring the progress of our schools and the children within them will all have to be carefully managed. We will need to be able to communicate effectively with professional colleagues both inside and outside the school as well as with a range of other audiences including the increasingly significant parents and governors. In short, if our children are to obtain the maximum benefit from their experience of primary education then that education has to be effectively managed by those who provide it.

REFERENCES

ACAS, (1986) *Agreement on Teachers´ Pay and Conditions of Service*, Coventry

Adair, J. (1983) *Effective Leadership. A Staff Development Manual*, Gower, Aldershot

Adelman, C. and Alexander, R.J. (1982) *The Self-Evaluating Institution*, Methuen, London

Alexander, R.J. (1984) *Primary Teaching*, Holt, Rinehart and Winston, Eastbourne

Anning, A. (1983) "The Three Year Itch", *Times Educational Supplement*, 24th June

Beckhard, R. and Harris, R.T. (1977) *Organisational Transitions: Managing Complex Change*, Addison-Wesley, New York

Bell, L.A. (1979) "A discussion of some of the implications of using Consultants in Schools" in *British Journal of Educational Research*, vol. 5, no. 1, pp. 55-62

Bell, L.A. (1985) *Teacher Attitudes to Appraisal: a survey of conference members*, University of Warwick, Department of Education mimeo., Coventry

Bell, L.A. and Maher, P. (1986) *Leading a Pastoral Team. A Staff Development Approach*, Blackwells, Oxford

Bell, L.A. (1986) *The Organisation of Primary Schools : A Survey of Headteacher Perceptions*, Education Department, University of Warwick, Coventry

Bell, L.A. (1987) "Appraisal and Schools", in *Management in Education*, vol. 1, no. 1, pp.30-4

Bell, L.A. and Arnold, F. (1987) "Introducing Staff Appraisal to Schools" in *School Organisation* vol. 7, no. 2, pp. 193-208

REFERENCES

Bell, L.A. (1988) The Appraisal of Staff in Schools: A Practical Guide, Routledge, London

Blackburn, K. (1986) "Teacher Appraisal", in M. Marland (ed.), School Management Skills, Heinemann, Organisation in Schools series, pp. 51-60

Blake, R.R. and Mouton, J.S. (1964) The Managerial Grid, III: The Key to Leadership Excellence, Gulf Publishing Co., Houston, Texas

Bradley, R., Chesson, R. and Silverleaf, J. (1983) Inside Staff Development, NFER - Nelson, Windsor

Broadfoot, P. (1979) Assessment, School and Society, Methuen, London

Brunt, M.P.C. (1987) "Marketing Schools" in I. Craig, (ed.) Primary School Management in Action, pp. 210-26

Bunnell, S. and Stephens, E. (1984) "Teacher Appraisal - A Democratic Approach", in School Organisation, vol. 4, no. 4, pp. 291-302

Burns, T. and Stalker, G.M. (1966) The Management of Innovation, Tavistock, London

Bush, T., Glatter, R., Goodey, J. and Riches, C. (1980) (eds.), Approaches to School Management, Harper and Row, London

Butterworth, I.B. (1985) The Appraisal of Teachers, Educational Management Information Exchange Paper, NFER, Slough

Campbell, J., Ridley, K. and Saunders, T. (1987) "The National Curriculum: Primary Questions. A Report of the 1987 National Primary Conference" Junior Education Special Report, Scholastic Publications, Leamington Spa

Campbell, R.J. (1985) Developing the Primary Curriculum, Holt, Rinehart & Winston, Eastbourne

Carter, A., Morgan, V. and Bell, L.A. (1980) "A Study of Innovation and Change in a Primary School", in Educational Change and Development, vol. 2, No. 3, pp. 13-23

Clift, P. (1982) "LEA Schemes for School Self-Evaluation" in Educational Research, vol. 24, no. 1, pp. 262-70

Coulson, A.A. (1977) "The Role of the Primary Head", in Peters, (ed.), The Role of the Head, pp. 92-108

Coulson, A.A. (1987) "Recruitment and Management Development for Primary Headship", in G. Southworth, (ed.), Readings in Primary School Management, pp. 16-29

REFERENCES

Craig, I. (1987) (ed.), Primary School Management in Action, Longmans, London

Croydon LEA (1984) A System of Professional Performance Appraisal, Discussion Document, London Borough of Croydon, Croydon

Cumbria LEA (1985) The Appraisal and Professional Development of Teaching Staff, Cumbria Education Committee

Day, C., Johnstone, D. and Whitaker, P. (1985) Managing Primary Schools: A Staff Development Approach, Harper and Row, London

Dean, J. (1985) Managing the Secondary School, Croom Helm, London

Dean, J. (1986) "Teacher Appraisal: some questions to ask", in Inspection and Advice, vol. 22, no. 1

Delaney, P. (1986) "Teacher appraisal in the Primary School: One School´s Experience", Junior Education Special Report, Scholastic Publications, Leamington Spa

DES (1972) Teacher Education and Training (The James Report), HMSO, London

DES (1975) Language for Life. Report of the Committee appointed by the Secretary of State for Education and Science, (The Bullock Report), HMSO, London

DES (1977a) Ten Good Schools, HMSO, London

DES (1977b) Education in Schools: A Consultative Document, HMSO, London

DES (1978) Primary Education in England. A Survey by HMI, HMSO, London

DES (1979b) A Framework for the School Curriculum, HMSO, London

DES (1981) The School Curriculum, HMSO, London

DES (1982) Education 5-9: an Illustrative Survey of 80 First Schools in England, HMSO, London

DES (1982) Mathematics Counts: Report of the Committee of Inquiry into the Teaching of Mathematics in Schools, (The Cockcroft Report) HMSO, London

DES (1983) Teaching Quality, HMSO, London

DES (1985a) Better Schools, HMSO, London

DES (1985b) Education Observed 3: Good Teachers, HMSO, London

DES (1985c) Quality in Schools: Evaluation and Appraisal, HMSO, London

DES (1985d) The Curriculum from 5 to 16: Curriculum Matters 2, HMSO, London

DES (1986) The Education Act, HMSO, London

REFERENCES

DES (1987a) The Education (School Teachers Pay and Conditions of Employment) Order, HMSO, London

DES (1987b) Financial Delegation to Schools: A Consultation Paper, HMSO, London

DES Welsh Office (1987) The National Curriculum 5-1 16: A Consultation Document, HMSO, London

Dockrell, B., Nisbet, J., Nuttall, D., Stones, E. and Wilcox, B. (1986) Appraising Appraisal, British Educational Research Association, Birmingham

Dror, Y. (1963) "The Planning Process: a facet design", in International Review of Administrative Sciences, vol. 29, no. 1, pp. 51-63

Dror, Y. (1968) Public Policy Making Re-examined, Chandler, San Francisco

Drucker, P. (1968) The Practice of Management, Pan, London

Easen, P. (1985) Making School Based INSET Work, Open University Press, Milton Keynes

Elliot, G. (1981) Self-Evaluation and the Teacher, Schools Council (mimeo), London

Elliot-Kemp, J. (1981) Staff Development in Schools. A Framework for Diagnosis for Individual Teacher Development Needs, Pavic Publications, Sheffield

Everard, K.B., and Morris, G. (1985) Effective School Management, Harper and Row, London

Everard, K.B. (1986) Developing Management in Schools, Blackwell, Oxford

Fayol, H. (1916) Administration Industrielle et Generale, Translated by C. Storris, (1949) as General and Industrial Management, Pitmans, London

Fellows, A. (1985) Survey of Responsibilities of Deputy Headteachers in First Schools, Rugby Teachers' Centre, Warwickshire LEA

Field, D. (1985) "Headship in the Secondary School", in Hughes, et. al., Managing Education, pp. 308-24

Friedmann, J. (1967) "A Conceptual Model for the Analysis of Planning Behaviour", Administrative Science Quarterly, vol. 12, no. 2, pp. 205-52

Goodworth, C.T. (1979) Effective Interviewing for Employment Selection, Business Books, London

Goodworth C.T. (1984) How to be a Super-Effective Manager, Business Books, London

Griffith, F. (1979) Administrative Theory in

REFERENCES

Education: Text and Readings, Pendell Publishing Co., Midland, Michigan

Gulick, L. and Urwick, L.F. (1937) Papers on the Science of Administration, Columbia University Press, New York

Handy, C. (1984) Taken for Granted? Looking at Schools as Organisations, Longmans, London

Harling, P. (1980) "School Decision Making and the Primary Headteacher", in Harling, P. (ed.), New Directions in Educational Leadership, pp. 221-30

Harling, P. (1984) (ed.), New Directions in Educational Leadership, Falmer Press, Lewes

Havelock, R.G. (1970) The Change Agent's Guide to Innovation in Education, CRUK, University of Michigan, Ann Arbor

Heller, H. (1985) Helping Schools Change. A Handbook for Leaders in Education, Centre for the Study of Comprehensive Schools, York

HMSO (1986) House of Commons Education Arts & Science Select Committee Report on Primary Education, London

Hoyle, E. (1974) "Professionality, Professionalism and Control", London Education Review, vol. 3, no. 2, pp. 15-17

Hoyle, E. and McCormick, R. (1976) Innovation and the School, Open University Course E.203, Curriculum Design and Development, Open University Press, Milton Keynes

Hughes, M. (1985) "Theory and Practice in Educational Management", in Hughes, et.al., Managing Education, pp. 3-39

Hughes, M., Ribbins, P. and Thomas, H. (eds.), (1985) Managing Education. The System and the Institution, Holt, Rinehart and Winston, Eastbourne

Humphrey, C. and Thomas, H. (1983) "Making Efficient Use of Scarce Resources", Education, 26th August, p. 125

Humphrey, C. and Thomas, H. (1986) "Delegating to Schools", Education, 12th December, pp. 513-14

Inner London Education Authority (1977) Keeping the School Under Review, London

Inner London Education Authority (1985) Improving Primary Schools. Report of the Committee on Primary Education, Chaired by Norman Thomas, London

REFERENCES

Joseph, K. (1984) Speech to the North of England Education Conference, 6th January, Sheffield

Joseph, K. (1985) Speech to the North of England Education Conference, 4th January, Chester

Leiberman, M. (1956) Education as a Profession, Prentice Hall, New York

Lewin, K. (1947) "Force Field Analysis", Human Relations, vol. 1, no. 1, pp. 5-41

Lindblom, C.E. (1959) "The Science of ´Muddling Through`", Public Administration Review, vol. 19, pp. 170-80

Lloyd, K. (1985) "Management and Leadership in the Primary School", in Hughes, et. al. Managing Education, pp. 291-307

Lyons G. and Stenning, R. (1986) Managing Staff in Schools: A Handbook, Hutchinson, London

Lumb, D., Gillis, R., Roberts, H. and Robinson, R. (1984) Primary Mathematics: Critical Appraisal Instrument, Longman Resources Unit for SCDC Publications, York

Marland, M. (1986) (ed.), School Management Skills, Heinemann Educational Books, London

Maslow, A.H. (1943) "A Theory of Human Motivation", in Psychological Review, vol. 50, pp. 370-96

Maslow, A.H. (1954) Motivation and Personality, Harper and Row, New York

Mason, A, (1987) "The Headteacher´s role in the Development of Staff" in Craig, I. (1987) (ed.), Primary School Management in Action pp. 30-40

Maund, D., Pountney, G., Scrivener, T. and Ward, C. (1982) Management in the Primary School, Coventry LEA

Maw, J., Fielding, M. and Mitchell, P., White, J., Young, P., Ouston, J. and White, P., (1984) Education plc?, London Institute of Education and Heinemann, London

McMahon, A., Bolam, R., Abbott, R. and Holly, P. Guidelines for Review and Internal Development of Schools. Primary School Handbook, Longman Resources Unit for SCDC, York

Millerson, G. (1964) The Qualifying Associations, Routledge & Kegan Paul, London

Mintzberg, H. (1973) The Nature of Managerial Work, Harper and Row, New York

Morgan, C. (1981) The Selection and Promotion of Staff, Course E323, Management and the School, Block 6, The Management of Staff, Open University Press, Milton Keynes

REFERENCES

Morgan, C., Hall, V. and Mackay, H. (1983) The Selection of Secondary School Headteachers, Open University Press, Milton Keynes

Morgan, C., Hall, V. and Mackay, H. (1984) A Handbook on Selecting Senior Staff in Schools, Open University Press, Milton Keynes

Moore, H. (1988) "Appraisal and the Headteacher", in Bell, L. (1988) The Appraisal of Staff in Schools: A Practical Guide

Musgrove, F. and Taylor, P. (1969) Society and the Teacher´s Role, Routledge & Kegan Paul, London

National Union of Teachers (1982) Memorandum of Guidance to Heads Number 16, Students on Teaching Practice, London

National Union of Teachers (1985) Teacher Appraisal and Teacher Quality, London

Nias, J. (1980) "Leadership Styles and Job Satisfaction in Primary Schools", in Bush, et. al., (1980) Approaches to School Management, pp. 225-73

Nuttall, D. (1986) "What can we learn from Research on Appraisals?", in Dockrell, et. al., Appraising Appraisal, pp. 20-8

Open University (1982) Case Study One. An Oxfordshire School, Course E364, Curriculum Evaluation and Assessment in Educational Institutions Open University Press, Milton Keynes

Oxfordshire County Council (1979) Starting Points in Self-Evaluation, Oxfordshire Eduction Department, Oxford

Paisey, A. (1981) Organisation and Management in Schools, Longmans, London

Paisey, A. (1984) "Trends in Educational Leadership Thought", in Harling, (ed.), New Directions in Educational Leadership, pp. 25-38

Peters, R.S. (1977) (ed.), The Role of the Head, Routledge & Kegan Paul, London

Plant, R. (1987) Managing Change and Making it Stick, Fontana/Collins, London

Poster, C. (1976) School Decision-Making, Heinemann Educational Books, London

Pountney, G. (1985) Management in Action, Longman Resources Unit for SCDC Publications, York

Rawlinson, J.G. (1981) Creative Thinking and Brainstorming, Gower, Aldershot

Richardson, E. (1975) Authority and Organisation in the Secondary School, Macmillan, London

REFERENCES

Rose, M. (1954) The Intelligent Teacher's Guide to Preferment, Chatto and Windus, London
Rust, W.B. (1985) Management Guidelines for Teachers, Pitman, London

Salford Education Department (1979) The Role of the Headteacher, Salford
Sallis, J. (1988) Schools, Parents and Governors, Routledge, London
Scott, B. (1981) The Skills of Negotiating, Gower, Aldershot
Sharpe, R. and Green, A. (1975) Education and Social Control: A Study in Progressive Primary Education, Routledge & Kegan Paul, London
Shipman, M. (1979) In-School Evaluation, Heinemann Educational Books, London
Shipman, M. (1983) Assessment and Evaluation in Primary and Middle Schools, Croom Helm, London
Shipton, D.G. (1987) How are the Needs of Primary School Teachers to be Identified?, Unpublished Report of a Headteacher Fellowship, University of Warwick, Department of Education, Coventry
Sidwell, D.M. (1987) Staff Appraisal in Education: an analysis of practices and principles in UK, France, Federal Republic of Germany and USA, Unpublished MA Thesis, University of Warwick, Coventry
Solihull LEA (1980) Evaluation of the Primary School, Metropolitan Borough of Solihull
Strauss, B.W. and Strauss, F. (1964) New Ways to Better Meetings, Social Science Paperbacks, London
Southworth, G. (1987) (ed.), Readings in Primary School Management, Falmer Press, Lewes
Suffolk LEA (1985) Those Having Torches...Teacher Appraisal: A Study, Ipswich/Suffolk

Tannenbaum, R. and Schmidt, W. (1958) "How to Choose a Leadership Pattern", Harvard Business Review, vol. 51, no. 3, pp. 162-75 and 178-80
Thomas, N. (1987) "The Appraisal of Primary School Teachers", A paper prepared as a result of discussions in The Primary Education Study Group, and published in Education, 28th August
Tomlinson, J.R.G. (1986) Crossing the Bridge: Addresses to the North of England Conferences, Sheffield Papers in Educational Management No. 54, Sheffield City Polytechnic, Sheffield
Tomlinson, J.R.G. (1987) "The Purpose of Primary Education", The Opening Address to the National

REFERENCES

Conference on Primary Education, Scarborough, April

Trethowan, D.M. (1984) *Delegation*, Education for Industrial Society, London

Trethowan, D.M. (1985) "To appraise teachers, not to bury them", in *Times Education Supplement*, 8th March, p. 21

Trethowan, D.M. (1987) *Appraisal and Target Setting: A Handbook for Teacher Development*, Harper and Row, London

Warwick, D. (1983) *Staff Appraisal*, Education for Industrial Society, London

Waters, D. (1979) *Management and Headship in the Primary School*, Ward Lock Educational, London

Waters, D. (1983) *Responsibility and Promotion in the Primary School*, Heinemann Educational Books, London

Whitaker, P. (1983) *The Primary Head*, Heinemann Educational Books, London

Whitfield, D.R. (1975) *Creativity in Industry*, Penguin, Harmondsworth

Wilcox, B. (1986) "Context and Issues", in Dockrell et. al., *Appraising Appraisal*, pp. 1-9

Winecoff, L. and Powell, C. (1979) *Seven Steps to Educational Problem Solving*, Pendell Publishing Company, Midland, Michigan

Winkley, D. (1984) "Educational Management and School Leadership: An Evolutionary Perspective" in Harling, P. (1984) (ed.), *New Directions in Educational Leadership*, pp. 205-20

Wirrall Metropolitan Borough (1986) *Staff Training Profile and School Curriculum Expertise Profile, Primary Education*, Department of Education Municipal Offices, Birkenhead

Woodcock, M. (1979) *Team Development Manual*, Gower, Aldershot

INDEX